Agents of the Welfare State

List of Previous Publications

Jewell C. "Assessing Need in the United States, Germany and Sweden: The Organization of Welfare Casework and the Potential for Responsiveness in the 'Three Worlds.'" *Law & Policy* 29, no. 3 (2007): 380–406.

Jewell C. and L. Bero. "Public Participation and Claimsmaking: Evidence Utilization and Divergent Policy Frames in California's Ergonomics Rulemaking." *Journal of Public Administration Research and Theory,* Advance Access published on December 27, 2006; doi: 10.1093/jopart/mo/023/

Jewell C., L. Davidson, and M. Rowe. "The Paradox of Engagement: How Political, Organizational and Evaluative Demands Can Hinder Innovation in Community Mental Health Services." *Social Service Review* 80, no. 1 (2006): 3–26.

Jewell C. and B. Glaser. "Towards a General Analytic Framework: Organizational Settings, Policy Goals and Street-Level Behavior." *Administration and Society* 38, no. 3 (2006): 1–31.

Sells D., L. Davidson, C. Jewell, P. Falzer, and M. Rowe. "The Treatment Relationship in Peer-Based and Regular Case Management Services for Clients with Severe Mental Illness. *Psychiatric Services* 57, no. 8 (2006): 1–6.

Karukstis K., K. Birkeland, B. Babusis, K. Kasal, and C. Jewell. "Chlorophyll Fluorescence Characterization of the Photosystem II Electron Transport Inhibitors." *Journal of Luminescence* 51, nos. 1–3 (1992): 119–28.

Karukstis K., M. Berliner, C. Jewell, and K. Kuwata. "Competition of Anthraquinones for the Q_B Binding Domain." In *Current Research in Photosynthesis,* edited by M. Baltscheffsky, vol. I, pp. 579–82. Dordrecht, The Netherlands: Martinus Nijhoff Publishers (1990).

Karukstis K., M. Berliner, C. Jewell, and K. Kuwata. "Chlorophyll Fluorescence Measurements-to Assess the Competition of Substituted Anthraquinones for the Q_B Binding Site." *Biochimica et Biophysica Acta* 1020, no. 2 (1990): 163–68.

Agents of the Welfare State

How Caseworkers Respond to Need in the United States, Germany, and Sweden

Christopher J. Jewell

palgrave
macmillan

First published in 2007 by
PALGRAVE MACMILLAN™
175 Fifth Avenue, New York, N.Y. 10010 and
Houndmills, Basingstoke, Hampshire, England RG21 6XS.
Companies and representatives throughout the world.

PALGRAVE MACMILLAN is the global academic imprint of the Palgrave Macmillan division of St. Martin's Press, LLC and of Palgrave Macmillan Ltd. Macmillan® is a registered trademark in the United States, United Kingdom and other countries. Palgrave is a registered trademark in the European Union and other countries.

ISBN-13: 978-1-4039-8411-1
ISBN-10: 1-4039-8411-5

Library of Congress Cataloging-in-Publication Data

Jewell, Christopher J.
  Agents of the welfare state : how caseworkers respond to need in the United States, Germany, and Sweden/Christopher J. Jewell.
    p. cm.
  Includes bibliographical references and index.
  ISBN 1-4039-8411-5 (alk. paper)
  1. Public welfare—United States. 2. Public welfare—Germany.
  3. Public welfare—Sweden. I. Title.

HV95.J48 2007
361.3'2—dc22   2007001625

A catalogue record for this book is available from the British Library.

Design by Macmillan India Ltd.

First edition: September 2007

10 9 8 7 6 5 4 3 2 1

Printed in the United States of America.

To my mother and good friend, Sharon Sue Alexander

Table of Contents

List of Figures

List of Tables

List of Acronyms

ABE	Association of Bremen Employers (Verband Bremer Beschäftigungen)
AFDC	Aid to Families with Dependent Children
AGAB	Unemployed Citizens Action Group (Aktionsgemeinschaft Arbeitloser Bürgerinnen und Bürger)
ALMP	active labor market policy
ARBIS	"work instead of welfare" (arbete istället socialbidrag)
AU	assistant unit
AUCOOP	Trade and Vocational Training Cooperative (Handwerks-und Ausbildungscooperative)
BSHG	Federal Social Assistance Law (Bundessozialhilfegesetz)
CalWORKS	California Work Opportunity and Responsibility to Kids
CBO	community-based organizations
CIA	comparative institutional advantage
CII	City Investment Initiative (Storstadssatsningen)
CLA	Cost-of-Living Assistance (Hilfe zum Lebensunterhalt)
CME	coordinated market economy
CW	GAIN caseworker
CWD	county welfare department
CWPDP	California Work Pays Demonstration Project
DG	Development Guarantee
EDD	Employment Development Department
EO	Employment Office
EU	European Union
EW	Eligibility Worker
FES	Federal Employment Services
GAIN	Greater Avenues to Independence
GED	General Educational Development
GEFAS	General Plan for Work and Employment (Generalplan för Arbete och Sysselsättning)
GNP	gross national product
HRD	human resource development
HSC	Help in Special Circumstances (Hilfe in besonderen Lebenslagen)

HSO	human service organization
HtW	Help to Work (Hilfe zur Arbeit)
JC	Job Club
JD	Job Developer
JOBS	Job Opportunity and Basic Skills
JTPA	Job Training Partnership Act
LMA	labor market attachment
LME	liberal market economy
MAP	maximum aid payment
MBSAC	minimum basic standard of adequate care
MCR	Malmö's communal rules
NBHW	National Board of Health and Welfare
OECD	Organisation for Economic Co-operation and Development
SCC	supplemental child care
SIP	self-initiated program
SSA	Social Security Agency
SSL	Social Service Law
TANF	Temporary Aid to Needy Families
U27	Under 27
UBI/II	unemployment benefit I/II
UC DATA	University of California Data and Technical Assistance
W-2	Wisconsin Works
WB	Werkstatt Bremen
WDC	Work and Development Center (Arbets- och Utvecklingscentrum)
WDS	Workforce Development System
WIA	Workforce Investment Act
WIC	Work and Integration Center (Arbete och Integration Centrum)
WIN	Work Incentive Program
WTW	welfare-to-work

Acknowledgments

Many have helped me and made life enjoyable along the long and meandering path to this book, so I have a lot of people all over the place to thank. Christopher Ansell, Leslie Green, Jonah Levy, and Kristen Luker provided me many of the intellectual resources I needed for conceiving a comparative, organizational, welfare policy project. Ed Barnes and the East Bay Community Law Center gave me my first hands-on knowledge of welfare in the United States and sparked my interest in finding out if other civilized nations might tend to the needs of their most vulnerable citizens in a more civilized manner. I had many fruitful discussions with Bonnie Glaser and Karin MacDonald about how California welfare offices do business as part of the process team for UC DATA's California Work Pays Demonstration Project evaluation, an experience that formed the basis for the subsequent doctoral work on which this book is based.

In Bremen, Germany, Stephan Leibfried and Uwe Scharze helped me to understand the German system and find my way through the confounding complexity of the welfare bureaucracy. For my time in Sweden, thanks to Kerstin Hansen, whose tutelage in Swedish eased the transition into a new language considerably; to Lena Persson, for keeping me intellectually and socially integrated in Lund and Malmö; and to Tapio Salonen, for his generous assistance in helping me organize my Swedish fieldwork.

Thanks also to my dissertation committee Margaret Weir, Henry Brady, and Lauren Edelman. I would especially like to thank my advisor, Robert Kagan, who has always actively engaged me and my material and whose casual, profound insights were instrumental to the development of the conceptual framework that was needed to contain so much complex information.

I would like to express my gratitude to Lisa Bero for hiring me as a postdoctoral research fellow at U.C. San Francisco, employment that afforded me the opportunity to complete this manuscript. Converting a dissertation into a book turned out to be a very confounding and opaque process, and I owe a great deal to several colleagues for their valuable advice: Paul Frymer, Joel Handler, Bronwen Morgan, Jennifer Reich, and Susan Sterett. Many individuals were kind enough to provide helpful manuscript comments and remind me of the needs of the gentle reader who one day might pick up this text: Dorie Apollonio, Elizabeth Boyd, Evelyn Brodkin, Petra Buhr, Anders Giertz, Zoe Hammer, Jonas Olofsson, and two anonymous reviewers. Thanks to Jeffrey Burke for designing a book cover that both I and this book can wear.

Thanks to all the welfare agency officials in dozens of offices across California, Bremen, and Malmö for sharing some of their limited time with me. The opportunities to talk with them and observe the work they did is the bedrock of this study.

I would also like to acknowledge the generous support of the Deutscher Akademischer Austausch Dienst (the German Academic Exchange Service [DAAD]) and the Foreign Language and Area Studies (FLAS), who made it possible for me to gain adequate proficiency in German to chat with Bremen caseworkers; the Berkeley Vice Chancellor Research Fund for providing me translation/transcription support; and the German Marshall Fund and the Scandinavian Studies department at U.C. Berkeley, who made it possible for me to spend a year in Germany and Sweden doing my field work for this project. I would also like to express my gratitude to the editorial staff at Palgrave Macmillan for their diligent assistance throughout the publication process.

Finally, I would like to thank my mother and my sister, who provided me encouragement like only loving family members can do; and, of course, my partner, Tony, for his unflagging editorial and emotional support through nigh on a decade of my preoccupation with this endeavor.

Some sections and ideas in this manuscript have appeared in various guises in previous papers. The descriptions of caseworkers and organizational conditions in the United States chapters (3 and 6) draw on a paper with Bonnie Glaser that was published in *Administration & Society* in 2006 under the title, "Towards a General Analytic Framework: Organizational Settings, Policy Goals and Street-Level Behavior." Some of the arguments and cross-national analysis of responsiveness among welfare caseworkers that appear in summative form, particularly in chapters 1 and 9, appeared in a paper previously published in 2007 in *Law & Policy* under the title, "Assessing Need in the United States, Germany and Sweden: The Organization of Welfare Casework and the Potential for Responsiveness in the 'Three Worlds.'"

1

Book Overview: Responding to Need in Diverse State Settings

Providing state assistance to the poor raises fundamental questions about the minimal level of public support individuals should receive and about the obligations that can be required of recipients to help themselves. At the same time, policymaking in different countries is grounded in diverse histories and political philosophies regarding appropriate relationships between states and their citizens. Yet little comparative research has been conducted on how these national traditions shape and become embedded in local administrative practices. The following cross-national, street-level study analyzes how caseworkers make needs assessment decisions and promote self-sufficiency in welfare and welfare-to-work agencies in the United States, Germany, and Sweden.

One of the major achievements of the modern welfare state has been the dramatic rise in the standard of living brought about, in part, by the establishment of various income support programs. By partially sheltering people from the financial burdens associated with predictable life events such as unemployment, childcare, disability, and old age, these programs ensured that individuals and their families were better maintained when wage labor and other private means of support were insufficient or unavailable (Leisering and Leibfried 1999). Meanwhile, this increased role of government in the provision of individual economic security imbued officials with considerable authority to affect both the quality of life of a large portion of the population and the levels of public spending.

In designing and managing this administrative state, policymakers have been faced with the difficulty of balancing individual responsiveness and program integrity. The ability to adapt policies to individual situations facilitates both the fit of organizational responses to specific claimant needs and the targeting of limited resources in an efficient manner (Tweedie 1989). But the institutional capacity for responsiveness is often associated with increased costs and complexity. Administration is expensive, especially where organizational tasks require staff with specialized knowledge. Political accountability, fiscal control, and legal consistency can also become attenuated as decision-making processes become more intricate and, therefore, difficult for policymakers and administrators to monitor and direct (Lipsky 1980).

While all forms of public income support raise such programmatic issues, for social assistance or "welfare," a context in which often desperate individuals encounter state officials on the basis of their need alone, these tensions are particularly significant. In the last 20 years the salience of this type of aid has grown considerably in many welfare states, as family forms and employment trajectories have increasingly diverged from the full-time male breadwinner model implicit in the traditional array of social security programs. As the "program of last resort," welfare becomes, in effect, the minimum level of support provided by society to many of its most vulnerable members. This poverty-prevention function is complex and difficult to implement as need is an amorphous and contentious concept to operationalize, multifarious in the forms it can take and the conditions under which it arises. At the same time, the morally problematic status of recipients—as the presumably able-bodied, yet nonworking poor—is often used to justify administrative intervention to engage in the moral work of "rehabilitating" recipients off public support. How, then, do welfare states strike the balance between ensuring that officials are dispensing resources in a consistent and fiscally responsible way, while also furthering the program's primary purposes of addressing legitimate, unmet need and moving people toward self-sufficiency? And how do these choices affect the way frontline officials deliver client services?

One line of argument is that the political dynamics of social assistance combined with the organizational requirements of public benefits programs will result in common policy choices and administrative structures. As a program serving a stigmatized and therefore politically marginal group, and one often substantially financed by subnational levels of government (with comparatively limited tax base), policymakers will be most concerned with maintaining strong oversight and minimizing fiscal costs. The general response will be to institute low, flat-grant benefit programs. While setting support levels according to the average claimant means that many will not receive adequate support appropriate to their situation, a system based on such a rough approximation is comparatively cheap, controllable, and easy to administer. Welfare can be organized as a rule-bound bureaucracy with relatively straightforward procedural requirements and implemented by comparatively low-skilled, low-cost technicians. Instituting self-help obligations could be organized using a similar, cheap, mass-processing approach. Rather than developing a range of costly service offerings and hiring a cadre of professionals, the labor market can itself act as the primary assessor and provider with program staff serving largely as monitors of recipients' independent job search activities.

A variant of this functionalist view argues that there has been a recent convergence in program design in the 1980s and 1990s owing to the adjustment difficulties of many countries to a postindustrial economy and the increased mobility of capital globally.[1] A rise in structural unemployment and a heightened fiscal austerity, combined with a large increase in the numbers of social assistance recipients, create strong political and administrative pressures to develop more standardized, controllable, and often restrictive practices (Gough et al. 1997; Bradshaw and Terum 1997). One sign of convergence has been a general trend toward expanded self-help obligations for recipients of welfare and other income programs cross-nationally (Handler 2004; Lødemel 2000).

On the other hand, the social function of policy in constituting state-society relationships varies among nations. While in some countries the state is a major, integrated institution in society with redistributional impact, in others social policy operates as a form of social insurance, designed to maintain existing occupational and class distinctions; and in still others the state only intervenes in market outcomes in cases of extreme hardship (Titmuss 1970). Esping-Andersen in *The Three Worlds of Welfare Capitalism* (1991) described countries clustered into three groups embodying the different roles the state can play. Countries with the most substantive social policy tradition consisted primarily of the Scandinavian countries; social insurance states included most of continental Europe; and the states that played a residual role resided largely in the Anglo-Saxon world. In broader political economy terms, states vary in the importance of market versus relational networks as coordinating mechanisms among economic actors. As a result, occupational structures and employment opportunities are markedly different between so-called liberal market economies and coordinated market economies (Hall and Soskice 2001). More generally, past political choices have been shown to result in country-specific, institutional trajectories in an array of policy areas that affect both how common challenges to the modern state manifest in particular national settings and the range of solutions that are feasible and politically appropriate (Rothstein and Steinmo 2002).

How these national differences in policy orientations and traditions might relate to the organization of social assistance is not immediately clear because most welfare state and political economy literatures are based primarily on mainstream social insurance system features and labor market institutions, rather than safety-net programs. One could imagine, however, that countries in which social policy and nonmarket institutions play a more substantive role would display greater efforts and capacity for the inclusion of those at the margins (Bradshaw and Terum 1997). Such commitment could occur, for example, through greater availability of both general and targeted resources for lower income populations and through greater programmatic efforts to individualize support for vulnerable groups.

Many important works of scholarship have examined welfare policy and administration (Meyers, Glaser, and MacDonald 1998; Bane and Ellwood 1994; Melnick 1994; Brodkin 1986; Lipsky 1980; Handler and Hollingsworth 1971), yet most have remained limited to the U.S. context. Scholarship that has looked specifically at social assistance policy from a comparative perspective provides important information about how policy choices and administrative structures vary (Lødemel and Schulte 1992; Eardley et al. 1996; for activation see also Handler 2004; Lødemel 2000; Van Voorhis and Gilbert 2001), but they rely primarily on formal policy descriptions. As a result, there is inadequate information to examine how needs assessment and self-help service decisions are structured and if they are structured differently cross-nationally.

This lack of comparative street-level data is understandable. Language barriers and resource limitations make it difficult for individual scholars to gain personal experience in and perspective on the literature, policies, institutional arrangements, and daily practices of programs in multiple countries. But unlike many other public income programs, ... social assistances' more basic, poverty-prevention function and its often highly interventionist nature mean that the absence of this information represents a significant gap in understanding. To be clear, welfare receipt differs from other, more traditional income-support programs in which claimants are treated as citizens and the state remains at arm's length. For those on social assistance, claimants are relegated to a status of dependency that permits the state and its workers to investigate the details of their lives and aggressively attempt to change their behaviors. As a result, the way welfare workers execute state policy constitutes much of the *actual* content of welfare policy. Not only are the discrepancies between rules and practices a well-documented general feature of organizational behavior in a variety of settings (Lipsky 1980; Prottas 1979; Maynard-Moody and Musheno 2003), it is also often in the details of implementation where many of the most crucial and interesting features and variations emerge. What may look like convergence at the level of political discourse or formal policy decisions may belie very different practices and interactions that occur between state officials and citizens (Pollitt 2002).

Agents of the Welfare State begins to fill in this gap in scholarship through case studies of welfare office practices in three countries that have been identified as the archetypes of Esping-Andersen's "Three Worlds," namely, the United States, Germany, and Sweden. Based on interviews and observations conducted in administrators' native languages, this book provides detailed portraits of caseworker decision making and administrative supervision. As mentioned, welfare programs are mandated to carry out multiple and sometimes contradictory goals—to meet people's material needs as well as move them toward self-sufficiency. Not surprisingly, adequately and simultaneously meeting both goals has proven to be a thorny organizational issue. As a result, agencies in all three countries examined here have frequently established separate organizations for benefit assessment and the provision of employment-related services. This book therefore involves two parallel comparative organizational studies, with chapter-length cases of welfare eligibility workers in each of the three countries and separate chapters describing welfare-to-work (also known as "activation") programs and staff in each national setting.

In brief, it argues that there are significant cross-national differences in the policy orientations and administrative practices of social assistance programs. U.S. welfare policy[2] is rarely able to respond to individual claimant situations due to the constraints that the policy puts on those it asks to carry out its goals. More specifically, the bureaucratic organization of casework that predominates in the United States significantly hinders the ability of frontline staff to tailor support to individual need and assist their clients to become self-sufficient—rules constrain them, and service options are limited. In Sweden and Germany, by contrast, caseworkers have greater authority and more choices, giving them a substantial role to play in tailoring resources and services to the circumstances of recipients. This book demonstrates how the maintenance of responsiveness in these European public service organizations is institutionalized through nationally distinct legal foundations, professional traditions, and resource networks. It also shows how the chronic condition of inadequate resources can easily erode these organizational capabilities, often in ways that similarly reflect country-specific dynamics.

Methods

Case selection

This book addresses the question of how the organization of social assistance at the state level shapes the capacity of program caseworkers to provide client services. Thus, while the focus of the investigation is at the street level, the unit of analysis is the nation state.

Since each case study represents only one possible configuration of the political, economic, and administrative conditions under which welfare programs may operate in each nation, I chose sites that would illuminate well the effects and interactions of various institutional forces, and the potential trade-offs and pitfalls present within each system. Case study sites ideally needed to be organizationally developed, and therefore urban rather than rural (where administrative structures often occur in truncated forms because of their small scale). They couldn't be so poor that the agency and its staff were overwhelmed and had little opportunity to realize their programs' potential; nor could they be so rich that the trade-offs of providing individualized services with limited resources was only of limited programmatic concern. On a more pragmatic level, sites couldn't be so large that it would be too difficult for one researcher with limited resources to develop a working familiarity and overview of them. Given that I was studying organizations with which I had relatively little working familiarity, I chose locations with local researchers who studied social assistance policy. Their expertise in the policy area and their familiarity with the local system greatly facilitated my ability to develop the necessary background policy and linguistic knowledge, and to gain access to agency officials.

The U.S. case study consists of four counties in California—one urban southern county, one urban/rural mixed southern county, one urban northern county, and one rural northern county. These choices were a result of my involvement with the process study team for the California Work Pays Demonstration Project (CWPDP) conducted by the University of California Data and Technical Assistance (UC DATA) program at U.C. Berkeley (Snow et al. 1995; 1997). The project selected four counties along the distinctions of northern/southern California and urban/rural settings in order to obtain as diverse a sample as possible of local economic and political conditions. This was important in part because of California's unusual welfare program structure, in which counties are responsible for the administration of welfare services. As most of my U.S. data was collected as part of my CWPDP fieldwork, I have retained the four-county sample. This choice provides me a good overview of welfare practices within the state of California.

The German case study is the city of Bremen, a medium-sized city of 500,000 located in northwestern Germany near the border with Denmark. It is a "port" town (though most of it is 30 miles from the coast) that has never recovered from the downturn in the economy in the 1980s and consistently has one of the highest unemployment rates among former West German states. It is also politically left by German standards, being a social democratic stronghold. Bremen is an unusual political territory in being one of only three "city-states" (in a country with a total of 16 federal states). As such, local and state governmental functions are often merged, with policy responsibility falling to a centralized administrative agency. Given Bremen's autonomy, it represented a medium-sized German city in which I could obtain a good overview of the entire "state." At the same time, owing to its distinctive political and economic features it may not be the strongest representative of the "typical" German city, if such exists. I also chose Bremen due to the presence of a very active local research program on social assistance policy at the University of Bremen. Researchers at the Special Research Unit 186, Project D3—"Social Assistance Careers" had devoted considerable scholarly attention to Bremen's welfare population and program. In particular, Professor Stephan Leibfried, well known in this area, provided me with considerable assistance.

Administration for Bremen's government programs is divided into four city districts—South, East, North, and Middle West-though there are multiple offices in each part of the city. The welfare-to-work agency, Werkstatt Bremen, on the other hand, is more centralized, with one main office and two smaller branch offices. While I originally intended to survey offices in two districts in Bremen, I encountered considerable, unexpected difficulties even getting permission to do interviews with welfare caseworkers, so that most interviews occurred only in one district—Middle West, one of the poor harbor areas. In hindsight choosing Bremen, as well as necessarily relying on welfare interviews from a relatively poor district, places this case a little too far on the poor end of the spectrum. Program staff likely faced unusually difficult work conditions and therefore were less able to complete their work in all its complexity compared to other districts and cities.

The Swedish case study is the city of Malmö, the smallest of Sweden's three large cities, with a population of 250,000, located in the southern region of Skåne. It is large by Swedish standards, but more comparable in scale to the other case study sites, and closer in size to the large numbers of smaller cities (100,000–200,000) than Sweden's two largest cities (Gothenburg at 500,000 and Stockholm at over 1,000,000). It, too, is somewhat atypical in that it consistently has the highest unemployment and social assistance rates among big cities, as well as the highest proportion of immigrants in the country, at approximately 35 percent of the population. Here, too, I was able to utilize the resources and expertise of the nearby School of Social work at Lund University, with which I was affiliated. Professor Tapio Salonen, an expert in Swedish social assistance and my primary advisor, provided me with relevant literature and introductions into the welfare administration.

Welfare policy and funding in Sweden is predominantly the responsibility of municipal governments. In Malmö, administration and, to some extent, policymaking responsibilities are further devolved to the city district level, with ten separate district offices (and corresponding activation offices) in all, each with its own local political committee and varying economic conditions and recipient levels. I selected three city districts to investigate in-depth—two were among the three districts with the highest recipient populations in the city (Havdal and Boklunden), and one was considered a moderately impacted district (Lönnäng). While I intended to add a fourth relatively "light" district office with low recipient levels, I ran out of time at the beginning of May, when most regular caseworkers left for four to six weeks of vacation, leaving the offices filled with temporary workers. This lack is unfortunate, as this district would have perhaps provided an example of caseworkers more able to realize their social work potential.

Data collection and analysis

My sources of data were primarily interviews I conducted with caseworkers and administrators in their native languages and participant observations of caseworker-client interactions and office operations. The data for California was collected primarily in 1996 and 1997 with approximately 90 interviews and 70 observations. An additional 16 interviews were conducted in late 2000, with most occurring in one county. Data for Bremen, Germany, was collected from November 1999 to January 2000 and in May 2000 and consisted of approximately 40 interviews and 30 observations. The data for Malmö, Sweden, was collected in March through May 2000 and consisted of approximately 50 interviews and 15 observations (See appendix for more detailed breakdown). Interviews were semistructured and covered a variety of topics, including: education and employment history, perceived roles and functions, daily activities, interorganizational relationships, and areas of discretionary activity and decision-making criteria.

The data collection strategies differ somewhat between the U.S. and the European sites both in methods and dates. The data for California was largely collected earlier than the data for the European sites, being primarily from the CWPDP study. This California data was also considerably more extensive, occurring over a longer period of time, and with greater opportunity to do "naturalistic" observations. It was, in fact, from this detailed knowledge of California welfare programs that this cross-national project developed.

Typical of this kind of fieldwork, neither the officials I interviewed nor the clients I observed were randomly selected, creating limitations in terms of representativeness. Administrators selected the caseworkers. This selection could have resulted in some positive sampling bias, as the more competent or compliant staff were likely chosen to present the organization in the best possible light. Also clients could refuse to be observed (though only one ever did, in the United States). But being observed could easily change the nature of these caseworker-client interviews, which was sometimes readily apparent in the United States, for example, when caseworkers began to awkwardly discuss work-related policies with which they had little familiarity.

While I originally planned on conducting a balance of interviews and participant observations in the European offices, comparable to my U.S. fieldwork, the opportunities I had to observe caseworkers meeting with clients were limited in several program settings. In Bremen, the welfare-to-work agency (Werkstatt Bremen) was very amenable to my spending time with staff, while welfare caseworkers were incredibly difficult to gain access to even for interviews. Therefore, all German observations are of clients in the welfare-to-work agency context. In Sweden, on the other hand, caseworkers in both program settings were readily available. Welfare caseworkers, however, rarely met with clients, and many clients failed to attend their scheduled appointments. As a result, I was only able to observe five meetings. And because of time constraints I was only able to spend a few afternoons in two welfare-to-work group activity settings. Thus, caseworker interviews are the only consistent form of data collected across all sites and programs, and therefore, this book rests most solidly on caseworker descriptions of how they perform and understand their work.

Since my project was based primarily on qualitative data, I needed to be sufficiently fluent in the appropriate languages so that interviewees could express themselves as naturally and spontaneously as possible, and so that I could make full use of observations. I therefore studied German intensively before starting my European fieldwork and spent the first several months in Bremen becoming familiar with the technical language associated with welfare casework while developing a German questionnaire. In Sweden, I relied on my prior knowledge of Norwegian, and, with the help of a language tutor, I was able to communicate comfortably in Swedish and develop a Swedish questionnaire after six weeks.

In the United States, all interviews and observations were documented by handwritten notes written during the activity. Greater detail was filled in as soon as possible after the activity was concluded. These notes were later transcribed. The observations in the European cases were handled similarly. For the European interviews, all but four with staff in Bremen and Malmö were taped in order to give me the most opportunity to comprehend and guide conversations taking place in a foreign language. I translated and transcribed all Swedish interviews myself. Some German interviews were also translated/transcribed by me, but over half were completed by two graduate students, one a native German speaker and the other a doctoral student in the Berkeley German Studies department.

Using the initial framework of topics provided by the interview questionnaire, and with the aid of N5 (Nudist) qualitative software, I analyzed each interview separately to identify emerging themes around, for example, work conditions, discretion, and role perceptions. I then compared the information obtained for each individual to identify commonalities and variations among individuals and offices in each case study, writing memos for each key theme to condense the data to its most important aspects (Patton 2002). These analyses were also compared with information obtained from other sources, including observations, and secondary analysis of documents about office regulations. Out of these initial distillations, I developed the case studies for each country. In addition, I triangulated information by sending case study drafts with follow-up questions to selected informants for commentary. In the second step, I compared major themes across national sites in order to identify how the roles of caseworkers differed and how these differences related to nationally specific regulatory, structural, and cultural conditions. These ideas were then further refined and corroborated with relevant secondary literatures.

What a Cross-National Study of Street-Level Bureaucracy Can and Cannot Tell Us

There are many challenges to conducting a comparative study of social policy and administration, and therefore it is important to clearly set out the questions this project asks and the limitations to the answers it can provide. This book examines how individuals imbued with state authority in public organizations make decisions and complete their work, and what they do to, provide for, and require of citizens. And by doing so from a cross-national perspective, it tackles a more general question, namely, How are common issues raised by the plight of the able-bodied, nonworking poor dealt with politically and administratively in different national settings? This focus distinguishes it from policy research that is primarily concerned with claimants' experiences and interactions with social service agencies and staff (e.g., Edin and Lein 1997). While in some places caseworker-client observations were a significant part of the data collection, this was not consistent across all settings, and recipients' own perspectives were never assessed directly. Thus, any discussion of how differences in the organization of casework affect recipients must be largely indirect and speculative.

An emphasis on organizational processes also sets this book apart from research that is primarily about program outcomes or effectiveness (e.g., Behrendt 2002). While this book does refer to existing research on effectiveness, the "which is best" inquiry implies some consensus on the selection criteria (best at what?). As mentioned, social policy and its administration comprehend a wide variety of values, and it is the institutionalization of different trade-offs, specifically, between efficiency and responsiveness, that are of primary interest here. Additionally, a narrow inquiry into "effectiveness" overlooks the interesting ways in which the problems and solutions of these systems are not entirely equivalent. Differences in political traditions and economic systems can mean that a seemingly common goal such as "integration" is instituted through distinct normative orientations and policy instruments (Taylor-Gooby 2005). Whereas requiring job search for virtually the whole recipient population may be an acceptable choice in one national setting, it may be viewed as inappropriate and/or ineffective in another. "Thick" descriptions of the caseworker experience in different office settings provide a suitable and textured method for examining how values and goals become institutionalized in street-level processes.

But there are risks involved in attempting to identify national administrative styles based on examples limited to one site or area in each country. Such an approach presumes that many of the observed programmatic features transcend locality and therefore can give us a deeper insight into larger systems of governance and their impact on how caseworkers shape policy. Studying street-level bureaucracy, however, is necessarily about the processes that develop at the individual, interpersonal, and office level, and the danger is that key characteristics may turn out to be largely a product of locally specific conditions. Adding to this research challenge is the fact that social assistance is also more greatly shaped by subnational forces than many other policy areas. Policymaking and financing responsibilities are often devolved to local governmental levels, though to varying degrees in these three countries, leading to significant official variation within a country. Additionally, this has been a very dynamic policy area in all three countries, so things can change quickly.

Given these limitations, theoretically informed case studies can illustrate how broader institutional features—features corroborated by country-specific and comparative literatures—impact and come to be embodied in local program practices. For example, Bremen's welfare-to-work program, Werkstatt Bremen, illustrates, among other things, how sustained funding from the national employment office for job-creation schemes and the central role of public welfare organizations in civil society can lead to a highly developed sheltered employment sector that is a major feature of casework and service delivery there. The case does not imply that all German activation programs look like this; rather this program example emblematizes and concretizes crucial features of the German welfare state, features that appear in striking contrast when compared across cases.

Additionally, because the comparative approach requires the generation of relatively generalizable concepts, the researcher can reframe many intracountry differences in terms of nationally distinct policy problems or approaches to which localities represent variations in response. For example, on the welfare side, in the United States there are certainly big interstate differences in grant levels (varying by a factor of eight at one time), which is often pointed to as an indication of how diverse the policy environment is in the United States. But at the same time, there are significant common institutional features that emerge in juxtaposing the American system to the Swedish and the German systems, namely, an emphasis on programmatic control via a low-skill, bureaucratic, flat-grant system, highly fragmented means-tested programs, and a focus on documentation. Also, knowledge must begin somewhere, and scholarship is at an early enough stage that detailed case studies are still very significant (Yin 2003). Given such foundational work, subsequent scholarship could then look more closely at how such contextual influences varied within countries.

Findings and Book Overview

Chapter 2 provides a more detailed presentation of the theoretical context for this comparative study, discussing the issue of responsiveness in public organizations and the variable role frontline staff can play in providing client services. It also provides an overview of the comparative welfare state and social assistance policy literatures, demonstrating the contribution of this project to political economy and socio-legal scholarship. Chapters 3–5 each present a national case study of caseworkers in social assistance programs. Chapters 6–8 do the same for caseworkers in welfare-to-work/activation programs. Chapter 9 examines more systematically the factors affecting caseworker responsiveness in both welfare and activation program settings and the origins of some of the differences in administrative practices that have been presented in the case study chapters.

While each case study is based on regulatory and administrative conditions that existed in the late 1990s or 2000, I have utilized the present verb tense as much as possible for ease of reading. The final section of each chapter places the case study in a broader context through an overview and update of policy and practices in the particular country. Also, the reader can assume that, unless otherwise noted, all quotes come from caseworkers or their supervisors. Only when the speaker's role provides necessary context for the quote have I clarified the speaker's position.

Welfare caseworkers (chapters 3–5)

Welfare caseworker ability to make individualized assessments of claimant needs is a product of two important dimensions, legal authority and organizational capacity. Authority to be responsive reflects the extent to which a caseworker can consider particular claimant facts to ensure that need is met in the individual case. This concept tracks in some ways the bureaucratic-professional distinction that Mashaw (1983) and others (Nonet and Selznick 2001) have identified. The second dimension, organizational capacity, names the varying ability an agency has to enable caseworkers to utilize their discretion to make thoughtful, individualized assessments, while at the same time ensuring that decisions are legally correct, consistent, timely, and fiscally responsible. This dimension reflects the balance achieved between work requirements defined by regulations and the means available to agencies to help caseworkers meet them.

Where an organization has sufficient resources to develop skilled officials with adequate time and supervision, caseworkers can be expected to utilize their available discretion to take full consideration of agency rules in light of underlying programmatic goals. But as the gap widens between demands and resources, the more likely it is that staff will make superficial and error-prone decisions. Similarly, as caseworker discretion increases, so too do the resources required to facilitate and control this process. Too few resources will lead to increasing rates of unused or inappropriately-exercised discretion. Thus, increased caseworker responsiveness may be graphically represented along the diagonal of figure 1.1.

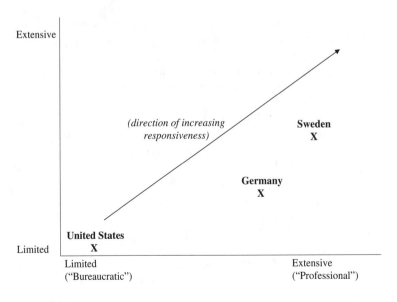

Horizontal Axis
Legal Authority for Responsive Decision Making: formal ability of caseworker to consider individual circumstances in assessing need

Vertical Axis
Organizational Capacity for Responsive Decision Making: ability of agency to enable and control official decision making

Figure 1.1   Comparing responsiveness among welfare caseworkers

In California (chapter 3), U.S. welfare caseworkers have neither the authority nor the resources to provide anything resembling individualized services. Caseworkers administer multiple, overlapping programs with complex and frequently changing regulations, primarily aimed at aiding only the "deserving" poor through low standardized grants. Quality control measures keep caseworkers focused on processing errors and detailed case documentation. Thus, in the United States, officials' restricted authority keeps their attention on managing regulatory complexity in the completion of routine eligibility tasks (see location in figure 1.1).

By contrast, both European programs are more explicitly intended to ensure recipients maintain a reasonable standard of living. This goal is operationalized through several programmatic features, including a two-tiered system of aid with a basic standard grant and a more discretionary area of one-time payments for exceptional expenses; a requirement that decisions be, in principle, individualized assessments; and full decision-making authority for officials after initial training. In each European case, legal frameworks, expertise, and work arrangements have evolved in nationally specific ways to contend with the challenges frontline discretion pose to program integrity.

In Bremen (chapter 4), the German approach involves considerable articulation and continual regulatory development to define the parameters of basic need. The administration of this complex set of rules is delegated to senior-level careerist public officials with extensive training in regulatory interpretation, an expertise and (top-down) basis of authority I call "regulatory entitlement scholarship." Granting recipients support for "special needs" and helping recipients access more secure, alternative forms of public support are central activities. The utilization of this discretion, however, is significantly constrained by the demands of their work. They contend with a unique level of regulatory complexity stemming from the continued generation of new guidelines for one-time payments; the unusually broad range of needs over which they have jurisdiction, including complicated areas of disability and institutional care; and the distinctly difficult task of identifying alternative, precedential forms of public support in Germany's larger social security system. With little staff specialization and no clerical support, caseworkers are also forced to address the full range of client demands, including many routine problems that absorb much of their time. However, recent policy reforms in Germany that transferred large numbers of recipients into a new national unemployment program and radically simplified the welfare benefit structure have likely brought work demands into better alignment with organizational capacity.

As in Bremen, Swedish caseworkers in Malmö (chapter 5) have the authority to consider the particular circumstances of claimants in determining levels of support. But by contrast, the Swedish approach is characterized by more limited regulatory codification. National regulations consist of a "frame law" of general principles, while most program guidelines are developed by local government with comparatively limited operational details. This challenge of "rule scarcity" is addressed through a reliance on the social pedagogical training of staff within a well-developed consultation culture, a (bottom-up) constitution of program authority that I call a "social work ethos." And, in general, they have greater organizational resources and opportunities to make individualized decisions. They administer a single program narrowly focused on daily living needs, and clerical staff conduct most routine assessments. Still, high caseloads and the increasingly administrative nature of their work have limited the ability of staff to make involved assessments and to utilize their social work training more directly in working with clients. Such constraints have contributed to short staff tenure, a situation that undermines the agencies' ability to maintain the integrity and effectiveness of its largely informal forms of guidance and control.

Activation caseworkers (chapters 6–8)

The central task of caseworkers in activation programs is to change client behaviors and capacities so that they become independent from welfare. Unlike eligibility workers, welfare-to-work caseworkers are ostensibly able to respond to client needs more dynamically. The capacity of activation staff to provide recipients with individualized services depends on two important dimensions: (1) the range of program offerings and (2) the nature of caseworker-client contact.

The variety of services affects the ability of staff to address recipients' particular needs and to offer choices that coincide with recipients' own interests and goals. Where there is a range of options and greater client choice, responsiveness is a more integrated aspect of casework. There is both the opportunity and necessity to interact with and assess clients in an in-depth manner in order to provide the most appropriate forms of assistance. Where offerings are limited, the caseworker's role is more routinized and bureaucratic, as evaluations require less information or involvement.

Opportunity for client contact affects caseworkers' ability to develop rapport with participants and become familiar with their particular situations. More frequent and continuous contact facilitates the ability of frontline staff to select and adapt intervention services to the changing situation of the

Table 1.1   Comparing responsiveness among activation caseworkers

Program offerings: range of options available to caseworker	Nature of client contact: opportunity to develop rapport and provide direct services	
	Processing (short-term contact) −	Engaging (longer-term contact) +
Extensive +	"Resource Broker" (medium)	"Counselor" (high)
Limited −	"Monitor" (low)	"Facilitator" (medium)

individual. A trusting relationship allows a caseworker to provide direct services in the form of motivation and counseling (skills allowing), addressing daily material and psychological struggles associated with making the transition to employment or study, thereby promoting client commitment to the process. Where client contact is infrequent, the capacity to identify a client's particular needs and interests and to have a personal impact is degraded.

The resulting 2 × 2 table has four quadrants that represent different caseworker roles and corresponding degrees of responsiveness (table 1.1). In a setting where a program has few offerings and client contact is restricted, the caseworker is limited largely to bureaucratic interactions, fulfilling the role of "monitor," and the capacity to respond to client needs is low. In a program that offers a wide array of activities and where the staff have the ability to meet with participants on an ongoing and frequent basis, caseworkers may function as "counselors," and their ability to provide individualized services is high. Where either one of these conditions is missing, the role of the caseworker is abridged. When program choices are limited but there is a longer-term contact, the caseworker performs the role of "facilitator." This cell in the table is an awkward one but may occur, for example, where recipients are required to participate in a standard, discrete activity, during which time they have frequent contact with the activity leader. And where there are a variety of options available, but client contact is short term, the caseworker acts only as a "resource broker," providing relatively individualized service, but hindered by limited contact and without a more meaningful personal connection.

The activation case studies highlight differences in the strategies different welfare states have pursued for "activating" their social assistance recipients. These nationally specific approaches arose from political choices that informed program ambitions, funding commitments, the creation of appropriate activation measures, and the corresponding development of organizational capacity to counsel clients and broker services. Different state institutions and labor market structures create different kinds of employment integration problems as well as different organizational actors with which an agency can coordinate provision of resources. Caseworkers are at the crux of these institutional forces, and the resources with which they are provided and the demands made of them determine the role they play in shaping policy.

Despite four decades in operation, activation programs in California (chapter 6) have remained largely limited to a narrow range of employment-related activities, due to little agency development during their first 30 years and current political demands for high participation rates in "work first" activities. As a result, the most readily available program options center on moving clients as quickly as possible into the low-skill, low-wage private sector service jobs produced in great numbers by a weakly regulated labor market. In this setting, activation caseworkers have a very limited role to play. Contact with clients is infrequent and primarily concerned with technical issues around support services and recipient noncompliance. Only a special set of caseworkers who run the job search activities have some opportunity to interact with clients on a more frequent and individualized basis; but their ability to respond to individual need is greatly circumscribed by the narrow focus of the program mandates and activities in which such contact happens.

As in California, most U.S. state welfare-to-work programs following federal welfare reform focused on a rapid expansion of a narrow range of short-term job readiness activities. In many instances this strategy required building large new service provider networks. Having little prior experience with this process, many states experienced significant implementation problems including poor service quality and high rates of improper sanctioning. This combination of a limited mix of program options that were nonetheless difficult to implement led to a situation of "complexity without variety."

In Bremen (chapter 7), chronic high unemployment has made labor market integration of welfare recipients a much more difficult task than in the United States, and agencies have had to turn to alternative routes to self-sufficiency, namely, placements in the nonprofit sector and vocational training programs. Despite this constricted economic context, activation caseworkers play a more substantive role in determining what services clients receive due to their social work training, the marginal role of regulation in their work, and their lack of responsibility for supportive services. What's more, a vast network of existing public welfare organizations, which have well-established ties with the activation agency that has been in operation for 15 years, creates opportunities for developing programs that are suitable to the interests and capacities of their clients.

Caseworker impact, though, differs between the two major program divisions (programs targeted to youths and programs targeted to adults) due to differences in resources and aims. Manageable caseloads (a result of a smaller recipient population and additional national funding for staffing) give caseworkers in the youth section (U27) the opportunity to develop familiarity and rapport with their clients. The program goals are also relatively modest—preparing clients to select and enroll in vocational programs that are readily available to this group due to national funding commitments and training entitlements for most youth. The 19.2 division caseworkers work toward placing older recipients in 1- to 2-year employment contracts in the "sheltered labor market." However, the limited resources of this purely locally funded program means that client demands far outstrip available placements. The resulting high caseloads severely limit caseworkers' contact with clients, reducing their work primarily to rapid brokering of contracts for the few participants they can help.

With the implementation of the so-called Hartz IV reform in 2003, however, all work-capable social assistance recipients have been incorporated into a new national unemployment benefit program. It remains to be seen how the new job centers, jointly managed by federal and local governments, will compare with the municipal activation programs like Werkstatt Bremen they have come to supersede.

Malmö's activation programs (chapter 8) had the least established form in 2000 due to their very recent establishment in the mid-1990s. Decentralized authority for program design among ten different offices (in a city of 250,000), along with a reliance on short-term local funding, has led to a very dynamic and chaotic development. Still, there were signs of a coalescing strategy in several districts toward large-scale programs with a wide variety of offerings. Practica in the large public sector are increasingly utilized to provide a range of work experience opportunities for recipients. Increased national funding for adult education, as well as the easy accessibility of inexpensive national student loans for higher education, have also made vocational counseling toward study another key integration strategy. A variety of in-house motivation courses and job search activities to take advantage of the recent upswing in the economy represents yet a third option clients can choose. The most important advance in activation institution-building in Sweden comes from recent national funding commitments allowing local agencies to combine their resources and expertise with those of the national Employment Office (EO) by co-locating staff with shared caseloads. Staff in currently operational programs of this nature have both a wide variety of activities to offer participants and the time and skills (being trained social workers) to become familiar with their clients' situations in order to offer direct individualized services.

2

Linking Welfare Caseworker Decision Making to State Institutions

Responsiveness in Public Programs—the Varying Role of the Caseworker and the Problem of "Legality"

Public benefits programs share common features with other large public bureaucracies that carry out many of the regulatory and distributive functions of modern life. Such organizations must balance a variety of policy purposes and values, both substantive and procedural, in a managerially complex structure. At least in principle, program administration is supposed to strive to be efficient, accurate, timely, consistent, and fair in its decision making, giving equal consideration to each claim, treating individuals in a humane and respectful way, and giving claimants as much information and participatory effect in the process as possible. The inscription of these procedural values presumably provides legitimacy to decision making, a fundamental requirement of "administrative justice" (Mashaw 1983). However, these organizing principles are often competitive in nature, so that trade-offs are inherent in organizing how services are provided and claims are processed.

An intrinsic dilemma in the organization of public programs is balancing the aims of distributing limited resources in the furtherance of social goals while meeting the particular needs of individual recipients, what Tweedie (1989) calls collective welfare and individual client orientations, respectively. How do agencies create frontline staff who respond to the particular situations of individual claimants, while at the same time safeguarding fiscal responsibility and procedural fairness? The regulatory and administrative challenge this balancing act represents concerns how frontline officials interpret rules and directives in light of the underlying goals of an institution. This "problem of legality" is one of "[establishing] procedures and attitudes that will prevent inconsistent and arbitrary decisions but that will also promote the rational adaptation of regulatory policies to the requirements of specific cases" (Kagan 1978, p. 85).

But the difficulty with creating responsive decision makers is not equal for all organizations. The nature of an organization's central function, its "critical task" (Johnson 1998), affects the role of frontline staff by determining the information demands made on them, their discretion for making decisions, and the nature of the contact they have with their clients. Organizations vary, for example, in the authorized responses they have to a claimant's situation. In the simplest case, the official makes a dichotomous (yes/no) decision, such as is approximated by eligibility decisions for the standardized cash grants of most public benefits programs. In contrast, where there exists a wider array of potential responses to a case situation, the official must select from among different alternatives that affect the quality and fit given a particular claimant's characteristics. This occurs, for example, when a social worker chooses among program providers for a child with special education needs (Adler 2000), or a prosecutor decides what charges to pursue against a defendant (Johnson 1998). Under such circumstances, staff need considerably more specific, nonstandard information about the available choices, the claimant, and how to match them most effectively.

The complexity and intractability of the problems organizations are mandated to address can also vary, therefore affecting the extent to which frontline staff intervene into individuals' private lives. A program may be intended, for example, to meet a particular need or maintain the well-being of a client, what Hasenfeld (1983) calls "people-sustaining" activities. Such is the case when community-based mental health teams provide medication and other supportive services to people with mental illness to help them remain in the community, or when a social security caseworker determines an applicant's eligibility for disability. For "sustaining" activities, clients are relatively passive, serving primarily as a source of information for frontline staff to collect and evaluate. The issue being addressed is relatively circumscribed and requires only limited interaction with individuals.

In contrast, an organization may be designed to alter a person's behavior, motivation, or other attributes (such as marketable skills), what Hasenfeld (1983) calls "people-transforming" activities. This is the case, for example, when a government agency enforces regulations requiring enhanced corporate environmental management and training (Bardach and Kagan 1982), or when an Alcoholics Anonymous program leader helps members achieve and maintain sobriety. Where an organization is not simply "providing things for someone," but rather "doing things to someone" (Glisson 2000), the intervention requires the direct participation of the targeted individual, so that outcomes are jointly produced in the interactions between frontline staff and claimants. The knowledge needed to change human attributes is incomplete because people are not inert or passive and may react in unanticipated ways (Meyers, Glaser, and MacDonald 1998). The attributes targeted for intervention also vary from person to person and may interact with other personal or environmental features in ways that cannot be readily isolated or controlled (Hasenfeld 1992). Transformative activities tend therefore to be more indeterminate in their effect and to require longer-term, more intensive interactions. Typically caseworker-claimant contact involves an iterative process of assessment, monitoring, and adaptation to the individual's changing response and situation.

The range of choices a caseworker has available to them and the nature of client contact can vary independently of one other.[1] This relationship can be summarized in a 2 × 2 table of the variable role officials can play in providing services in different kinds of organizations (table 2.1).

Table 2.1   Variable role of frontline staff based on organization's "critical task"

Organizational responses available to caseworker	Nature of client contact (organizational goal)	
	Short-term and one-sided ("sustaining claimant") (low)	Longer-term and dynamic ("transforming claimant") (high)
Wide repertoire of responses (high)	(moderate role) social assistance caseworker determining benefit adequacy (Germany, Sweden)	(significant role) activation caseworker facilitating client participation in range of activities (Germany, Sweden)
	*staff maintaining person with mental illness in community *caseworker selecting services for a child with special educational needs	*Alcoholics Anonymous leader helping individuals achieve sobriety *regulatory official enforcing regulations requiring enhanced corporate management and training
Limited repertoire of responses (low)	(minor role) social assistance caseworker determining benefit eligibility (United States)	(moderate role) activation caseworker monitoring client participation in job search activities (United States)
	*caseworker determining eligibility for disability	*regulatory official enforcing effluent limits for routine technology

Organizations whose critical tasks are relatively "simple" (where front-line staff play a correspondingly minor independent role) can be organized according to a "bureaucratic rationality model" (Mashaw 1983) that emphasizes accuracy, consistency, and cost efficiency through the hierarchical organization of work and a well-developed system of rules that limit caseworker discretion. But as activities become more complex and require more substantive engagement with clients, relying on rules to calibrate frontline decisions eventually comes up against organizational and cognitive limits, where neither caseworkers nor supervisors can adequately attend to additional guidelines (Diller 2000). Rather, there tends to be a greater reliance on frontline judgment (Kagan 2006). In some cases this dependence involves a formal delegation of authority justified by particular expertise (such as social work training), a basis of decision making that Mashaw refers to as the "professional model" of program legitimacy.[2]

In others, often in spite of efforts to institute a bureaucratic organization, the conditions of work lead to the de facto devolution of some discretion to frontline staff in how they perform their jobs. In such "street-level bureaucracies" (Lipsky 1980), which include most human service organizations (like welfare offices), organizational rules and goals are often ambiguous or even at odds with one another. Limited resources generally preclude completion of all tasks, and administrators have difficulty monitoring and evaluating caseworker performance because much of the information about their decisions and interactions with clients is filtered through the caseworkers themselves.

Greater reliance on individual caseworkers' judgments for implementing program goals makes it more difficult for an organization to ensure the integrity of the process. Frontline behavior can more readily degenerate into unrestrained discretion and runaway costs than in an organization in which hierarchy and regulations are able to govern worker behavior. Responsiveness can also fall victim to shortcuts, as organizational tasks that require such nuanced decision making are more sensitive to the conditions under which work is performed.[3] Where resources are inadequate, workers often develop simplifying procedures to cope with the demands placed on them, including redefining client needs to align with more immediate, attainable goals (Brodkin 2006) and limiting client interaction to the extraction of information necessary for the completion of paperwork (Brodkin 1997; Hagan 1987; Lipsky 1980).

Characterizing responsiveness

Organizations can function more or less effectively as adaptive institutions depending on officials' orientation to rules and program purposes.

The most responsive "culture of rule application" incorporates both rules and goals into the decision-making process (table 2.2, modified from Kagan 1978 and Meyers, Glaser, and MacDonald 1998). Ideally case assessment is a two-step process: (1) "looking backward"—determining which rules apply to a given fact pattern, utilizing the concepts and definitions provided in the rules and through analogies; (2) "looking forward"—determining the consequences of applying the appropriate rules as conventionally understood and whether issues of fairness or other public policy issues warrant against it. Where the current rule interpretation seems inappropriate, officials decide whether creating an exception is worth the costs involved—including a more complicated interpretive framework, threats to consistency, future resulting expenditures, and legitimacy erosion.[4] This "judicial mode" of decision making makes it possible for organizational members to adapt rules "to produce the results that are consonant with [an institution's] purposes" (Kagan 1978, p. 90). Less responsive, "deviant" modes of rule interpretation can also occur in three other forms, depending on whether the rules, the organizational goals, or both are disregarded in the process. "Legalism" occurs where staff focus exclusively on the conventional meanings of rules and procedures without considering how decisions relate to a program's primary objectives, referred to elsewhere as "goal displacement" (Blau 1963). "Unauthorized discretion" occurs when decision makers focus entirely on program purposes with little regard for procedural propriety. And "retreatism" occurs where officials avoid making decisions altogether or do so on entirely personal grounds, such as personal gain or convenience.

In organizations where the central task involves engaging clients and/or providing the appropriate resources, orientation to rules is less central. The deliberations of frontline staff increasingly shift from rule interpretation to direct considerations of how well assessment and choice of intervention take client needs and interests into account, in light of organizational goals. This change in the mode of reasoning reflects a shift in organizational function from one of "enforcing laws" to one of "solving problems" (Bardach and Kagan 2002, p. xxi). Utilizing a table from Meyers, Glaser, and MacDonald (1998) depicting how information on "work first" welfare reform policies was conveyed by welfare caseworkers (the organizational goal in this case), we see the conceptual correspondence to Kagan's table. For example, transformational interactions were ones in which caseworkers informed clients about work and self-sufficiency and did so in a way that individualized the message, helping clients to understand how the new policies applied to their particular situation.[5]

Table 2.2   Modes of decision making

Organizational goals pursued (Kagan)/(*Meyers*)	Rules followed (Kagan)/ *High personalization* (*Meyers*)	
	−	+
+	Legalism/ *Routinized*	Judicial/ *Transformational*
−	Retreatism/ *Instrumental*	Unauthorized discretion/ *Particularistic*

The Special Administrative Case of Social Assistance

Needs assessment

In most public income programs, contending concerns of individualization and accountability can be reasonably managed by organizing work along traditional Weberian lines, as eligibility is relatively unproblematic, both as a technical issue and as a political one. Most benefit programs have comparatively clear "event criteria" (such as old age, disability, and unemployment) and a solid foundation for claiming public resources, either through prior contribution or recognized incapacity to work. And most of these programs also have bounded support purposes, generally consisting of standardized amounts for future income loss, sidestepping the more complicated issue of whether the grant level is sufficient (Ochoa 1997). Responsiveness and administrative control are fairly easy to achieve concurrently, as information and interpretive requirements can be relatively standardized and are amenable to routine, verifiable procedures for decision making.

Social assistance, or "welfare," though, differs markedly from mainstream income programs in terms of its basis for entitlement and underlying social welfare function. Those who receive welfare are deemed able-bodied but insufficiently employed or entitled to be self-sufficient. Lacking any of these more stable bases of entitlement instigates significant political attention to claimants' personal responsibility for their plight and leads to considerable regulatory and administrative efforts to define "genuine need." As a result, eligibility determination is generally more comprehensive and intricate than for other income programs because the adequacy of all other sources of support must be evaluated. Documentation requirements may also be considerable, reflecting less trust in claimants' statements as compared to less stigmatized programs. Regulations often also further restrict support to a subset of the income poor based on other "deserving" characteristics, such as having a dependent child. And recipients are often required to fulfill behavioral requirements associated with "help to self-help" and other aspects of "good citizenship."[6]

As the "program of last resort" welfare also becomes, in effect, the minimum level of support provided by society to its members. Its purpose is therefore both more fundamental and more contested than for other support programs, being directly tied into larger debates about individual desert, the distribution of resources and opportunities among groups, and government's responsibility for the inclusion of citizens in societal life. Given such a nebulous and readily contested underlying program function, determining the conditions of appropriate support in the individual case can be a complex political and administrative task.

One way to simplify the organizational work of providing social assistance is to offer set benefits based on the typical needs for a household of a given size. Establishing a flat grant system allows program delivery (and decision making) to be organized along bureaucratic lines, with caseworkers possessing little independent authority over how they make decisions or in the kinds of support they can provide, having been effectively reduced to "technicians." This is the program design followed in the United States and is the reason for its location in the lower left quadrant of table 2.1. A welfare caseworker in California, for example, is primarily concerned with ensuring claimants provide all appropriate documentation to establish eligibility. Amounts are determined by legislated schedules, mechanically calculated from clear criteria like prior income. A family of three could receive a maximum cash grant of $723 in 2005, regardless of their particular circumstances. The issue of the *sufficiency* of aid is beyond the caseworker's purview.

Decoupling benefit eligibility from benefit adequacy presumably provides greater program predictability and control (though as we shall see in the U.S. case, other programmatic features seriously undermine this capacity). The price, though, is less assurance that claimants receive adequate benefits appropriate for their particular situations. Where benefit levels are set at a low level, many individuals do not get what they actually need. As standard benefit levels are increased, more individuals get what they need, but many also get more than they need, increasing fiscal costs and creating a looming moral hazard problem[7] as the grant amount begins to approach entry-level wage rates. Thus, giving officials substantial discretion over the amount paid to recipients is another approach to organizing aid assessment. Wide discretion over aid is characteristic of many southern European welfare programs. Such program conditions, though, lead to wide variations in eligibility criteria and benefit levels, as caseworkers tend to allocate benefits based on ad hoc criteria and personal judgments (Garcia and Saraceno 1998). Such an institutional design fails to provide even the most rudimentary procedural protections of modern legal institutions (Nonet and Selznick 2001).[8]

An intermediate institutional strategy that incorporates legal safeguards while also acknowledging that "in individual cases life plays very different melodies,"[9] is to create a two-tiered system with a rule-bound, standard grant level ensuring some basic level of support for the typical case, and a second, discretionary level of support available for exceptional needs. Authorizing frontline officials to provide for the unusual needs of particular claimants (above the standard grant) would better ensure that eligible recipients achieve some actual minimum standard of living. Increased individualization, however, also makes a bureaucratic organization of work a more problematic fit. Both the goal (benefit adequacy rather than eligibility) and the means for achieving the goal (idiosyncratic rather than standardized claimant information) are more ambiguous and complex.

Both German and Swedish social assistance programs employ this more difficult, two-tiered design, and it is for this reason that they appear in the upper left quadrant of table 2.1. In both countries welfare caseworkers are charged with ensuring clients maintain "a reasonable standard of living," and program decisions must be based, in principle, on individualized assessments. In their daily work, then, caseworkers must contend with complex issues of benefit adequacy. For example, When should a client be granted a special allowance for a winter coat, a child's bike, or a washing machine? When does the possibility of improving a client's employment prospects justify providing additional public funds? Would financing a recipient to take a truck driver's course be an appropriate investment even if it cost several thousand dollars?

"Help to self-help"

Welfare is intended to be only a temporary means of support, and while there are often a wide range of personal and structural reasons individuals come to rely upon it, there is an implicit programmatic assumption that people often need to be made to help themselves. Social assistance policies address the behavior of recipients to a greater extent than programs in any other area of social security (Bradshaw and Terum 1997), and this additional, more in-depth focus on claimants' situations further highlights welfare's exceptionality.

Changing client outcomes generally requires a different kind of skill and knowledge base than welfare caseworkers have and a more sustained kind of interaction with clients than staff are generally able to develop in an eligibility-oriented setting (Jewell and Glaser 2006; Meyers, Glaser, and MacDonald 1998; Hvinden 1994).

Moving people toward self-sufficiency can necessitate an involved and flexible worker-client relationship—to evaluate a recipient's capacities, interests, and needs; to develop adequate rapport in order to counsel and motivate them; and to identify and coordinate services, from childcare to education, that are typically under the jurisdiction of a wide variety of organizations. The complexity and improvisational nature of providing and brokering services in an individualized manner make it difficult to carry out such activities in a heavily regulated organizational setting, as meeting procedural requirements can easily become a substitute for organizational goals (Blau 1963; Simon 1983; Brodkin 1997). The recognition of the difficulties in providing both "cash" and "care" by the same officials has generally led agencies to establish separate programs with activation caseworkers whose sole purpose is getting people off welfare.

The entrance of local government into the area of employment policy has occurred in many countries in part because of the limited ability of national and state employment offices to assist the unemployed who receive social assistance, a population whose financial needs fall more heavily on local government (Salonen and Ulmestig 2004; Empter and Frick 2000). Insufficient employment office resources often result in preferential assistance for those with unemployment insurance entitlements. Employment office services also tend to be targeted to those with marketable skills and recent employment histories; welfare recipients as a group are generally "further from the labor market," requiring more substantial forms of intervention, which employment offices do not traditionally offer.

As a result, local welfare agencies often face a distinct set of challenges in moving recipients off the rolls and into work. They contend with a recipient population with a wide range of needs—behavioral, educational, physical—and many of the necessary resources and services must be developed through collaboration with other kinds of organizations, often requiring them to overcome significant interorganizational barriers created by differences in funding streams, target populations, and organizational cultures.

Developing activation services raises different kinds of trade-offs than providing material support, due to their nonessential (optional) nature and the uncertainties inherent in interventions meant to change people's behavior. Services themselves are expensive to develop, yet they may not improve participants' prospects of finding employment. There are, in addition, the administrative costs associated with monitoring and ensuring the quality and consistency of in-house and contracted-out services, as well as matching clients with appropriate programs. Administrators must also be sensitive to recipients' capacities to meet program demands, as sanctioning for behavioral noncompliance can have serious consequences. One way of dealing with these trade-offs is to limit a program's focus to facilitating recipients' efforts to find employment directly, the so-called labor market attachment (LMA) approach (Trickey 2000). In this way, the costs and risks of providing expensive, potentially ineffective, and difficult-to-manage services are largely avoided. The market itself becomes the means for assessing people's employment prospects as well as the primary provider of "services" in the form of wage work. The California case represents an example of the LMA approach, with the primary program option being "Job Clubs" to help clients search for employment. The emphasis on this program component makes U.S. activation a transformative effort, but with a very limited repertoire (lower right quadrant in table 2.1). A caseworker in a California welfare-to-work office would have a correspondingly limited role to play in moving people off the roles, primarily by monitoring their clients' independent job search activities. At least in principle this standardized approach is an efficient way to implement general self-help obligations among welfare recipients. There is obviously less assurance that claimants receive services that address their particular problems or that help them achieve long-term economic self-sufficiency.

An alternative service model involves a broader programmatic focus on education and social integration, an acknowledgment that for some people a move directly into work is unrealistic, the so-called "human resource development" (HRD) approach (Trickey 2000). Both Bremen and Malmö provide a considerably wider range of program options, including training, education, and job placements, though also in both cases to a smaller percentage of the recipient population. These HRD-focused programs, therefore, have greater capacity to provide services tailored to participants' particular needs and interests, and caseworkers play a more substantive role in identifying and providing clients appropriate services. As a result, activation programs in both countries are located in the upper right quadrant of table 2.1. Achieving this goal often requires staff to function as counselors, to help their clients articulate their interests and goals, address personal problems as they arise and, when necessary, remind them of their obligations to participate. At the same time, they must identify and, in some cases, develop a wide range of career preparation and work experience programs that give clients opportunities to develop vocational interests, learn social skills and work habits, and become more confident. This resource-brokering function can require maintaining close ties with an extensive network of nonprofit, governmental, and private employment organizations in a variety of occupational areas, including construction, gardening, restaurant work, metalwork, retail services, and health care.

Linking Macro (Political Economy) and Micro (Administration/Social Policy) Literatures

Explaining how the organization of welfare at the state level affects how caseworkers make decisions and deliver services draws on many disparate areas of scholarship—political economy, U.S. welfare administration, comparative social policy. Each literature provides insights about institutions and processes that are important in any effort to situate and link street-level operations to their larger national and regime context.

Welfare state regimes

The choice of the three countries for this book emerged out of a large comparative literature of the welfare state. This scholarship points to significant differences in the availability, generosity, and equality of benefits provided by different states' social security systems and in the impact of state institutions and policy choices on the structuring of labor markets. An early effort to distinguish different kinds of state-society relationships is provided by Titmuss (1970) who identified three different functions of social policy, a framework that would prove influential in subsequent comparative scholarship. A "residual" state intervenes only when people are unable to help themselves, for example, only after market and family breakdown. In a "handmaiden" state, policy serves other institutions, so that need is met on the basis of merit, work performance, and productivity. In the most substantive form, an "institutional-redistributive" state is a major, integrated institution in society, providing universal services on the basis of need.

Esping-Andersen applied Titmuss's model in *The Three Worlds of Welfare Capitalism* (1991). In this work he distinguished among welfare states on the basis of "decommodification," that is, on the extent to which they freed individuals from a primary identification as a commodity by assisting them to live at a socially acceptable level without having to rely on the selling of their labor. This concept was operationalized as an aggregate score of the availability, generosity, and equality of pension, disability, and unemployment benefits. Countries clustered into three groups based on their decommodification scores, with high scorers being primarily Scandinavian countries (the "Social Democratic" regime), middle scorers, continental Europe (the "Conservative" regime), and low scorers, primarily the Anglo-Saxon world (the "Liberal" regime). Esping-Andersen posited these clusters as embodying the three different roles of the state that Titmuss had identified. These differences were, in turn, seen to directly structure labor markets by setting the conditions of entry and exit.

The *Liberal* welfare state (of which the United States is a member) is characterized by a minimal, residual role in society. Eligibility for public support is based on a restrictive interpretation of need. Market outcomes are allowed to persist, with only limited, usually targeted, state intervention. Insurance against most disruptions to working life is acquired through private provision in the market. Liberal states are therefore distinguished by a large number of private pension systems and a heavy emphasis on means-tested benefits.

The *Conservative* welfare state (of which Germany is a member) is characterized primarily by the maintenance of occupational status. Eligibility is based on contribution. Funding is primarily through employer and employee contributions to a large number of occupationally based funds, with benefit levels maintaining the status and wealth of one's occupation. The state's welfare role emphasizes income transfers rather than service provision, reflecting the Catholic value of "subsidiarity." Caring service, in the Catholic model, is to be provided primarily by the family and to some extent by private charitable organizations. Thus, workers are explicitly conceived as male breadwinners earning a family wage.

The *Social Democratic* welfare state (of which Sweden is a member) is characterized by universal benefits based on citizenship status, redistributive income policies, generous replacement rates, and relative equality among benefit levels. The social democratic state is also committed to full employment policies for both men and women, which has resulted in a distinct set of government responsibilities, in particular, a highly developed system of public employment and service provision and active labor market policy measures.

Esping-Andersen's work spawned a large comparative welfare state literature that developed and complicated his "three worlds" framework. For example, scholars found that states often took alternative working class or welfare state strategies that could be effective at reducing inequality, both by reducing pre-tax and transfer inequality through labor market policies and by targeted benefits (Bonoli 1997). Other researchers have investigated the role the welfare state has played in structuring women's autonomy both in the family and in the market (e.g., Orloff 1993; Lewis 1992; Sainsbury 1994; Gustafsson 1994; Gornick, Meyers, and Ross 1997). While the analytic utility of this typology has been qualified to some extent (e.g., Abrahamson 1999), the notion of the "three worlds" has endured.

Because social assistance recipients generally represent state/family/market failures, there is an evident relationship between the larger welfare state program environment and social assistance. The more protective the rest of the social security system is, the fewer the recipients on social assistance. Thus, for example, in liberal welfare states, where the safety net is relatively thin, the salience of welfare (in terms of the percentage of population receiving it and its proportion of social security expenditures) is much higher. Existing comparative literature (Eardley et al. 1996) also demonstrates different "tendencies" in terms of standard welfare benefit levels provided by countries from different welfare state regimes, with social democratic countries being the most generous, liberal ones tending to be the most meager, and conservative types lying somewhere in the middle, though these correlations are not entirely consistent.[10] But whether there exists more specific relationships between the organization of welfare and national or welfare regime context is unclear.

Varieties of capitalism, skill formation regimes

Other scholarship has examined the welfare state in broader, political economy terms, analyzing how a variety of interlocking financial, industrial, and vocational institutions affect the incentive structures and strategies of business firms in different national settings. This "Varieties of Capitalism" (Hall and Soskice 2001) approach distinguishes between "liberal market economies" (LMEs) in which market and hierarchical arrangements prevail, and "coordinated market economies" (CMEs) where more collaborative arrangements play a significant role in how economic actors interact.

In brief, in CMEs (primarily northern and western Europe and Japan), dense networks of relationships in which firms are embedded, including business associations, labor unions, and cross-shareholding among companies, facilitate sustained cooperative behavior among economic actors due to their capacity for information exchange, monitoring, and sanctioning. As a result, financing is generally geared toward long-term performance, technology is often produced and shared through intercompany arrangements, and production processes depend on a skilled workforce. These features provide firms from these countries with "comparative institutional advantages" (CIA) in particular types of production in global trade, namely those based on established areas of technology in which the market share is based on high quality and continuous incremental improvements and product differentiation (so-called diversified quality production [Streeck 1991]).

By contrast in LMEs (the Anglo-Saxon countries), where associational institutions are limited and market mechanisms of coordination predominate, financial incentives are geared toward short-term profitability, companies can readily acquire new technologies through the purchasing of other firms, and labor can be hired and fired with relative ease. Such a combination of factors allows firms to take advantage of new technologies by mobilizing resources rapidly and to adapt large organizations to new product lines and strategies. At the same time, weak labor market protections are also favorable to the production of standardized goods and services that depend upon lower labor costs.

From this perspective, social policy can act to support and reinforce development of particular skill profiles in the workforce by shoring up commitments among economic actors, with CMEs having institutionalized specific-skill systems and LMEs general-skill systems (Estevez-Abe, Iversen, and Soskice 2001).[11] Skills that are specific to a particular firm or industry are risky for both employers and employees to invest in because of the uncertainty of future employment or income loss based on that investment. Employment protections (in the form of job security legislation and company policies) enforce employer commitment to retain hired workers. Unemployment policies (reflected in high replacement ratios and narrow suitable job definitions) protect a worker's high-skill wages even when the worker is out of a job. Income protection through wage-determination systems similarly provides assurance against a serious drop in wages for particular skills. Specific-skill systems are associated with and supported by developed vocational systems in which business associations and labor unions collaborate to ensure high quality, consistent training programs, as well as good employment prospects for graduates. In countries without such protections, individuals are better off investing in general skills that are transferable between jobs. Educational systems in these countries similarly reinforce this pattern of human capital development with limited vocational and company training but a highly developed system of general, university-level education (Iversen 2005).

These differences in labor market and vocational features have a significant impact on the employment opportunities of individuals who are academically weak. In specific-skill countries, vocational schools provide an alternative educational system for young adults not able to or interested in university education. For weaker students in general-skills countries, by contrast, there is little opportunity to acquire useful training outside of the education system. Poorly performing students therefore tend to have fewer opportunities to acquire marketable skills and much lower income levels in LMEs than in CMEs. Given the poor educational levels of most of those on welfare, these educational resources may be a significant feature of welfare-to-work program efforts in specific-skills countries (such as Germany and Sweden). In general-skills countries where such education systems are neither well developed nor central to labor market entry at the lower end, we could expect education to be less relevant or important in welfare-to-work approaches.

The post-industrial service sector trilemma

Since the 1970s there has been a gradual, but inexorable shift in the developed world from manufacturing to the service sector as the driving force of economic growth. Many explanations have been given for this change, including increased productivity and resultant market saturation, international competition from countries with lower labor costs, as well as affluent societies' increasing demand for services. While global trade facilitated the development of an international division of labor between manufacturing firms in different countries, most services remain largely restricted to domestic markets. The limited demand, as well as the generally lower productivity and the more labor-intensive nature of most services, means that private sector service growth is significantly impacted by associated labor costs. Where coordinated wage-setting institutions have tended to keep low-skilled workers' wages comparatively high, this shift in the economy has created a steeper trade-off between employment growth and wage equality.

Anglo-Saxon, Scandinavian, and continental European countries responded to the transition to a post-industrial economy in different ways, pursuing policies that in each case were able to meet two of the three goals of employment growth, wage equality, and budgetary constraint that Iversen and Wren (1998) have characterized as the "service sector trilemma." These different approaches also further reinforced the distinct trajectories they have taken. Liberal economies, such as the UK and the United States, already characterized by low levels of labor market protections, continued a strategy of labor market deregulation as well as a weakening of union power. Such market clearing efforts have enabled the low-skilled, low-paid private sector to grow dramatically, but at the same time has allowed wage inequality to continue to grow and remain at the extreme of Organisation for Economic Co-operation and Development (OECD) countries.

Scandinavian/Social Democratic countries responded through an expansion of government-funded caring services. This strategy provided both the means for women to juggle their responsibilities as mothers and workers and good-paying, protected state jobs that helped keep unemployment low and labor force participation rates among the highest in the world (as well as among the most gender segregated). Further public employment growth, though, is no longer a viable strategy, due to the significant financial burden it already places on government budgets.

By contrast, in Continental countries with strong Christian Democratic parties, expanding public employment was neither fiscally nor politically acceptable, as policymakers were reluctant to expand government involvement in the traditional jurisdiction of family and charitable service providers. Instead, unemployment was managed through retirement and disability programs that facilitated early exits of older workers. While this strategy helped alleviate some of the most immediate employment pressures, it did not address the underlying problem of high labor costs, resulting in tenaciously high levels of chronic unemployment.

In the last decade, there have been some common policy efforts to encourage low-skilled private service sector growth while protecting workers from extreme poverty wages, for example, by deregulating part-time and temporary employment, reducing the labor costs for low-wage jobs, and introducing tax credits for low-wage earners. However, during the 1990s these strategies have had little impact on most European economies where there has been virtually no employment growth. As a result, the differences in the volume and distribution of employment between regimes have largely continued, and the differences and gaps between regime clusters persist. This combination of similar recent policy approaches with continued national differences has been referred to by Iversen (2005) as "lasting divergence with convergences at the margins" (p. 263).

These differences in economic environments and labor market structures have implications for activation programs because the policy instruments for achieving client self-sufficiency look quite different between, for example, a context of high chronic unemployment (in Bremen) and one with low unemployment and a growing low-skilled service sector (in Southern California). How these features of labor market systems become articulated in program practices and casework, though, has not been well documented.

Social assistance policy and administration

Public assistance is a highly stigmatized and conditional form of public support. Nowhere has its low status been more evident than in the United States where there exists a large body of scholarship that has charted and problematized its controversial development (e.g., Handler and Hollingsworth 1971; Piven and Cloward 1971; Brodkin 1986; Bane and Ellwood 1994; Handler 1997; Munger 1998; Riccucci 2005; Lurie 2006). Yet these studies have focused on U.S. agencies and therefore have been limited in their ability to connect national culture, institutional history, and agency organization to ground-level practice.

Growing caseloads of social assistance programs in most Western welfare states in the last two decades have resulted in increased political attention to and research interest in social assistance policy more generally, with comparative studies beginning to appear in the 1990s (Lødemel and Schulte 1992; Eardley et al. 1996; Garcia and Saraceno 1998; Puide and Minas 2001). Because social assistance programs have many operational and politically changeable details, though, efforts to classify them based on similar administrative or policy dimensions have been difficult (Gough et al. 1997). For example, the survey of 24 OECD countries by Eardley et al. (1996) led to eight distinct groupings.[12] While the United States, Germany, and Sweden remained in different social assistance categories,[13] many countries from the three welfare state regimes fell into other categories, sometimes with countries from two or more worlds grouped together.

Greater conditioning of welfare receipt on explicit self-help efforts has also emerged as an important recent policy development in most OECD countries (Handler 2004; Van Voorhis and Gilbert 2001; Lødemel 2000; Trickey 2000; Hanesch, Stelzer-Orthofer, and Balzter 2001).[14] However, there are no definite trends as to whether the new programmatic focus is on increasing recipient opportunities or on simply discouraging receipt in order to reduce expenditures. A few key dimensions along which activation programs vary have been identified, including centralized/decentralized program design and range of program offerings. But, as might be expected in a policy area generally less than a decade-and-a-half old, wide variations were observed in strategies and coverage with no correspondence to any traditional welfare state classifications (Lødemel 2000).

These comparative studies of social assistance and activation provide important information about how policy choices and administrative structures vary cross-nationally. But there are several limitations to most such comparative projects. They generally rely on separate contributions from experts describing individual countries. As a result the country chapters often do not have the same kind of information, and there is no one person familiar with all cases. These studies also tend to rely on policy descriptions rather than information about actual office practices. And in covering anywhere between 7 and 24 countries, it becomes difficult to synthesize information across so many cases. As a result, conclusions tend to be few or relatively general in nature.

This book addresses many of these limitations through a smaller, more in-depth comparative approach. In recognizing that it is often at the point of delivery where we see how welfare states actually work and how they work differently, it utilizes street-level observations and interviews in addition to policy-level data. It also looks at social assistance as a whole, examining how program officials contend with complicated issues raised both by needs assessment and the promotion of recipient self-sufficiency. Most importantly, the choice of three countries from distinct political traditions provides a manageable sample with sufficient variation to enable the articulation of how broader state policy relates to day-to-day office practices in regime-specific ways.

3

Welfare Caseworkers in California, the United States: Eligibility Technicians and the Regulation of Desert

> Why can't I ever get hold of my caseworker?
> You don't have a caseworker anymore, you have eight.[1]

Introduction

Historically, targeted, means-tested programs have been a dominant policy response in the American welfare state, with its emphasis on distinguishing between the deserving and the undeserving poor (Esping-Andersen 1991; Skocpol 1988). The development of the welfare state since the time of the New Deal has involved, in part, a movement toward greater inclusion of vulnerable populations into the more generous, protected, and federalized social security programs, in particular the disabled and the elderly. In contrast, general protection for the able-bodied nonelderly has always been comparatively weak, with limited government involvement in the funding or direct provision of childcare, the development or coordination of employment and training programs, or the design of unemployment insurance (Weir 1988).

Similarly, American social assistance is a fragmented and contingent form of entitlement. In contrast to Germany, Sweden, and most other developed countries that have instituted a single comprehensive cash-assistance program for the income poor, in the United States there are multiple, partial forms of assistance. The program traditionally identified as "welfare" is the state-based income program for families with dependent children, Temporary Aid to Needy Families (TANF). Agency officials in TANF offices are also responsible for assessing eligibility for a variety of other targeted programs, the two most important being a federal food voucher program, Food Stamps,[2] and federal health insurance for the poor, Medicaid.

For claimants without disabilities and without children, the only available income support is the more meager and stigmatized benefits provided by some localities, known as General Relief. As a result, entire segments of the population who are poor—namely, single adults and childless couples—do not have an entitlement to cash aid in much of the United States. Given that these groups (especially young, single adults) often make up the majority of the recipient population in most European programs (including Germany and Sweden), this is a significant baseline difference between American and European welfare programs.

In an earlier era, American welfare caseworkers had considerably more discretion in how they made support decisions, and there was even a brief effort to professionalize its administration as the domain of social work. However, frontline discretion came to be seen as the cause of exclusionary practices as well as unauthorized generosity. A confluence of political and legal forces in the face of rising caseloads in the late 1960s led to the transformation of the welfare program into a highly regulated and bureaucratic endeavor. As a result of these reform efforts, issues of benefit adequacy were removed from street-level jurisdiction leaving caseworkers focused primarily on assessing when claimants were entitled to standardized grants. Extensive regulations minimized caseworker discretion and provided agencies with clear information for evaluating the correctness of decisions. Claimants were held to a high burden of proof, requiring the submission of very specific kinds of documentation in order to verify their assertions of need. And reassessments were made monthly, so support was provided only as long as and to the extent recipients were legally eligible.

Such a well-developed system of legal constraints would seem to represent a finely tuned administrative apparatus for distributing limited resources to assist the truly needy, but several systemic problems plague the American arrangement. Benefits are generally inadequate and do a poor job of tracking actual need, and the discretion states have to define their own benefit levels results in large inter-state variations. A comparative study of social assistance policy (Eardley et al. 1996) found that social assistance for most family types in the United States varied between 10 and 80 percent below the OECD average.[3] The regulatory burden also significantly hinders caseworkers from fully performing their so-called technical role of case processing. Each of the multiple programs caseworkers administer has its own set of complex regulations with different requirements for different kinds of partial aid. And the complex distinctions that are made between the deserving and undeserving income poor require a demanding *degree* of assessment.

In combination with high caseloads and inadequate frontline training, agencies struggle to ensure that officials make legally correct eligibility assessments. Procedural checklists and forms facilitate structuring casework into discrete activities. Worker specialization and automation also give organizations some ability to limit the range of knowledge and variety of tasks with which individual frontline workers contend. At the same time, the high level of routinization that results also makes it difficult for caseworkers and agencies more generally to respond to situations or program mandates that have not been incorporated into the case-processing script (Lurie 2006). As a result, early efforts to institute new policies meant to encourage work among recipients, such as earned-income disregards and childcare subsidies, were often underutilized or led to significant errors and delays in benefit issuance (Snow et al. 1995; 1997).

Ensuring accurate aid determinations became an even more significant organizational task after the 1996 welfare reform that contained both new eligibility restrictions and expanded employment-related and transitional benefits. As individuals found employment, were sanctioned, or reached lifetime limits, transitional benefits and noncash forms of aid became crucial to prevent serious economic hardship. Yet it was exactly these kinds of dynamic case situations that welfare agencies were poorly equipped to manage. As a result there were drops in take-up levels for Food Stamps and Medicaid (Lurie 2006), as well as high levels of sanctioning due to administrative errors in many places in the United States (Brodkin 2006).

This chapter begins with a brief history of the development of American social assistance into its current bureaucratic flat-grant form and an overview of the regulatory challenge of extreme targeting this poses for caseworkers. It provides examples of how specialization and automation have been utilized in an attempt to manage the workload, as well as the challenges involved in incorporating new employment-related tasks. It then presents the primary features of the major federal welfare reform that occurred in 1996 with the passage of TANF and California's state plan, the California Work Opportunity and Responsibility to Kids (CalWORKS). These changes led to a devolution of a certain kind of discretion to the street-level—to make exemptions to the new restrictions on eligibility and to maintain access to employment-related and transitional benefits. At the same time, the organizational capacity to enable and control frontline decision making remained limited due to even greater program fragmentation, regulatory density, and changing recipient situations. While the California experience is atypical in terms of the leniency of some policy parameters, the literature on American welfare reform demonstrates many common features and challenges across states stemming from an overloaded, bureaucratized setting.

The Development of U.S. Welfare Law and Administration—The Rise of the Eligibility Technician

Starting in 1935, Aid to Dependent Children (later Aid to Families with Dependent Children (AFDC)) was enacted by the federal government as Title IV of the Social Security Act, a federal bailout of state mothers' pension programs. AFDC was a joint federal-state program from its inception ("cooperative federalism"), with the federal government providing grants-in-aid (at 50–80 percent of program costs, with poor states receiving proportionately more) as long as states met broad statutory requirements.[4] Beyond these general conditions, though, states had significant discretion over program rules, leading to wide variations in eligibility conditions, benefit levels, and forms of administration.

This lack of oversight began to change in 1962, when federal officials tried to institute a greater programmatic focus on "rehabilitating" recipients and ensuring that children were being taken care of properly. This "caseworker model" (Simon 1983) envisioned an army of trained social workers deployed in the community. Through their professional expertise and their close and frequent contact with clients, they would be able to better evaluate their clients' situations and provide individualized assistance in the form of cash aid, counseling, and service referrals. However, this ideal was never realized in practice, as comparatively few social workers were hired, and few new services developed. Responsibility for both cash and care also put caseworkers in a conflicted and powerful position. Being agents of social services, they could activate the coercive power of the state by calling in child-protective services, making relationship building difficult. Often, then, in an effort to develop rapport with recipients, caseworkers would also grant more than their clients were legally entitled to (Bane and Ellwood 1994). Large caseloads also often led to very limited use of discretion, resulting in simple, categorical determinations (Diller 2000) and infrequent and superficial contact between caseworkers and their clients (Handler and Hollingsworth 1971).

During the latter half of the 1960s and early 1970s, a two-pronged effort of grass roots and legal aid organizations led to a doubling in the number of recipients, overwhelming staff and resulting in high overpayment error rates. Welfare rights organizations began mobilizing poor people to assert their rights, especially for discretionary special needs aid, like furniture and clothing (Piven and Cloward 1971). At the same time, legal aid services brought dozens of cases throughout the court system in an effort to strike down discriminatory and restrictive state rules and to narrow the discretion of caseworkers who were seen as exercising their authority in capricious and often racially exclusionary ways. The courts responded. A "window of opportunity," created by a political climate temporarily attentive to poverty and equality issues, gave the legal system an opportunity to develop the law of due process and equal protection that injected some measure of procedural fairness into the AFDC program. The Supreme Court, as well as numerous lower federal and state courts, used statutory interpretation of Title IV of the Social Security Act to strike down various state administrative restrictions on eligibility,[5] including the "man in the house" rule (*King v. Smith* [1968]) and long-term residency requirements (*Shapiro v. Thompson* [1969]), thereby expanding program access and limiting state control[6] (Melnick 1994).

Adding to the momentum for more rigorous oversight of decisions, state and federal officials responded to the unprecedented growth in expenditures and error rates. The caseworker model fell into disrepute as an abuse of discretionary authority—from the left, for its potential use for moralistic and racist ends; from the right for its ability to circumvent the law to provide illegitimate, overly generous support. In 1967 cash aid and social services were formally separated, and in 1969 the degree requirement was dropped. States began developing objective eligibility criteria and more stringent verification procedures. Social workers were replaced by "eligibility technicians," people who could think, "like bank tellers" (Bane and Ellwood 1994, p. 26). The introduction in 1970 of federal "Quality Assurance" measures backed by sanctions for high state-error rates also contributed to this "quiet administrative revolution" (Brodkin 1986).

These legal and administrative changes resulted in a new kind of organization. Whereas Germany and Sweden continued to develop and institutionalize discretionary need decisions, the United States left this path almost entirely. Caseworker discretion and work tasks became increasingly inscribed in regulations, and leeway to provide for exceptional needs was all but eliminated. Quality control led to the introduction of explicit criteria for evaluating worker performance and enhanced the ability of administrators to monitor and control worker behavior. Correct documentation rather than determination of actual need became the focus of staff in order to ensure that federal officials would not find errors during their case audits.[7] Casework moved from a discretionary professionalized activity to one solely devoted to verifying forms for flat grants based on family size and income. While establishing eligibility became less moralistic and more generally accessible, it also became more complex, opaque, less individualized, and less concerned with actual need (Simon 1983).

The regulatory challenge of extreme targeting

At first glance, then, social assistance appears to be organized and operated like other income-maintenance bureaucracies, such as unemployment insurance or disability, dispensing standardized grants according to clearly delineated regulations (Ochoa 1997). However, several programmatic features readily distinguish welfare and create a much more significant challenge for caseworkers and administrators to ensure a well-functioning organization.

Welfare caseworkers, or "eligibility workers" (EW), are responsible for a number of programs that together provide a mix of cash and in-kind benefits, most importantly, AFDC/TANF, Food Stamps, and Medicaid. This "program diversity" means staff assess claimants according to several different sets of eligibility requirements, with often complex interactive effects. Eligibility is also not based on material need alone, but on additional status and behavioral criteria meant to distinguish among the poor. The most obvious example is that AFDC/TANF support requires a child's "deprivation" due to the death, incapacity, or continued absence of a parent, or (for two-parent families) the unemployment of the principal wage earner. As a result, large numbers of single adults and childless couples are ineligible for cash aid but are eligible for Food Stamps. There are also distinctions between the "assistance unit" and the "family," between the state's "need standard" and its "maximum aid payment," and, in California, further differences in benefit levels based on ability to work.[8] Frequent additions and revisions from multiple levels of government and court orders also require caseworkers to modify the way they make assessments and hinder their ability to develop proficiency and decision-making certainty.[9] The regulatory system becomes, in effect, an accumulation of political and administrative efforts to inscribe distinctions and gradations of deservingness. The degree of elaboration over *threshold conditions* to receive any form of public support sets the American system far apart from its European counterparts. This point is made very clear simply by comparing the 3–4 page applications in Germany and Sweden with the American "application package," which includes two separate 14-page versions for cash aid and Food Stamps as well as two to three dozen supporting forms and documents.

As we shall see, in Germany and Sweden the challenge of caseworker decision making is primarily one of evaluating whether claimants' circumstances merit additional support, that is, whether the basic level of aid is *adequate*. By contrast, U.S. caseworkers have little authority to respond to individual need, with grant amounts set by formulas. The difficulty for U.S. officials is instead applying the complicated rules designed to narrowly target standard grants to particular types of poor people.

California county efforts to promote efficient/accurate decision making

I have to do 225 redetermination interviews in the next two weeks. That means I have to do more than 20 appointments a day, about 4 an hour. Then many don't show up and I have to reschedule them for a second appointment. You have to be really efficient to get through all the material, reading through the Rights and Responsibilities, confirming the information in the applications. Hopefully they've brought all the docs I marked off for them in the notice I sent. If not it just causes more delays. (continuing eligibility worker)

Starting in the early 1990s, welfare caseloads in California increased dramatically, growing more than 50 percent between 1990 and 1994 and reaching their peak in March 1995 (Klerman, Zellman, and Steinberg 2001). By the time federal welfare reform was passed in 1996, recipient levels were still far above the 1980s' levels. Chronically high caseloads, caseworkers' limited skills and training,[10] and a program setting with strong incentives to minimize error rates created persistent pressures for agencies to find new methods to streamline the process and ensure that the most critical eligibility tasks were completed. Specialization, task-based structuring of work, and automation were strategies agencies pursued to address their excessive work demands.

Case specialization
Because of the difficulty involved in administering all the regulations and varied tasks of multiple programs, agencies often utilized extensive staff specializations—between intake and continuing aid; along program lines (Food Stamps or health insurance only); and based on regulation-driven distinctions, such as working households, or two-parent or single-parent nonworking households. In this way, caseworkers had a more limited set of regulations to administer and fewer variations in case fact patterns. This division of labor worked well as long as cases remained static. But when recipients' situations changed—especially when they started or stopped reporting earned income—new problems emerged. Managing the relocation of files between different specialized caseworkers became an additional, complicated administrative activity. Transferring cases also meant several caseworkers often had to become familiar with the same recipient file, an inefficient use of scarce staff attention.

Banking systems
Banking systems are arrangements where cases are kept in a central area and handled by a team of workers, rather than being assigned to individual caseworkers. It represents, perhaps, the purest manifestation of a task-oriented,

mass-processing approach to welfare casework. The emphasis is on completing assignments as they arise, rather than handling cases as a whole. The result of this new arrangement was a substantial increase in efficiency. In one county where a banking system was implemented, it was estimated that 20 percent fewer staff were required than what had previously been considered minimum staffing levels, leading, for example, to units with 1,900 cases staffed by six workers. For administrators, there could be increased accountability for certain tasks, especially where a computer system was utilized for assigning tasks to workers and for tracking their completion. This arrangement no longer relied on the independent judgment of workers to determine what should be done for each file; rather it was the agency that dictated the content and priority of work. For the workers there was increased predictability in daily workload, as client access to workers became extremely regulated and restricted. At the same time, workers' knowledge of clients became more superficial and ad hoc, and they were less informed about individual circumstances because cases only remained in their hands for the duration of the task to be completed.

The transfer desk
In another county a banking system, of sorts, emerged inadvertently. The "transfer desk" was intended as a temporary site to which cases without workers (due to transfers, promotions, sickness) could be temporarily transferred and minimally maintained until the cases could be reassigned. Caseworkers at this site were only held responsible for the work they did on cases, but not for keeping cases up-to-date. As caseloads increased in the mid-1990s, few cases ever left, so that over half of the county caseload was located there with caseloads averaging between 450 and 500 per worker. Staff became increasingly unable to keep client records accurate, and client complaints increased dramatically. To handle the situation, the county promoted more workers from eligibility technician II to III, eliminating the caseload restrictions on these workers (required by union agreements in this county for lower-level staff) and increased the staffing of the transfer desk. A new level of clerk was also created to handle routine tasks. Owing to the extreme caseload sizes, there was especially little worker-client contact, and caseworkers did very little more than handle the most urgent tasks. As the office director commented, "Under such circumstances the work incentives have to be very simple to understand in order for them to be effective."

Automated systems
Given the complexity and workload involved in maintaining client files, information technology became an important management tool for

California county administrators. But the extent to which it was utilized in the mid- to late-1990s varied considerably across counties. In two counties where IT was not well integrated into casework, caseworkers did not have desk terminals. All case changes had to be entered manually onto forms that were then sent to a data-entry unit, resulting in delays to case updating, especially when forms with errors were returned to be corrected. This arrangement made monthly case processing an especially cumbersome task.

All four counties were moving toward more automated systems that would allow client applications to be completed online. This arrangement was intended both to reduce paperwork involved in the application and to guide caseworkers through the various steps of the eligibility process to ensure they completed it correctly. One county implemented such a system during fieldwork. Such a significant organizational shift required enormous training and resulted in slower initial processing as workers became familiar with the system and subsequent system changes. In the middle and long run, automation could result in more efficient case processing, allowing workers to devote more attention to each case. However, in this county, any resulting organizational slack was immediately absorbed in higher caseloads for workers. Automation also appeared to alter the nature of client contact by making the process more opaque and increasing the passivity of clients. Forms that had earlier been filled out by clients were replaced by a series of questions the caseworker asked, prompted by a screen usually unseen by the client. While applications could sometimes be processed more quickly, caseworkers were often absorbed in navigating through the complicated sequences of screens, shifting the focus of the meeting from the client to the technological requirements of processing. In addition, frequent rule changes absorbed considerable caseworker attention, as they had to keep abreast of the discrepancies that developed between the online eligibility procedures and the current regulatory requirements, thereby limiting the ability of automation to simplify the process.

Efforts to automate case processing also led many agencies to move back toward generic caseworkers as a more efficient utilization of staff resources. Caseworkers would then be able to complete all applications more readily online. This development led to significant additional demands on agencies to train caseworkers in new program areas and for caseworkers to be able to develop proficiency in a relatively short time. Inadequate training resources, as well as delays in the implementation of automated systems after the reorganization to generic caseworkers, however, created, in many instances, staff who were even less able to contend with their newer, heavier regulatory responsibilities.

Bar coding CA-7s

Recipients were required to send in a monthly report form (a "CA-7") reporting any changes in their situation, including, for example, income, childcare expenses, and family household. From these reports, caseworkers make adjustments for future AFDC/TANF and Food Stamps payment amounts. Because of the high caseloads, however, staff were not processing a significant percentage of these forms. As a result, many recipients were receiving incorrect grant levels, especially overpayments to those who had stopped sending in monthly reports. During the mid-1990s, the three largest counties automated the process in order to ensure that all monthly reports received by the agency were recorded. Under this new procedure, every check that went out included a CA-7 with a bar code. When the check was sent, the case went into a hold status until the next CA-7 was received and scanned. Scanning was done by unit clerks, and only forms with changes were sent on to caseworkers. While this new procedure may have created a more effective way to monitor clients' reporting, it did not guarantee that caseworkers would act on any of these changes. Furthermore, bar coding fundamentally altered recipients' default eligibility status, as a late CA-7 meant an automatic discontinuance unless the caseworker intervened.

Promoting employment in the shadow of welfare reform

Income maintenance and supportive services are critical to welfare recipients' transition to employment. Clients, for example, confront new work-related expenses immediately—transportation, childcare, clothing—that are difficult to manage on welfare. In an effort to encourage clients to find employment, California welfare policy provided additional economic assistance to recipients through various income disregards and supplements. These policies were meant to address the added costs associated with employment, as well as reduce the implicit "tax rate" on benefits (below 100 percent) so that clients would have more money if they worked. Often, though, these resources were administratively cumbersome and required separate applications.[11]

In preparation for impending federal welfare reform, agencies made considerable efforts to shift the focus of casework and caseworker interactions with clients from eligibility determination to promoting self-sufficiency. However, caseworkers were generally unable and/or unwilling to incorporate these new additional mandates into their work. The strategies meant to ensure efficient and accurate decision making also reinforced standardized forms of processing. Caseworkers neither had the time nor were they evaluated on these new supplemental tasks (Meyers, Glaser, and MacDonald

1998). As a result, more individualized assistance, such as informing clients about welfare reform, or helping them access available, targeted childcare benefits, or even correctly determining changes in monthly grant amounts for recipients with earned income, were poorly implemented.

In the AFDC program EWs' contact with clients was infrequent, rigidly structured, and primarily about eligibility and documentation requirements. After spending several weeks in welfare offices observing the routines and interactions of AFDC EWs with recipients, it was clear why communication and coordination around employment goals was so difficult. Often, intake workers would rush through the interview reading a script and gathering the immense pile of information necessary for determining eligibility, packed into a large room with other workers, clients, and conversations. There was little opportunity to discuss additional issues like employment or inquire about the client's own work situation. Clients also generally struggled simply to understand how to apply for benefits. As one caseworker observed, clients were often "burned out" after 20 or 30 minutes of discussing technical questions around eligibility requirements, leaving little opportunity for broader discussions about a recipient's situation.

Because of high caseloads (typically over 200 cases per worker), continuing eligibility workers were often doing six or seven redetermination interviews in a row, with each one lasting no more than five minutes, or group redeterminations with very little individual interaction. And this interaction was the only statutorily required, face-to-face contact between caseworker and recipient. The caseworkers' role as cop/gatekeeper for program funds also meant that nonroutine interactions with clients were predominantly about money—missing checks or reductions/denials of benefits—situations which created a level of urgency and often hostility that overshadowed other issues. Caseworkers also had clear disincentives to help clients find employment, as employed clients had frequent changes in case information that resulted in more complicated budgeting work for EWs.

Given the limited capacity of eligibility workers to discuss employment-related issues with clients and often their failure to correctly implement "work first" policies, administrators had to develop alternative routes for conveying employment-related information between the agency and clients. Agencies had the most significant impact on this worker-client relationship through fostering worker specialization, in which case processing and employment-related tasks were divided between different types of workers. In this way, many of the hindrances to a more general transformation of office practices could be overcome for a certain subset of frontline workers. A separation of the cop and counselor roles allowed these employment specialists to focus on the most relevant program resources and expectations rather than on regulations and procedural checklists.

In one county, for example, AFDC offices pursued this strategy by creating two new kinds of positions—child care coordinators and work pays coordinators.[12] The *child care coordinator* positions were designed to increase client utilization of existing childcare resources by increasing client knowledge of and ability to maneuver through the complicated rules for accessing these resources. Coordinators also made efforts to ensure that applications were processed correctly, training caseworkers in how to use childcare forms, and, in some cases, taking over responsibility for all childcare applications. *Work pays coordinator* positions were designed to increase client knowledge of employment-related policies and the impending welfare reform, and to convey the agency's expectations about the importance of work. These coordinators also often developed additional resources for their individual clients, including job listings, resume workshops, and the coordination of community services to assist welfare recipients in becoming employed. Thus, through specialization, information about certain employment-related program expectations and rules became a routinized, integrated part of client processing for a larger part of the client population and one usually separate from interaction with case workers.[13]

TANF and CalWORKS

Following decades of political stalemate and incremental changes to the policies and practices of welfare, the program was fundamentally overhauled in 1996, a political bargain struck between a Republican Congress and President Clinton in his bid for a second term as president (Brodkin 2006; Weaver 1998). While most states had already begun incorporating many reforms into their programs under a waiver process during the early 1990s,[14] TANF represented a significant break with tradition. It eliminated the federal entitlement to welfare assistance, gave states significantly more fiscal authority, and instituted new methods of accountability for achieving federal objectives. TANF reform represented a combination of "pressures and flexibility" (Lurie 2006).

Selected TANF requirements

1. *Entitlement eliminated.* Under AFDC, anyone who met the eligibility requirements of a state welfare program was legally entitled to benefits for as long as they continued to meet those requirements. Under TANF, federal funds could be used to support clients for a total of 60 months during their lifetime (though with a 20 percent caseload exemption). States could also change a wide range of basic

eligibility conditions. In general few states altered their benefit levels, but made working on welfare more attractive by increasing income disregards, as well as income and asset limits (Martinson and Holcomb 2002). At the same time states instituted tougher non-compliance policies (including full-family sanctioning in 36 states [GAO 2000]), and half the states introduced shorter time limits than the federal law required.

2. *Block grant funding.* Previously the federal government matched state expenditures at a set rate. Under TANF, federal monies were now dispensed as block grants,[15] giving states considerable discretion in how they chose to spend the funds,[16] while also shifting the fiscal risk to the states. As a result of this formula, most states experienced a huge initial windfall because of almost universal and significant drops in caseloads in the years following.[17] This formula, however, preserved the skewed expenditure differences among states (Lurie 2006).

3. *Work requirements.* TANF also created new kinds of performance standards. The federal policy change that impacted state spending decisions most was the unprecedented levels of work participation required of program recipients. In the first year, 25 percent of lone parents and 75 percent of two-parent families were required to participate in a work activity for 20 hours/week. This rate increased to 50 percent and 90 percent respectively and 35 hours/week during the following five years. At the same time, states were credited toward meeting their participation requirements through caseload declines on a point-for-point basis. This trade-off was intended to give states credit for both continued program participation and successful transitions of clients off the rolls. To prevent the most egregious kinds of disentitlement practices that might arise from such an incentive system, caseload reductions would not count if they were a result of greater restrictions in eligibility conditions (one reason benefit levels may not have been widely changed). (See chapter 6 for more details.)

4. *Behavioral requirements.* In addition to new workfare participation demands, clients could also be assessed on additional new behavioral requirements, including ensuring that any child under age 6 was properly immunized; verifying that any child up to the age of 17 was regularly attending school; and submitting to fingerprinting at the time of application. TANF also set goals to promote marriage, two-parent families and to reduce out-of-wedlock pregnancies (Lurie 2006).[18]

5. *Coverage limitations.* TANF created new status restrictions on who could receive aid, including an optional "maximum family grant" (no additional TANF support is provided for children conceived and

born during a household's continued receipt of aid); the permanent exclusion of convicted felons; and the optional exclusion of most legal immigrants.

CalWORKS

California's state welfare reform plan—CalWORKS—was passed in August 1997. California was unusually "generous" in many of the policy choices it made in implementing TANF. Families remain entitled to benefits for 60 months, and it is one of only six states that eliminates only the adult portion of a household's grant when the lifetime limit is reached, with the remaining grant being paid through state funds. California also retained its previous sanctioning policies for recipient noncompliance with welfare-to-work participation requirements, eliminating only the adult from the grant. The state did not choose to end aid to legal immigrants in most cases, and, in fact, created a state Food Stamp program to offset new immigrant exclusions introduced into the federal program.

New regulatory challenges: enhanced conditionality and concentration of informal street-level discretion

Welfare reform was first and foremost about enforcing a general obligation for virtually the whole recipient population to participate in work or work-related activities. As a result, much of the emphasis in the CalWORKS program was on enrolling claimants in job-readiness programs, coordinating supportive services, and monitoring compliance—activities primarily carried out by staff in the rapidly expanding welfare-to-work programs.

The new approach, though, also involved creating strong behavioral incentives through regulations. And EWs were central to this process through their proper application of a complicated bundle of carrots and sticks. For example, conditions for receiving aid became far stricter, and with these new restrictions came new exceptions so that the most vulnerable recipients would not be subject to the full brunt of the program. Under certain conditions, then, clients could be exempted from participation requirements, referred to more appropriate social services, or their months on aid not counted toward their time limit.

Income disregards provided a valuable additional support to the large numbers of recipients who found employment while remaining on aid. But access to noncash forms of assistance, including Food Stamps, Medicaid, and new employment-related supportive services, also became more important in the post-TANF world. While many recipients found employment that made them income-ineligible for cash aid, these jobs tended to be low wage, often part-time, and without benefits (Brock, Nelson, and Reiter 2002). In other states besides California, time limits and full-family sanctioning could lead to a loss of cash benefits for large numbers of recipients, and, in many cases, potential claimants chose to withdraw their TANF application in order to save up their months. In all of these cases where poor families were unable to or chose not to receive cash aid, the other components of the safety net system could be crucial to prevent severe deprivation.

Thus, frequent changes in grant level (from earned income)[19] and new gradations of eligibility status were to characterize large numbers of recipients in the new system. Yet, as we have seen, welfare case processing is designed to contend with routine case patterns. The implementation of these new variable tasks required their incorporation as monitored features in the daily work of frontline staff. In most instances, though, these kinds of assessments were not evaluated (Diller 2000), making them, in effect, "optional." Under these circumstances, caseworkers accumulated considerable new decision-making discretion to provide individualized support *of a kind*. Officials could now use the possibilities provided by the law to selectively assist *particular* recipients—either to assess whether they should be exempted from new eligibility requirements or to cobble together an array of administratively cumbersome partial aid programs.

Organizational conditions under CalWORKS

With CalWORKS there's a lot more work, too much paperwork. There are more rules and they are constantly changing with all these temporary directives. Plus a lot more people are employed which makes the budgeting piece a lot more complicated. And then there are the different laws for immigrants and the new Food Stamps program . . . and those budgets have to be done manually and you have to overwrite things because that whole thing hasn't been added to the computer system yet. It's really difficult for workers to keep up with especially the new ones who are barely trained and are constantly asking questions. (caseworker)

While federal welfare reform in 1996 fundamentally altered many features of American welfare, the bureaucratically organized eligibility apparatus endured (Klerman, Zellman, and Steinberg 2001; Diller 2000). During the first years of CalWORKS work conditions became even more onerous for caseworkers for several reasons. Rules changed even more frequently than before, as state and county officials continued to draw up and revise new instructions to complete the implementation of an entirely new program. Even in late 2000, several years after the introduction of the new framework, caseworkers commented that "regulations change all the time," even "daily, hourly." A new state Food Stamps program had been introduced to offset the loss of entitlement for legal immigrants to federal Food Stamps included as part of the new welfare reform, requiring a new set of status-based determinations and budget calculations. Several supervisors complained that many caseworkers didn't know the rules for the new program, didn't understand the distinction between the federal and state versions, and didn't bother with the necessary manual budget calculations it required. Legal actions again proved disruptive to organizational operations. An injunction against a new fingerprinting and photo requirement necessitated a flurry of new instructions suspending the procedure, and caseworkers had to remove all previously collected material from their case files. More clients were now working, with estimates of one-third to two-thirds of all recipients (vs. 15 percent earlier), making casework more time consuming to process and determinations more prone to errors.

The rapid expansion of welfare-to-work programs led to a "brain drain" in welfare offices, as many of the most experienced caseworkers moved over to higher-paying jobs as "employment counselors." This migration created huge challenges for agencies to rapidly hire and train new staff to fill caseworker vacancies. Training times were shortened, and qualifying exams often eliminated; error rates increased substantially. While federal quality assurance had been eliminated for welfare under TANF, this practice continued for the federal Food Stamps program, resulting sometimes in large sanctions against counties, keeping agencies still focused on error rates (Polit et al. 2005).

Welfare Reform Developments in the United States

Other research on post-TANF America has found similar program developments across the states. While employment-related goals have been incorporated into state programs (Lurie 2006; Martinson and Holcomb 2002), welfare casework is still governed by an "ineluctable core of case processing" (Jewell and Glaser 2006). Based on nearly 1,000 caseworker-client encounters at 11 sites in four states (New York, Texas, Georgia, and Michigan), Lurie (2006) found that eligibility work continued to be highly routinized, with staff having little discretion in how they made decisions—they collected and verified information, entered it into the computer, asked for signatures, and explained rules (see also Riccucci 2005). One of the remarkable examples of changed practices, however, was the communication of new reform messages and the imposition of work-related mandates as part of the application process. In many states, applicants were required to attend a work orientation class (and in some cases engage in job search activities) before their applications would be considered (Lurie 2006) (see also chapter 6).

Yet many other new activities tended to be neglected. The imposition of employment-related behavioral mandates as part of the application process was often carried out with few exceptions as caseworkers rarely inquired into the ability of applicants to work (Lurie 2006). And attention was not given to explaining conditions under which claimants could obtain noncash forms of aid, contributing to a widespread loss of access to and reduction in take up rates for Food Stamps and Medicaid benefits (Fossett, Gais, and Thompson 2003). Recipients also often had difficulties obtaining transitional benefits (Michaelopoulos et al. 2003). Inappropriate sanctioning caused by administrative errors in the verification process also resulted in significant loss of access to entitlements (Brodkin 2006; Brock et al. 2004). High rates of Food Stamps errors and the resultant federal sanctioning of many states were also indicators of the general difficulties agencies were having in carrying out even the most essential tasks given the more dynamic nature of clients' employment and program participation status (Polit et al. 2005; Riccucci 2005).

Conclusion

Welfare programs in the United States are bureaucratic organizations, staffed by nonprofessionals who make eligibility assessments based on extensive regulations. An earlier programmatic aspiration to utilize trained social workers who could provide material and therapeutic assistance tailored to the needs of their clients (as is the aspirational model in Sweden today) dissipated in the late 1960s. Concern with exclusionary state practices, unrestrained discretion by officials, and rising fiscal costs led to political and legal reforms for a more equitable, procedurally developed, and controllable administrative system.

The result today is a setting in which caseworkers have virtually no formal decision-making authority or control over the amount of support they grant, subject instead to program rules meticulously describing the considerable amount of information to collect and the ways to evaluate it. Limited official discretion and low standardized grant amounts mean that caseworkers have little capacity to be responsive to claimants' particular needs, and so they fall far to the left on the dimension of *legal authority* (figure 3.1). While this organization of work was intended to help administrators process cases efficiently and consistently, unmanageable levels of regulation combined with high caseloads generally prevent caseworkers from performing their work in the predictable and technically proficient manner envisioned. This situation of "overregulation" arises from several distinct program features.

Welfare officials are not responsible for a single, unified aid program, but rather for a number of programs that together provide a mix of cash and in-kind benefits. With the introduction of major welfare reform in 1997 in California, program fragmentation increased even further with the introduction of a new state Food Stamps program, and the rate of regulatory change accelerated for the first several years of implementation. Adding to the regulatory burden is the *degree* of assessment the program requires of officials. Eligibility is not based on material need alone, but on additional status and behavioral criteria meant to distinguish among the poor in order to provide support only to those who are judged legally deserving. Stemming from federal quality control requirements, and as a further measure to ensure only those with legally recognizable need receive support, caseworkers must evaluate whether claimants provide appropriate documentation for their assertions.

Such a targeted and procedurally dense system requires caseworkers to map clients' particular situations onto all of the programmatic, status, behavioral, and financial conditions the various aid programs require. Furthermore, such a system necessitates that administrators have the means to monitor and evaluate caseworker performance. However, organizational resources are far from sufficient to fully implement the rules on the books. Staff are generally inadequately trained, leading to errors in the application of rules. This knowledge deficit worsened after the introduction of welfare reform when large numbers of caseworkers left the agency for the expanding welfare-to-work programs that were the centerpiece of the new program. And chronically high caseloads have also made it difficult for staff to complete even essential tasks. With the passage of federal welfare reform in 1996, TANF, the federal entitlement to support was eliminated and the conditions for receiving support became even more complex, stringent, and punitive.

Agencies have responded to these problems by (1) utilizing caseworker specialization to limit the amount of regulation and variation in cases with which any one individual official must contend; (2) reorganizing work on a task- rather than case-basis; and (3) increasingly automating the system to guide caseworkers step-by-step through the relevant procedures involved in each claimant situation. However, these efforts have had only a limited effect on the disjuncture between the demands of the program's targeted approach to aid and the ability of caseworkers to effectively implement them.

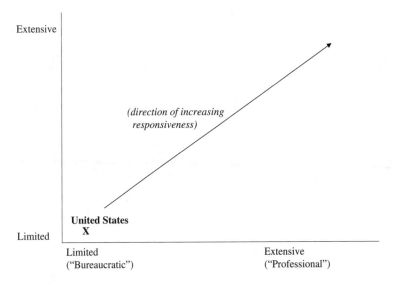

Horizontal Axis
Legal Authority for Responsive Decision Making: formal ability of caseworker to consider individual circumstances in assessing need

Vertical Axis
Organizational Capacity for Responsive Decision Making: ability of agency to enable and control official decision making

Figure 3.1   Comparing responsiveness among welfare caseworkers (U.S. example)

Thus, while limited caseworker discretion is an intentional feature of the U.S. welfare system as a way of ensuring consistency and efficiency, the organizational means for maintaining a smoothly operating bureaucracy have proven inadequate. Thus, caseworkers fall near the bottom left corner in figure 3.1, representing caseworkers' very limited capacity to be responsive and limited organizational control over caseworker decision making.

4

Welfare Caseworkers in Bremen, Germany: Entitlement Scholars in a Highly Regulated State

We have developed an organization here in which a single case worker is comprehensively responsible for the entire economic circumstances of the applicant . . . cradle to grave.[1]

Introduction

German social assistance is the first of two examples of a "needs-based" system, that is, one in which the program's mandate is to provide individualized assistance to enable recipients to participate in larger societal life. Such an approach contrasts with U.S. welfare, in which aid is dispensed in standardized amounts, and where there is a tenuous relationship between the assistance provided and the situations of claimants.

The German system has several programmatic features that create the possibility of providing more comprehensive and tailored forms of relief than in the United States. Standard benefits are more generous, including full coverage for housing and heating costs and an amount for daily expenses. In addition, clients can apply for one-time payments for any expenses not covered by the basic grant. Caseworkers have significant latitude to decide whether a particular one-time expense is a justifiable need, a discretion that is strengthened by their full decision-making authority. This ability to consider particular needs of claimants creates both the potential for responsive decision making and difficulties in monitoring and influencing frontline behavior.

The basis for officials' authority and the bulwark against its abuse reside in a highly regulated program staffed by skilled public bureaucrats trained in the general interpretation of government regulation. An institutionalized process of ongoing policy development, including the frequent incorporation of court decisions, provides a mechanism for increasingly articulating the considerations caseworkers must take into account in their decisions. High levels of staff education in administrative work, extensive traineeship for new caseworkers, and long-term tenure of most staff facilitate proficiency and common interpretive approaches for assessments. Supervisors are able to maintain some influence over caseworkers through case audits that keep staff attentive to grounding their decisions in the law, as well as through weekly meetings and individual consultations to discuss difficult cases. In Bremen, a strong advocacy presence also helps inform many clients of their rights and, through threat of complaints and appeals, makes caseworkers more careful in their assessments than they might otherwise be.

But while the regulatory process creates strong legal constraints on what caseworkers can do, staff often commented on the differences in the way similar kinds of decisions were handled among different caseworkers and between different offices. Residual discretion was viewed as inevitable, and by some as justified and legitimate due to caseworkers' regulatory expertise. More troubling, the intricacy and quantity of the work staff are expected to perform make it difficult for them to utilize their discretion, not least of all due to the regulatory structure itself. This situation is made even more challenging because social assistance in Germany covers a broader array of needs than traditional welfare programs, including areas of disability and institutionalized care. Local organizational conditions exacerbate this problem. Information systems are unable to provide caseworkers with the necessary assistance to locate and utilize relevant regulations. High caseloads resulting from financial constraints and a local government focused on cost savings through staff reductions have made it difficult to hire and retain the highly qualified staff needed to administer such a complicated program. Even supervisors carry at least half caseloads, limiting their ability to consult with staff and evaluate their cases.

The regulatory complexity of the larger German social security system also adversely impacts agency work. Caseworkers are required to identify and often seek reimbursement from a wide array of other income-support programs that have precedence over welfare. Because many of these agencies process claims inefficiently, the welfare office must often pay interim support to recipients. Seeking reimbursements from other government agencies, then, becomes another important responsibility of caseworkers. The difficulty and centrality of this "accounting" role appears unique among the three countries.

Such an immense workload, both in client numbers and in the evaluative intensity associated with each case, has led inexorably to superficial, legalistic, or incorrect treatment of many cases and the neglect of many program functions. Aid applications are granted without investigation or adequate documentation. Other forms of public support that take precedence over welfare are missed or not claimed, even if known. And activation efforts among Bremen caseworkers are marginal. The result is a considerable loss of agency control over its expenditures. Recent reforms, however, may lead to significant recovery of the program's operational capacity. The transfer of a large proportion of the recipient population to new pensions and unemployment benefit programs in 2003 and 2005 respectively, as well as the introduction of a more consolidated benefit structure, should significantly reduce the workload and greatly simplify some of the regulatory structure with which caseworkers contend.

This chapter provides an overview of German social assistance law and the areas of discretion it provides frontline staff in their assessment of claims prior to these major reforms. It then discusses the challenge caseworkers face in making individualized decisions under conditions of heavy regulation. Program features that contribute to individualized decision making are presented, along with the seemingly unassailable core of residual discretion that caseworkers maintain. This discussion is followed by a longer section on the conditions that hinder responsive behavior. Finally, after a brief discussion of the marginal role that activation efforts play in welfare offices, the chapter concludes with a look at some reforms that officials were considering at the time, as well as the actual, and in some cases profound, program changes that have since taken place.

Regulatory Framework

The modern form of German social assistance (*Sozialhilfe*) was established in 1961 with the passage of the Federal Social Assistance Law (Bundessozialhilfegesetz [BSHG]).[2] This program has been characterized as an "integrated safety net" (Eardley et al. 1996) due to its near-universal coverage, average benefit levels, and strong codification in national legislation.[3] In the German federated structure, the Ministry for Health and Social Insurance (today, the Ministry of Labor and Social Affairs) is responsible for policy at the national level, but states and localities implement the program and have some influence over the rules that govern it.[4] The states are responsible for setting grant levels, but within narrow limits defined by the federal government.[5] Social assistance is largely a locally financed program, with 80 percent of its costs covered by local government and most of the remaining 20 percent by the states. Yet localities have only limited independent taxation powers and receive most of their revenue from the central government through a system of vertical and horizontal revenue sharing (Leibfried and Obinger 2003).

German social assistance is much broader in scope than in the United States or Sweden. German caseworkers are, in some sense, "poverty generalists." Like these other income maintenance programs, most recipients receive general assistance to meet their daily needs, through a component known as cost-of-living assistance (CLA) (Hilfe zum Lebensunterhalt). A second area, known as help in special circumstances (HSC) (Hilfe in besonderen Lebenslagen), though, is intended to address a variety of special hardships. These situations include help for the blind, integration assistance for the disabled who are not entitled to social insurance,[6] "caring assistance" for those in need of nursing care,[7] and health care, areas of support that are generally covered by other agencies in the United States[8] and Sweden. Although some CLA clients also get HSC (especially health care), on the whole, CLA and HSC clients are different groups.[9] HSC law is complicated and, while not the focus of this study, increases the regulatory burden and diversity of claims with which social assistance caseworkers contend. In addition, while social assistance is intended to provide a last safety net for all in need, in 1993 policymakers created a separate program for asylum seekers (Asylbewerberleistungsgesetz), with lower benefit levels and more restrictive eligibility conditions. Social assistance caseworkers are also responsible for administering this program.

"Help to self-help" has been an official aim of social assistance since its inception,[10] though it remained largely unutilized by local agencies until the mid-1980s (Voges, Jacobs, and Trickey 2000). Work-capable recipients[11] are required to register with the employment office every quarter and to accept any work that is offered. Caseworkers can also require recipients to submit job applications as a way of showing self-help effort. Many clients are also referred to the local welfare-to-work agency. Those who refuse to make adequate efforts can be sanctioned by at least a 25 percent reduction of the standard rate. As part of the agency's activation efforts, social assistance caseworkers additionally are supposed to provide personal support services, either directly or by referral to private welfare associations and special counseling centers, with the social assistance agency bearing the costs.

Distinguishing Features of Individualized, Needs-Based Programs— German and Swedish Social Assistance

Both German and Swedish social assistance (chapter 5) share elements that set them apart from the U.S. program, including their explicitly stated intent to ensure recipients are able to participate in societal life. In Germany, the program's purpose is "to enable the assistance recipient to lead a life of human dignity" (Art. 1, Para. 2, BSHG), a mandate that originates in Germany's

Constitutional Law, which requires a uniformity of life chances throughout the country (Basic Law, Art. 1).[12] This goal[13] is operationalized through several programmatic features common to both countries' programs.

1. Aid is organized into a two-tiered system. A monthly standard grant is intended to cover reasonable housing and heating costs and daily living expenses.[14] This kind of support is analogous to the U.S. standard grant, though comparably more generous (Eardley et al. 1996). The European eligibility assessments are also much simpler than the American process in part because there are fewer conditions required to establish and maintain eligibility. A manageable level of regulation, even in detail, is much easier to achieve with a near-universal right to support based on income alone.

A second level of discretionary one-time payments is also available for some exceptional expenses. In Germany, it is estimated that one-time payments amount to between 10 and 20 percent of all benefit payments (Adema, Gray, and Kahl 2003; Behrendt 2002). Determining what items are covered by the basic grant and when additional aid (and the amount) can be granted based on a determination of a "special need" is a central regulatory and administrative challenge.[15] One unusual but illustrative example follows:

> If someone needs a driver's license and will get a job because of that, I can decide to approve the DM 3,000 it will cost, so that the person eventually will be able to get a job and no longer need public support.

2. Program decisions must be based, in principle, on individualized assessments. In German law this principle is articulated in the requirement that the nature, type and extent of social assistance should be geared to the specific features of the individual case, particularly toward the personal characteristics of the assistance recipient, the type of need and local conditions (Art. 3, Para. 1, BSHG). This principle provides a regulatory basis for officials to move beyond simply applying laws to assessing how granting support in a particular case relates to important organizational goals such as recipient self-sufficiency (example above), material adequacy, and expenditure control.

> We don't usually pay someone's rental debt, but a caseworker can use their discretion to consider whether the person can keep their apartment if we don't pay their debt. Because ultimately homelessness is more expensive than paying rent.

An individualized assessment may also be used to create an exception to a normally applicable prescription. For example, in Bremen, standardized conditions and payments for many household items act as presumptive rules from which caseworkers may deviate in individual cases to ensure actual needs are met:

> If DM 600 is the normal amount for a washing machine, but we see that the family has eight children, then we can approve DM 1500 for the washing machine instead. That is possible, although it creates more work for the caseworker.

> If someone suddenly needs a winter coat, the case worker might say, "You just got one two years ago. A winter coat is supposed to last you three years." But maybe the client fell and ripped the coat or got it so dirty that it can no longer be used; that is in the realm of the imaginable. Then he will get a new one. That is discretionary latitude.

3. The significance of this latitude in decision making is even more pronounced because caseworkers receive full decision-making authority after they complete an in-house traineeship. This coequal status of supervisors with their staff eliminates administrators' most direct methods for monitoring and influencing caseworker decisions.

In order to manage the challenges to program predictability and control posed by these programmatic features—a potentially open-ended aid category, a powerful exceptions clause, and a decentralized authority structure—German and Swedish social assistance administrations have evolved distinct configurations of regulation, frontline expertise, and organizational design. Germany's top-down regulatory design is described below, while Sweden's decentralized, consultation approach is presented in the following chapter.

Caseworker Decision Making and the Regulatory Challenge

> It is rarely the case that if I am training a new colleague . . . that I can say that if the instructions say such and such, then that will result in this outcome . . . Instead it is more like, this client can receive it for this reason and the other one, perhaps not. It is difficult but ultimately makes the work not so boring.
>
> (supervisor)

German caseworkers administer a law that is at once voluminous and "very in need of interpretation," imbuing caseworkers with "an insane amount of discretion." This seemingly paradoxical situation results from a combination of two contradictory impulses in the structure and mandates of the program, both responses to the fundamental programmatic question: What is required for a life with human dignity?

On the one hand, public administration in Germany is governed by a strong rule of law tradition ("Rechtsstaat"), to increasingly narrow discretion and systematize criteria in order to make decisions predictable and controllable. As such there are well-developed processes for formalizing political, administrative, and legal discourses (see Grunow 2001). Regulatory development for social assistance centers primarily on defining what the basic grant covers and under what conditions additional, exceptional support should be granted. Based on client appeals, case law from the administrative court system creates a powerful feedback that is incorporated by local government into program guidelines.[16] A tradition of intergovernmental conferring at the state and local level also provides a regular method by which program administrators learn from each other about emergent issues and attempt to harmonize policy development (Goetz 2000). But because court rulings concern very specific issues, legal decisions are often narrow, and particular judgments become difficult to maintain as a coherent and manageable regulatory scheme.

> There is always a problem of drawing the border between what is part of the basic grant and what is a legitimate additional need . . . There are [interviewee gestures to indicate thickness] volumes like this of court decisions concerning the question of whether, for example, an umbrella is considered covered by the standard monthly amount, or can be applied for separately as a one-time expenditure. One can philosophize about that for a long time. And that is a crazy system; it's insane, totally insane.
>
> (supervisor)

Such decisions are also often superseded because, as society becomes wealthier, the requirements of a decent standard of living change. "Basic need" is a moving target:

> Before, we always said, What about a television? Is that a basic need, or not? And then, we said, OK, one per household. But the court established that for people to be able to participate in the general life of the society, it was necessary each person had their own television . . . There should be a gap [between low wage earners and welfare recipients], but it shouldn't be too big. If the society becomes more affluent, the welfare recipient should be a beneficiary of this process.
>
> (agency administrator)

On the other hand, due to the special status of social assistance as the program of last resort and its commitment to ensuring that basic needs are *actually* met in the individual case, regulations cannot fully articulate all appropriate considerations or lines of reasoning a caseworker could take into account in a given claimant situation: "Everyone is different. No administrative guidelines can cover everything." In acknowledgment of this constraint, the system is designed to give officials discretion in assessing what is appropriate in the individual case. As one supervisor characterized a caseworker's scope of authority, "There are always a few things which I can't do. But basically we can make everything possible with these rules when it is necessary."

The German context of needs-based assessments thus creates a distinct challenge to responsive and consistent decision making. Caseworkers contend with a wide variety of claimant situations in which they must conduct substantial legal analyses and utilize their discretion to grant more individualized aid where situations warrant. The workability and legitimacy of this top-down regulatory approach is sustained primarily through the deployment of a cadre of long-term regulatory experts.

Program Conditions that Promote Responsive Decision Making

Standardizing practices through regulation

The policymaking capacity to develop additional guidelines as new situations emerge provides a powerful method to ensure that public officials make decisions well grounded in the law, while also providing targeted and appropriate relief to a wide variety of needs. For example, in an effort to better standardize decisions and control costs, many state and local governments (including Bremen) developed uniform payment levels and conditions for dozens of one-time special expense items that are not covered by the basic grant, from large household appliances and furniture,[17] down to a towel, mirror, or tea kettle.[18] Additionally, for some regular special expense items, automatic lump-sum payments are made periodically to claimants, such as a standardized clothing allowance every six months.[19] And it is clear this accumulation had an impact on how caseworkers do their work: "The work has become considerably more regulated through administrative instructions and case law from the administrative court system . . . and there is more consistent practice in Bremen now than there was earlier." (supervisor)

Education, training, and tenure

Although the German civil service ("Beamte") has been the object of criticism and debate (Hauschild 2001), it remains a defining institution of the German welfare state. The function and primary features of public administration are embodied in several principles defined in the German Constitution, including the idea that the sovereign authority of the state must be exercised only by entrusted officials. These special administrators act as the providers and guarantors of the public good, a mandate secured by educational requirements, clear career structures, lifelong tenure, and high levels of regulation both to restrict official discretion and to insulate them from direct political influence (Goetz 2000). It is this combination of educational background and professionalization as career civil servants that provides significant safeguards for ensuring consistent and sophisticated assessments by German welfare caseworkers (cf. Kaufman 1967).

The complexity and range of issues that arise under the BSHG mean that social assistance administrative work is classified as "executive" or "higher-intermediate" civil service work,[20] requiring university-level training in specialized administrative schools. Welfare workers' skills and understanding of their role as public servants centers therefore on interpreting regulations. Additionally, because most beginning caseworkers are only legal generalists and know little more than the fundamentals of the BSHG, new staff undergo a minimum six-month traineeship on-site, overseen by an experienced caseworker or the unit supervisor. During this time, they get practical guidance—a sense of how the work flows, what to pay attention to at intake, what to ask clients, and why aid is provided in particular circumstances and not in others. Depending on the individual's proficiency, the caseworker is assigned a small number of cases, first under supervision and later monitored through ongoing discussions. Her caseload is gradually increased until, after six or eight months, she has a full caseload (of about 180) and receives full decision-making authority. This mentoring process teaches staff not only program-specific regulations, but also informal knowledge such as conventional usages of legal terms and the handling of ambiguous situations.

The long tenure of many caseworkers is another important factor enabling offices to administer such complex regulations. Of the eight caseworkers interviewed, six had been there between 11 and 14 years (the other two, 5 and 7 years, respectively). A core of veteran administrators, acting independently, facilitates the maintenance of a high level of institutional memory about regulatory interpretations and approaches for complex cases. While fiscal constraints are making it increasingly difficult for social assistance to retain these types of workers, this "Beamte" tradition still plays an important role in maintaining the crucial feature of decentralized expertise in social assistance administration.

Supervision and consultation

Unit administrators are a central source of expertise in the office. They are all veteran staff who have been there for 15–30 years and know how the regulations and interpretive approaches have developed. Due to their responsibility for disseminating and explaining new regulations to their staff, they also have regular contact with other district offices and central administration. This boundary-spanning position gives them a broader perspective on the meanings and implications of new directives and the system as a whole. Supervisors also have their own clients, which is equivalent to half a normal caseload, a responsibility supposedly intended to keep administrators familiar with day-to-day decision-making issues.

While supervisors have little direct influence over their staff after caseworkers receive decision-making authority, they have two ways to keep caseworkers' attention on "the possibilities the law provides for assisting recipients"—case audits and consultation. Case audits[21] are relatively limited in scope, primarily a technical assessment to determine whether the caseworker has filled out all documents correctly, cited the appropriate rules, and constructed a logical argument for their decision. A supervisor cannot overturn a "properly justified" decision. This type of monitoring cannot guarantee that most cases are decided "correctly," though they may discourage the most egregious misuse of authority. Rather, these reviews reinforce the importance of a focus on rules and the development of solid lines of reasoning (Kagan 1978).

Supervisors also utilize their knowledge in advising individual caseworkers and through weekly unit meetings where difficult cases are discussed and new rules are explained. This regular forum also facilitates the voluntary exchange of information and ideas among staff, discussions that are all the more sophisticated due to the long history of case experience upon which most caseworkers draw. As one supervisor observed, "It helps the person to obtain a second opinion and for the colleagues to learn about potential situations in comparison to their own cases." This combination of initial training and ongoing interaction contributes to the development of similar working methods among caseworkers, at least within particular offices and city districts.[22]

Supervisors also often insist they oversee decisions in more difficult areas of the law, such as integration assistance, "because many colleagues grant things without being able to foresee the huge fiscal effects." In some cases, supervisors take over all such cases in their unit. This oversight, too, helps safeguard against incorrect and inconsistent decisions for some of the most complicated and expensive kinds of decisions.

Advocacy organizations and the well-informed client

Bremen has a developed network of government-funded and private welfare associations (Garcia and Saraceno 1998) that provide advice and support to individuals with a variety of problems. An advocacy group for welfare recipients and the unemployed known as AGAB (Aktionsgemeinschaft Arbeitloser

Bürgerinnen und Bürger—Unemployed Citizens Action Group) is especially active in this area, advising close to 5,000 people annually about their entitlements and available community resources. They produce a guide to welfare rights that explains social assistance law in great detail, including caseworker authority in various situations, observed patterns of bad caseworker practices,[23] and Bremen's list of standardized payments for various one-time expenses.[24] They also encourage clients who are dissatisfied with their caseworker's behavior or decision to complain to the supervisor or ultimately file an appeal.

This advocacy presence seems to have contributed to a high level of program knowledge among many clients in Bremen. Several staff mentioned the influence of AGAB and their yellow booklet, citing clients who sometimes come to the office with long lists of one-time expenses for which they wish to apply. Empowering clients in this manner is an important counterbalance to the structural disparity in information and power that naturally exists between public agency staff and their dependent clients (Handler and Hollingsworth 1971). Advocacy organizations may produce unhelpful adversarialism and lead to differences in treatment between those who are informed and assertive and the rest of the client population. But the presence of a watchdog organization also helps keep agencies and caseworkers more attentive to the way they utilize their authority more generally. Client complaints keep attention on officials who may be behaving inappropriately. Even more importantly, the threat of client appeals reinforces the importance of properly justifying decisions in the regulations. As one supervisor commented, "It is crucial to support your decisions with strong reasoning so that the appeals don't work. Otherwise you get a 'bombing effect.' Once word gets out among clients that a particular kind of claim worked, you will be inundated with such appeals. So we take a lot of time to support our decisions."[25]

Residual discretion and "weak" organizational culture

Despite extensive regulations, common educational background and training, and opportunities for consultation, staff readily acknowledged that caseworkers often assess basic need differently based on "life experience," "personal horizon," and "a certain affection or dislike for the client [that] naturally comes in." One supervisor noted that while she is quite generous in her interpretations of the law, at least one-third of caseworkers in the office were very restrictive in their approach. For example,

> When people apply for compensation for health care, for example orthodontics/dentures, which is very expensive. Some welfare workers might say

that the expense is too great, that the client does not need completely new teeth. Others say that every person should have good teeth and in those cases the costs are immediately accepted.

Some considered this discrepancy a significant problem, but largely unavoidable; others minimized the issue as purely theoretical because "there are almost no two cases that are really the same." The right to appeal was often cited as a way of ensuring "a society based on the rule of law and on rights," though it was also readily conceded that few clients actually appealed decisions.

A more interesting interpretation of this seemingly unassailable discretion was expressed by two supervisors. Caseworkers' authority is based on their mastery of a well-developed regulatory system and their proper utilization of the law to construct sound arguments. "While two identical cases could be decided differently . . . it doesn't mean it is arbitrary," as each caseworker could have legitimate reasons under the circumstances for their decision. The law creates constraints on what a caseworker can do, but it also provides the interpretive resources caseworkers utilize to select and incorporate the facts of a case in different ways. It sets limits on the form of the decision while the content remains less controllable. Unequal treatment is not simply a result of inadequate monitoring but is affirmed and reinforced in some sense by the rules themselves, in defining the area where officials are allowed to make decisions based on extralegal considerations. The differences in the way caseworkers make decisions, "confirms the discretion we have in the law."

Assuming officials are adhering to the program's legal requirements, can caseworkers utilize different lines of reasoning to arrive at different outcomes for similar cases and be considered judicial decision makers? Recall that judicial decision making is a two-step process, first identifying which rules apply to a given fact pattern, and then determining whether public policy considerations warrant against conventional applications of these rules. Consistent decision making within an organization depends on maintaining an ongoing and evolving consensus on legal interpretation and on the institutional values toward which officials' actions should be oriented in particular situations (Kagan 1978). Variations in how caseworkers respond to an application of dentures, for example, could be characterized as a kind of legalism because frontline officials follow their own interpretations of core program values, including what a reasonable standard of living requires, and how much emphasis is to be placed on controlling fiscal costs. These personal judgments inform, therefore, how stringent caseworkers are in making discretionary assessments of need. Caseworkers may be acting "responsively," but based on their own personal conceptions of the organizational mission.

This weak "culture of rule application" may be a result of many factors: (1) the difficulty of creating a detailed enough interpretive schema to handle the variations caseworkers encounter. In other words, the organization's central task of making individualized assessments may be too complicated to develop a thoroughly operational consensus (but see Sweden in chapter 5); (2) a regulation-heavy environment that channels organizational attention more toward the technical requirements of the work (i.e., the first step in the decision-making process) rather than on underlying institutional values; (3) a group whose professional status as senior civil servants creates a greater ethos of independence, where close supervision is considered less appropriate than in other occupational areas, especially after full decision-making authority has been granted; (4) a core of veteran workers who have developed their own particular practices and are resistant to collective efforts to change them, or are left alone by administrators; (5) supervisors who are unable to maintain strong influence over caseworkers, due to their own caseloads, and other work-related limitations; and (6) caseworkers being honest about a situation that plagues all organizations.

Program Conditions that Limit Responsive Decision Making

Each case worker . . . has too little time to use her discretion . . . The case worker is responsible for a huge policy area and a large number of cases. . . so that in day-to-day work she only gets around to approving payments to clients for living expenses.

Making decisions quickly is a source of constant pressure in an organization that serves indigent individuals with few other options for support. Where caseloads are chronically and unmanageably high, careful and comprehensive eligibility assessments are rarely possible (cf. Kagan 1978, chap. 8). The ability to influence officials' behavior also becomes less effective as the inundation of applications overwhelms usual integrative organizational processes, like supervision, training, and consultation. While Bremen's caseworkers may work under more strained conditions than what is typical in many German social assistance programs, their predicament sheds light on the many potential stress points and pitfalls of such a heavily structured program and welfare state.

Workload—personnel shortages and caseload pressures

Bremen has an especially precarious financial base and higher than normal demand for social assistance.[26] As a port town, it was hit particularly hard by the shift toward a postindustrial economy. Many manufacturing and shipping companies closed and were not replaced with other suitable forms of employment for many residents. Its status as a city-state also gives it less control over its tax base as many of the people who work in Bremen live in the suburbs, that is, in another state tax base. In an effort to deal with the difficult fiscal situation, the Bremen government has repeatedly reduced personnel costs in a variety of ways that have steadily increased caseload sizes. For example, the introduction of computers for entering and storing information and calculating budgets was purportedly to reduce the amount of time staff spent on routine work so they could keep better track of their clients. Instead, the increase in efficiency immediately led to a formal caseload increase from 92.5 to 116, and this official number has continued to rise to 127.

Many caseworker vacancies are also never filled or are converted to temporary positions. New caseworkers are then required to "float around for years" from one office to another, filling in wherever need is greatest. Only after an existing caseworker retires or is promoted, and the position remains, can a caseworker take over a permanent position. Needless to say, the high stress of the job, the precarious employment status, and the low pay in comparison with other, higher-status, public administrative jobs have made it difficult for social assistance offices to hire and retain qualified staff. Caseloads for empty positions are frequently redistributed among existing caseworkers, putting their actual numbers far above the official limit, often approaching 180.[27] As a result, staff often deal with clients with whom they have little familiarity, leading to an even greater tendency to treat such rotating cases in a cursory manner.

Recruitment problems have also led to an increasingly heterogeneous, less qualified mix of staff. Because individuals with senior civil service credentials are so difficult to find, offices have had to hire individuals with only a middle-level administrative expertise or from entirely different educational backgrounds, including social workers and teachers. These so-called side entrants receive special training in order to equip them as rapidly as possible with the knowledge and skills necessary for doing casework. While administrators maintained that many of these individuals performed just as well as more traditionally trained staff, several also voiced concern that the complicated nature of assessment in many kinds of cases required traditional public administration expertise.

The organization of work

A heavy reliance on high qualifications is also reflected in the organization of work. Bremen caseworkers are responsible for all the work associated with their cases.[28] This situation creates high levels of client contact (between 20 and 30 client visits per week). A lack of support staff means that a significant portion of caseworkers' time is consumed by tasks that require little skill or information to complete, leaving them less opportunity for attending to more complex issues. Under such conditions, the two-tiered benefit structure itself is a primary cause of work because of the heavy reliance it places on caseworkers as gatekeepers for itemized expenses:

> We have to evaluate every single application, and the client has to ask for each support separately. This is one of the most time consuming things about this job. We pay for rent, some living costs and health insurance. But everything else has to be asked for separately ... It is outdated and way too complicated.

As mentioned earlier, unit supervisors officially carry half a caseload, but these levels often approach the official full caseload limit. This high number most certainly limits their ability to perform their administrative functions. Disseminating information, conferring with caseworkers, and performing case audits all get short shrift. One supervisor commented that she views herself first as a caseworker, and only secondly as a supervisor, because her clients' needs must come first, and there is hardly any time left over to do anything else.

One important aspect of eligibility assessments in Germany that lessens the burden full case responsibility might entail is that, unlike in the United States and Sweden, after an initial assessment, eligibility is only reassessed annually, unless a client reports changes or is judged unreliable. As a result, much of the work associated with monthly reassessments that agencies in these other countries perform is eliminated. While the workload is more manageable without this recurrent task, agencies also have less ability to ensure that grant levels reflect actual client situations. Therefore, infrequent monitoring of client status likely leads to frequent errors of generosity, where clients receive more than they are eligible for because they become employed or eligible for benefits from other programs.[29] As we shall see, this lack of fiscal control is rampant in many areas of support.

Information management and training deficits

The regulatory complexity associated with the broad areas of support covered by Sozialhilfe, the continual development of special-needs guidelines, and the larger social security system make it impossible for an individual caseworker to keep all regulations in her head. Needed under such conditions is a sophisticated information management system, such as a search engine where "you could enter a keyword and get the information on the screen."[30] Unfortunately, the means by which caseworkers receive, learn, and navigate program regulations is too primitive to meet the challenge. Regular publications of new rules are disseminated to caseworkers in written form. It is both a lot of information and not well structured, "a jumble of rules," and it is largely left to the individual caseworker to learn and organize them. Continuing education seminars are also not typically offered. Rather than attempting to research the latest regulatory developments, to save time, caseworkers often simply decide to go on their own personal impression of rule meanings.

Accounting complexity—the welfare state environment

> In Germany, the welfare system is very complicated. Most people, even those who write the regulations, don't understand it.
>
> (agency administrator)

The dense thicket of rules found in social assistance is emblematic of the way programs are generally regulated in Germany's vast array of public benefits programs. And with fiscal pressures caused by chronically high unemployment levels and continuing costs of reunification, eligibility conditions in all the various entitlement programs change frequently. For officials who administer any one of these programs, such changes are likely manageable because of the limited scope of their jurisdiction. They only deal with a small slice of the regulatory world.

However, for social assistance caseworkers this political approach to budgetary concerns has a much more significant and deleterious effect. As administrators of the program of "last resort," they must establish that all other forms of financial assistance have been exhausted before an applicant may be considered for social assistance. Caseworkers and supervisors without exception described one of their most important functions as advising clients about accessing other benefits. In order to do this, caseworkers need to have both a working knowledge of the changing eligibility conditions of all precedential programs[31] and sufficient information about a client in order to evaluate their entitlements.

> When I began there was no alimony support, no child support allowance (Erziehungsgeld). When someone was approved here at that time we only had to look at children's allowance (Kindergeld), unemployment insurance, housing subsidy (Wohngeld) and pensions (Rente). In the meantime a lot has happened in the whole area of social security—many things have been added while other areas have changed. The newest, there is no more unemployment assistance for those who didn't first get unemployment insurance.

Asylum seekers benefits law didn't exist thirty years ago. There were no asylum seekers. That began in the 1980s. And that law has changed two or three times since, radically changed. And that means a total rethinking. There are always a lot of changes.

Applying these multiple regulatory systems has made casework increasingly complex and time-consuming, with "modalities of calculation changing constantly." Assessment and advising are also not the only accounting tasks. As one caseworker observed, "The work here is not just about giving out money . . . but also getting it back." Most income-maintenance programs are funded by sources other than the local government, most typically the federal government through a hierarchy of precedential entitlements. Local social assistance agencies, then, are entitled to reimbursement for any interim support they provide recipients while their claims in these other programs are processed. Inefficiencies and delays in processing claims in many government agencies are well-recognized problems in Germany (Breuer and Engles 1998). A study of Bremen social assistance clients, for example, found that 40 percent were receiving aid because other entitlements were pending (Leisering and Leibfried 1999). These back payments from other government programs are, thus, a potentially huge source of income for local governments and a huge amount of work for caseworkers, one that requires them not only to identify claims, but also to properly document them and follow up with other agencies.[32]

The centrality and intricacy of this function appears to be unique among the three countries due to differences in the development of social security programs, as well as in systems of regulation. There are few other public entitlements in the United States. In Sweden, program regulations are generally simpler and assessment comparatively easy.

Coping mechanisms under impacted work conditions

Shortcuts are structurally inevitable in a system of governance steeped in regulations without adequate organizational resources, "the most expensive form of savings," as one administrator lamented. Many aspects of case processing are eroded, and it becomes difficult for caseworkers to assess clients on an individualized basis. Caseworkers often grant applications without any investigation in order to avoid client contact and potential appeals, although some also simply deny the application. The nuances of the rules are also often ignored in favor of the most efficient decision. For example, several staff explained that when they received a one-time aid application, they simply checked to see if the client had ever applied for it before, and if not, granted it. Home visits to assess a client's situation more carefully were virtually unheard of. While such retreatist behavior is inappropriate, such methods fall within the discretion of caseworkers and are therefore difficult to detect or prevent. Or caseworkers may actually make individual assessments, but then fail to document their argument in the decision report, a "documentation" error that could be detected by supervisors during case inspections.

Quite often the workload simply results in careless mistakes—a missed income source or cost reimbursement application, a failure to verify client information, or a failure to consider the implications of a client's situation—errors that can be very costly.

> For example, there was a young woman who had a kid and never reported it. If I had had a normal caseload, I would have probably realized this because she had reported she was pregnant and received a special needs payment. I only discovered it in June through the annual questionnaire. The point is she should have applied for child allowance and child support, which was not done. The amount would have been so high for those two benefits, she wouldn't have had any right to welfare and in fact there would've been a reduction in rent subsidy. In effect there is a welfare overpayment. And such things slip through because of time.

As a result of the failure to advise clients properly about their precedential rights and to collect interim support costs, it was estimated by one official that the state of Bremen lost tens of millions of DMs annually.

The difficult work conditions also lead to very apparent burnout and cynicism among many staff. Several complained about their "stupid," "lazy," and "conniving" clients. In moments of scary frankness, a few discussed how they would simply shut their door and ignore the clients in the waiting room or make difficult demands on some disfavored client, such as turning in many job applications every month. Most staff, though, were more stalwart in their attitude (at least in the interview) and tried to remain professional in the face of the overwhelming demands of clients, many of whom could be extremely aggressive and unfriendly.[33]

Activation Efforts among Caseworkers

Activation, in the broadest sense of making clients independent of welfare, is supposed to be a central goal of social assistance caseworkers, and officials frequently expressed the importance of helping recipients become self-sufficient. But work conditions in Bremen's welfare offices largely preclude much involvement in clients' situations. There is little opportunity to meet with and counsel more than a few clients at any one time. While requiring job applications is a more standardized option, it appears to be infrequently used, as it also creates more work for staff.

The only definitive activation resource available to caseworkers is the local welfare-to-work agency, Werkstatt Bremen (see chapter 7), and referrals there were the only regularly used activation obligation. Werkstatt Bremen's mandatory activation program for "youth" (those under 27 years of age) means that all such recipients are automatically referred, and monitoring of participation appears very well enforced. For older recipients, there is a second division of the activation agency, but it is less well funded and unable to serve more than a relatively small percentage of the more work-capable recipients. While many caseworkers regularly send clients there, a large number are sent back without having received services. Thus, activation mandates tend to be neglected or only sporadically implemented by those caseworkers who choose to impose obligations on or help particular clients.

Local Reform Efforts in Bremen in 2000

At the time of this fieldwork in 2000, central administrators in Bremen were considering new ways to organize casework in order to gain greater programmatic control and increase activation efforts. In one pilot project, specialized caseworkers were assigned to one of the variety of expensive discretionary areas of support (eight in all) where caseworkers have generally failed to conduct accurate assessments. Including home visits, they were to investigate cases where, for example, a client applied to alleviate rent debt or for special one-time payments for appliances. While these pilot positions had proven to be self-financing, there were serious misgivings with such an approach, especially that such task-specialized staff would come to replace existing vacancies, leaving the entire office caseload to even fewer staff. One supervisor was also dismayed that such positions would change the nature of social assistance work. The variety, freedom, and challenge that makes the work so interesting would be effectively eliminated, turning caseworkers into "specialized idiots" (*fachidioten*) by "ripping everything apart."

A more systemic solution that was being developed would divide current case tasks among three different kinds of caseworkers. Straightforward support decisions could be handled by less qualified, middle-level civil servants, thus freeing time for more senior staff to provide real case management, "to follow a case as it develops." Her responsibilities would include the neglected duties of identifying precedential entitlements and a much more substantive activation role, not only encouraging clients to find work, but also developing familiarity and relationships with the city-district's employers. Due to the legal complexity involved, a third worker would take care of income (*Einnahmen*), specifically the establishment and collection of child support and alimony payments.

Subsequent National Policy Changes

Since 2003 German social assistance has been part of several policy reforms that have significantly altered basic parameters of the program, shifting large proportions of the population to different benefit systems and simplifying the benefit structure. These changes were fueled in part by concerns that welfare continued to provide long-term support for individuals whose problems arose from social risks that should already be met by the social insurance system, in particular, old age and unemployment. In 2003 a new needs-based benefit was introduced for persons with an insufficient entitlement to old age or disability pensions. This new benefit allowed the elderly with low incomes to obtain a supplement as part of their retirement program rather than having to apply for welfare (Aust 2003).

Unemployed social assistance recipients were a much more significant problem, representing an estimated 40 percent of all claimants (Adema, Gray, and Kahl 2003). This meant that work-capable individuals without jobs were being served by both the national employment office and local social assistance agencies. Given the differences in rights and rules applied by the two programs and the fact that individuals frequently moved back and forth between them, the result was significant administrative inefficiencies and inequities. In response, a radical benefit redesign called the Hartz IV reform led to the creation of a new integrated benefit program for all people without work who were employable, called "basic security income for the unemployed." Benefit levels would be set at the social assistance level, but it would be administered by the federal unemployment office and funded by the national government (see chapter 7 for more details). As a result of these two reforms, it was estimated that 1.8 million of the 3 million beneficiaries would be removed from the local welfare system (Aust 2003).[34]

Responding to arguments that the current program required too many decisions for nonstandard, exceptional needs, the social assistance program itself was also comprehensively reformed on January 1, 2005. The new social assistance law (now Book XII of the Social Code) largely retained the original goals and principles, but with significant consolidation in the benefit structure. The two-tier system of support was largely collapsed, with most previous one-time payments now considered to be covered in an increased basic grant rate. Nonrecurring expenses were only to be provided in three instances—setting up a household, initial outfitting with clothes, and school outings of two days or longer (FMH 2005). Any other special expenses would only be granted as loans. By simplifying the benefit structure it was hoped that casework would be less burdensome and less administrative and so allow caseworkers to focus more on their social service function. At the same time, a larger basic monthly amount was viewed as more respectful of recipients by giving them greater control over their finances (FMH 2005).

While results of the main reform have not yet been published, a less radical benefit restructuring had been previously tested and evaluated in some "model regions" (Univation 2004). The results show that most case workers were quite satisfied with the new regulatory approach because it simplified work and gave them more time for their clients. However, recipient surveys indicated that a large portion of claimants felt otherwise. Particularly households with children frequently experienced situations of accumulating debt they previously had been able to manage through periodic one-time need applications. The authors of this report recommended that program administrators devote greater resources to developing budgetary skills in recipients and creating procedures to ensure that particularly vulnerable groups are provided sufficient support.

Conclusion

German caseworkers have more decision-making authority than U.S. caseworkers to consider particular situations of claimants in making needs assessments. Caseworkers may grant special-needs payments to recipients for a wide variety of additional household items and other exceptional expenses not covered by the monthly grant, and they may also make individual exceptions to presumptive rules when deemed appropriate. Their discretion is also reinforced by their full decision-making authority, greatly limiting the ability of administrators to affect the choices they make. Therefore caseworkers have a considerable role to play in ensuring that recipients are provided adequate support to maintain a reasonable standard of living.

At the same time, this discretion is embedded in (and justified by) an extensive regulatory framework that continues to grow through the incorporation of legal and political decisions regarding what constitutes "basic need." This significant authority to make individualized assessments in the context of extensive regulations places German caseworkers toward the middle right on the dimension of *legal authority* (figure 4.1). This formal capacity to be responsive is in stark contrast to the United States. Caseworkers there have little independent formal role to play in determining claimant need because their task has been reduced to a technical determination of "eligibility" for a standardized grant, rather than a more complicated evaluation of benefit adequacy.

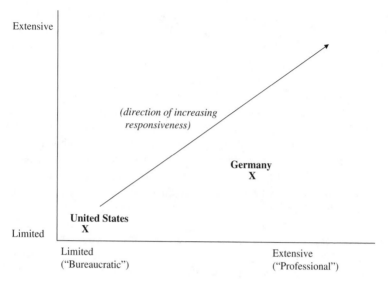

Horizontal Axis
Legal Authority for Responsive Decision Making: formal ability of caseworker to consider individual circumstances in assessing need

Vertical Axis
Organizational Capacity for Responsive Decision Making: ability of agency to enable and control official decision making

Figure 4.1   Comparing responsiveness among welfare caseworkers (U.S. and German examples)

The German system creates greater possibilities for individualized support, but it also engenders greater organizational challenges to ensuring consistent and equitable decisions. Detailed regulations and the regulatory expertise of caseworkers—due in part to their extensive on-the-job training and the long tenure of many careerist staff—create some built-in safeguards. But in some circumstances, caseworkers regularly make different decisions about similar cases. Many officials saw this discrepancy as an inevitable consequence of a system geared toward "individualized assessments." A few supervisors, however, also framed such discrepancy in a more positive light, as a manifestation of officials' legitimate authority to make such distinctions based on their personal judgments as regulation experts.

However, German caseworkers lose much of the capacity to utilize their discretion due to the demands created by legal complexity in light of their heavy workloads. As in the United States, German caseworkers have considerable regulations to apply, but generally these regulations come from different sources. In the United States this rule burden arises from distinctive features of determining eligibility for the basic grant—from multiple programs with different eligibility conditions, and detailed procedures and documentation requirements that assess not only material deprivation, but make additional behavioral and status distinctions for identifying only the deserving poor.

By contrast, in Germany, rules governing basic support are comparatively manageable, stemming from a "simpler," single universal welfare program, based largely on being income poor. Rather, German caseworkers must contend with extensive regulations from three other sources: (1) program "breadth" (rather than program "diversity" as in the United States), with program jurisdiction over special kinds of needs for which caseworkers in other countries are not responsible; (2) a formalized system for the continual production of new guidelines to operationalize the shifting requirements of participation in societal life (the United States has no analog to this mandate); (3) complex eligibility conditions for precedential forms of public support which caseworkers are responsible for identifying and helping clients access. (In the United States, there are very few alternative forms of public support.)

Caseworkers in Bremen must also deal with very high caseloads stemming from a public financial crisis that has cut staffing levels and made it difficult to fill vacancies. Additionally, the lack of clerical support means caseworkers face the full burden of client demands, absorbing much of their time with routine tasks, leaving little for difficult assessments. Relevant regulations are not computerized, requiring caseworkers to look among stacks of unorganized manuals. Finally, the ability of supervisors to monitor caseworker behavior and facilitate case discussion is very limited by their own half (to full) caseloads.

Under these conditions, caseworkers develop predictable shortcuts that often lead to considerable loss of fiscal control. Discretion is not utilized to make careful assessments, and so decisions become superficial and legalistic. Special-need applications are often granted without any investigation. Many alternative forms of public support to which a client may be entitled are not identified, or the caseworker fails to obtain reimbursement from other agencies for interim support. And the burnout caused by such work conditions causes some caseworkers to exercise their discretion by retreating from their casework, denying applications out of hand, or punishing clients with heavy job search requirements so they will leave caseworkers alone.

Thus, inadequate *organizational capacity* often reduces caseworkers to "technicians," with their capacity to tailor aid based on careful considerations overrun by the need for hard-and-fast rules of thumb to complete their work. Thus, Bremen's welfare program in 2000 fell far short of its potential for officials provided with this much decision-making authority (figure 4.1).

Reforms in 2003 and 2005 in social assistance policy and the larger German income maintenance system addressed several of the program conditions that limit efficient (and effective) administration. A large proportion of social assistance recipients have been transferred to new, needs-based income-security programs for pensioners and the unemployed, drastically reducing the caseloads of local welfare agencies. A simplified benefit structure with a higher standard grant and fewer opportunities to apply for special needs should eliminate much of the regulatory structure as well as the volume of one-time expense applications with which caseworkers have had to contend. At the same time, however, it is unclear to what extent such a change limits caseworkers' ability to ensure adequate support, especially for vulnerable populations.

5

Welfare Caseworkers in Malmö, Sweden: Social Workers and the Consultation Culture

The most challenging aspect for caseworkers are those things for which there isn't any kind of rule structure. It is difficult for them to accept sometimes and difficult for us to manage.[1]

Introduction

Swedish social assistance is a second example of a "needs-based" system, one that aspires to secure claimants a "reasonable standard of living," while also assisting them to "live an independent life." Like its German counterpart, it consists of a two-tiered system of support. A relatively rule-bound standardized grant is intended to cover most typical living expenses a household will incur. A second, more discretionary, area of support is available to cover a variety of exceptional needs, including longer-term and emergency expenses. Assessments are, in principle, individualized, and caseworkers have full authority over the decisions they make.

But beyond this basic programmatic and authority structure, the way caseworkers assess need is remarkably distinct, reflecting different traditions of regulation, organization, and expertise in this policy area. In Germany, highly skilled public administrators contend with an enormous array of regulations covering a broad set of needs, a "regulatory excess" in some sense. In Sweden, on the other hand, trained social workers make narrower (economic) support decisions, and their decision-making challenge is rather one of "rule scarcity," where legal constraints often take the form of general considerations and recommendations. Such a loosely structured program creates not only a potential to tailor aid based on careful deliberation about a claimant's particular life circumstances, but also makes it difficult for caseworkers to be certain about the decisions they make and for administrators to ensure some consistency in the way their staff provide support.

This "interpretive challenge" is largely met through specific features of the social assistance office: (1) A well-developed informal knowledge base is maintained by veteran administrators. Specialized staff, known as "method developers" (*metod utvecklare*), train caseworkers in these office practices and monitor their decision making by directly supervising new employees and acting as designated, ongoing "discussion partners." Caseworkers' social work training also gives them important skills for evaluating clients' situations in a holistic and sophisticated manner. (2) Caseworkers are also specialized to handle only cases requiring an individualized assessment. Clerical staff manage all routine tasks and regular contact with clients. This division of labor allows welfare officials to devote much of their time to difficult claims and to develop expertise in their evaluation.

At the same time, the ability to make individualized assessments is constrained by changes in the social assistance program. Dramatic increases in the number of recipients in the 1990s led to rising caseloads, forcing officials to make decisions quickly and leading to more superficial treatment of many cases. The increasingly bureaucratized nature of social assistance work also created dissatisfaction among caseworkers, contributing to high staff turnover. Short tenure puts added stress on agencies' efforts to maintain and instill the supplemental interpretive knowledge that is so crucial for decision making. There are also indicators that staff sometimes exploit the limited ability of administrators to monitor activities in order to provide certain clients more generous benefits than the law allows. Despite these impacted work conditions, Malmö social assistance caseworkers seemed to be more able than their Bremen or Californian counterparts to effectively individualize economic support, owing to their strong social work consultation culture, specialized positions, and limited legal constraints.

Caseworkers' roles in activating their clients has also changed noticeably in the last decade. Previously welfare staff focused on rehabilitation for a clientele with multiple social problems. But with the recession, the influx of the "simply unemployed" shifted the program's activation focus to moving these new recipients back into the labor market as quickly as possible. Caseworkers now focus primarily on the administrative tasks of referring clients to recently established local welfare-to-work programs while monitoring their participation. Administrative efforts are under way, however, to shift economic and activation responsibility for these clients to other organizations in order to allow some caseworkers to return their attention to the traditional social assistance clientele.

This chapter gives a brief overview of welfare law and administration in the past two decades in Sweden. A discussion of the regulatory framework and the interpretive and information challenges it poses for caseworkers follows. The chapter then presents the organizational features that contribute to individualized decision making: followed by a section on the features that limit this possibility. Finally, it briefly discusses the changing activation focus of caseworkers and the efforts to recoup the lost social worker role.

Local Self-Governance in Social Services

A unique combination of institutional features, distinguishing it from both Germany and the United States, characterize Swedish social assistance (*socialbidrag*). In keeping with its reputation for a generous system of protections, welfare benefit levels are among the highest in the OECD at 25 percent above the mean (Eardley et al. 1996).[2] At the same time there remains a stronger institutional connection between welfare and social services, and regulations are less extensive and systematic at the national level than in Germany or the United States. Central government has limited fiscal control over municipalities that raise close to 80 percent of their own income (through personal income tax and user fees) and spend 80 percent of all government revenue, including largely self-financing social assistance (Ditch et al. 1997).

A brief history of welfare law and administrative practices in the 1980s and 1990s[3] illustrates the impact of local governance in the area of social services—the tension between central and municipal government; the precarious status of social assistance entitlement; and the see-saw effect in institutional reform caused by financial pressures.

Prior to the passage of national legislation, municipalities had considerable discretion over the design of their social assistance programs. Welfare aid often involved several levels of support for different kinds of need (such as short-term, acute, and food grants), requiring caseworkers to assess the claimants' appropriate category of need. Benefit levels were often insufficient for basic needs, requiring claimants to apply separately for a variety of additional expenses and subjecting them each time to close scrutiny. Caseworkers were also generally responsible for income support and rehabilitative and other interventionist state services, creating coercive potential to demand and monitor behavioral compliance as a condition for aid.

In 1982, the first national social assistance law went some way toward correcting these weaknesses without making a radical break from past institutional arrangements. This legislation was constructed as a "frame law." It established a programmatic goal of helping people maintain a reasonable standard of living and delegated the ultimate responsibility for meeting this need to the localities. However, the individual's right to social assistance was not specified beyond this stated objective, leaving such determinations of support levels to local politicians and administrators. Individuals' right to support was to be ensured through the supervisory and corrective functions of the National Board of Health and Welfare (NBHW), through its non-binding policy recommendations and through the administrative court system, by granting individuals the right to appeal caseworkers' decisions. Johansson has characterized the widely held confidence among national legislators regarding the localities' ability and beneficence to administer this last entitlement as the era of the "hopeful definition" of a right welfare.

During the 1980s, many national and local politicians aspired to break with social assistance's charity tradition by developing it into a substantive right with the legal protections and limited means-testing associated with traditional social insurance entitlements. Johansson has characterized this time of locally initiated reform as the era of "borrowed universalism," referring to the modeling of new social assistance program features on the principles of many of Sweden's other, more accessible, and legally articulated entitlement programs, such as unemployment benefits and disability. Many localities introduced a single, standardized grant level that included the majority of daily living expenses. It was to be generous enough so that social assistance recipients could manage their own lives as much as possible without regularly applying for extra money.

The administrative relationship between the recipient and the caseworker was also to be as anonymous and formalized as possible, in order to maintain recipients' dignity and limit the caseworkers' power over their clients. The eligibility process was simplified, and claimant-caseworker contact was largely limited to the submission of applications and documentation via the mail. Caseworkers were often placed in centralized, social-assistance-only units, so that, for the first time, the same caseworkers were no longer responsible for both economic support and other social service functions. This separation of cash and care significantly eliminated the potential for "therapeutic coercion" from the caseworker-client relationship.

In the 1990s, however, economic conditions changed dramatically. Whereas the unemployment rate in 1987 was at 1.9 percent, by 1993 it had risen to an unprecedented 8.3 percent, the highest since the Great Depression. Increasing numbers of the unemployed lost their entitlement to social insurance or never qualified, with youth and recent immigrants hit particularly hard. Welfare receipt increased from 270,000 nationally in 1990 to 400,000 in 1996 (Salonen 2001). Costs for social assistance nearly doubled, with almost the entire fiscal burden falling on the municipalities. Social assistance suddenly became a central political question at the local level that overshadowed all others.

During the "crisis," local politicians made the conditions of welfare eligibility more stringent, reintroducing many of the old programmatic features. Many living expenses that had been included in the standard grant were once again separated out as "special needs," allowing localities to thereby reduce the general level of support. Clients were again required to make separate applications for these expenses, and caseworkers to make additional individual determinations. A variety of less generous norms were also reintroduced for clients in different situations. Many localities also reorganized the processing of social assistance cases again, decentralizing and reattaching them to other social service units. Specialized social assistance units were often created for particular client groups—especially youth—so that agencies could better supervise these clients' efforts at self-help. Later, this more "active" monitoring of clients was extended to the entire caseload. Thus, in this era of "recovered selectivism," the regulatory balance shifted away from institutionalizing social assistance as an entitlement and reverted to the prerogatives of local self-determination and budgetary control.

A revised social service law in 1998 affirmed many of these changes in municipal practices, including the right of welfare programs to require recipients' participation in local activation projects as a condition of eligibility (see chapter 8). At the same time, though, this law also set a common national grant level for the first time, as had been called for during the previous two decades by both the administrative court system and the NBHW (and fought by many localities for much of the 1990s) (Ditch et al. 1997). While national norms greatly reduced local discretion over basic support decisions, the law also created a category of "aid in other cases" over which localities had complete discretion and clients no right to appeal (a section that was subsequently repealed in the 2002 revisions).

Regulatory Framework

Building on the two-page national frame law, local authorities develop their own supplemental communal regulations (*tillämpningsbestämmelser*) to provide operational detail to the eligibility process. The forms of aid, the conditions under which they are granted, and the level of codification can therefore still vary quite dramatically among Swedish municipalities (Byberg 1998).[4]

Another important source of administrative guidance are the periodic reports published by the NBHW, the central government agency that supervises medical care and social services in Sweden. Although only advisory, these reports give a national overview of practices, providing general statements of interpretation and examples of their application. Claimants also have the right to appeal most decisions through the three levels of the administrative court system. While decisions are only legally binding for the particular case (and are not generally incorporated into administrative regulations as in Germany), these cases also provide a useful, though dispersed, source of interpretive guidance.

As in Germany, Swedish social assistance is intended to ensure some basic level of material support. The Social Service Law (SSL) provides that municipalities must support an individual "who cannot provide for their own need or cannot meet their need in another way" at a level that will secure a "reasonable standard of living." It is organized in a variation of a two-tiered system with a standard grant amount for daily living expenses (§6b.1).[5] Other additional expenses (so-called "6b" items) (§6b.2)[6] are also considered an entitlement but were deemed to vary too much by locality and individual circumstance to be packaged together as part of the basic grant, including housing and utilities that are "reasonable." A second area of discretionary support, "aid in other cases" or "6g" items,[7] is intended to cover any other possible expenses a person may incur. In contrast to the basic grant and 6b items, localities have great latitude over the kinds and amounts of aid they provide when the support falls under this category. As in Germany, then, Swedish caseworkers must often decide when an expense is covered by the basic grant and when this type of additional aid is justified.

> Take, for example, a gym card, so you can go and train at the gym and do something with your free time. Most are denied this because one considers this to be included in the normal monthly grant which is totally absurd. There are those who don't have anything to do temporarily. It can be because they are overweight, it can be because of other social problems, so if one can manage to find a way so they have something to do, so they can get going in something, perhaps it can help.

Assessments are also intended to be individualized. In Swedish law this administrative principle appears in many different instances, including in Malmö's communal regulations, which state that "the amounts are a guide for assessment, that, however, in principle must be individual." Swedish caseworkers, like their German counterparts, therefore make discretionary decisions to ensure adequacy of support, to promote recipients' self-help (example above), and to control claimants' long-term costs to local coffers.

> So one thing that can involve very different judgments is home furnishings . . . We have certain ceiling amounts that are the IKEA prices, but you can choose whatever amount you think.

> I had a person who applied for welfare who hadn't made his unemployment insurance payments for half a year. So this is in fact a debt, which we

normally reject, because debts are not a component of day-to-day living expenses. But if we do not approve payment, then he will become dependent on welfare in the future. So it might make sense to make an exception and pay his unemployment insurance payments.

Finally, as in Germany's social assistance administration, after 4–6 months of on-the-job training, caseworkers receive "delegation," that is, full decision-making authority.

Social assistance agencies are also expected to play an important role in making their clients self-sufficient, to "strengthen his or her resources to live an independent life." The SSL requires welfare recipients to participate in local "skill-enhancing activities" as a condition for receiving support, in order to develop "the individual's possibilities to become independent in the future . . . (and) strengthen the individual's possibilities to enter the labor market, or when appropriate, additional vocational training." The SSL also stresses the importance for agencies to tailor these activities to the wants and needs of the individual. If an individual fails to participate, however, his or her grant can be reduced or denied entirely.

Caseworker Decision Making under Conditions of "Rule Scarcity"

You get a good ground to stand on with the legislation, recommendations, communal regulations, but you have to learn still more, because there are always questions and things that aren't in the regulations in detail. It is so wide . . . Some practices, legal interpretation, those you have to learn and that requires that you have worked a while in order for you to "find your feet".

(supervisor)

Similar to characterizations in Bremen, caseworkers in Malmö are seen to possess considerable discretion in how they provide client support, what one supervisor characterized as "a fearful amount of power to sit with." But caseworker authority in Sweden is exercised under quite different programmatic conditions. Rather than the "regulatory excess" created by volumes of administrative guidelines as in Germany, Swedish caseworkers often face a challenge of "rule scarcity." Malmö's communal rules (MCR), the primary regulatory content of the program, were only 15 pages long in 2000.

Even where there is relatively extensive commentary, the local regulations provide only limited guidance. For example, in determining the eligibility for home furnishings, a "6g" discretionary area of support, caseworkers should consider the applicant's age and future support possibilities: "Persons who are considered likely to become independent within a reasonable time shall only be granted a smaller amount for immediate need." If an applicant is deemed eligible, the caseworker should then "consider carefully" the most economical means of purchase. In addition, if the support requested is extensive, the caseworker must make a home visit. Thus, for such an aid application, caseworkers are called upon to make a wide variety of difficult judgments about the actual need of a client for particular household items, the client's future employment prospects, and the local market for home furnishings—all of this with few additional specific procedural instructions.

Several administrators extolled the benefits of such a "loosely structured" system. It led to a more nuanced system of case evaluation than might occur were officials more constrained by, and could more readily rely on, definite rules. Caseworkers could consider ways of facilitating self-sufficiency based on a client's particular goals and abilities. They could also adapt their evaluations to changing societal conditions, such as a tighter housing market that made it more difficult for a client with existing rental debt to find an apartment.[8] Given such a flexible regulatory system, there were also advantages to a decentralized authority structure. The "burden of authority" was seen as a source of motivation, requiring caseworkers "to think more on their own . . . to become more creative and thoughtful in their consideration" than they might otherwise if their decisions had to be reviewed and approved.

But these same formal characteristics that give staff broad latitude also create significant challenges for caseworkers. While most "typical" decisions are covered reasonably well by the existing communal rules, all caseworkers and supervisors commented that they contend with novel issues all the time that they struggle to correctly assess:

> We are often confronted with entirely new situations that we have to take a position on which aren't found at all in any rules or provisions. Our job deals a lot with these kinds of situations . . . It is extremely frustrating here that there aren't clear guiding principles for certain things.

And under such circumstances, this authority can be difficult to manage, "like it is so big that you want to have someone to lean on sometimes."

In many situations, then, the rules do not set out the kinds of information that need to be collected or how to interpret this information in making decisions. Caseworkers are therefore often bombarded with the largely undistilled complexity of a new applicant and struggle to make sense of and translate her situation into assessment terms. Everything becomes potentially relevant and difficult to interpret.[9] Previous case patterns may have some precedential weight, but an individualized assessment means that even prior similar cases may be distinguished by particular unique facts in the present case.[10]

Because the rules are general and court cases only provide for analogous reasoning, there is often wide latitude for interpretation:

In one matter one might issue a denial based on the law—and it might have been possible to approve the application based on the same law. It depends upon one's interpretation which complicates matters.

There are different ways of thinking: should you take a hard line and reject the application now, or should you see mitigating circumstances, so to speak, and approve the application despite everything?

This legal ambiguity coupled with full decision-making authority can potentially lead to very different approaches among staff, and a number of caseworkers commented on the seeming arbitrary nature of many of the kinds of decisions they make: "They say here are the rules but don't forget that it is an individual assessment, and that is the reason that you can do almost anything you want to." Several situations were mentioned as being the most difficult to assess and therefore presenting the greatest risks of inconsistent treatment. These included debt, nonacute dental care, home furnishings, rental amounts higher than accepted norms, deciding who was work-capable, and the number of job applications one should require as a condition of eligibility.

The decision-making challenge for Swedish caseworkers, then, is to make individualized yet consistent assessments in the context of a regulatory framework that often provides only limited guidance for evaluating and balancing the particularities of claimants' situations. This interpretive difficulty is largely managed through particular features of social assistance administration, including caseworker education, intraoffice social arrangements, and task specialization.

Program Conditions that Promote Responsive Decision Making

Social work professionals

The continued links between welfare administration and local social services in Sweden have meant that all caseworkers are trained social workers. Swedish officials therefore have a different kind of knowledge and professionalization than administrators whose training is primarily legal or regulatory in nature. This social services orientation can affect the way they make decisions and relate to clients. It may make caseworkers more sensitive to client needs, more skilled at the consideration of people's situations holistically, and able to provide direct services in counseling and motivation. Their therapeutic expertise is therefore an important resource for making sophisticated evaluations that fill in where the law is inadequate. As one supervisor stated, "One can't think simply in terms of money . . . Sometimes there are a lot of things that must be taken into consideration like looking at what is in a client's background, and what their future options and intentions are . . . things that only a social worker can do."[11]

Method developers and the consultation culture

> It is . . . important that you have someone who has the same approach . . . that is what I can do as the one who hears all the different cases, to try to say that here we should try to think in this way.
>
> (method developer)

A well-developed informal knowledge base at the office level also provides crucial supplemental detail to the general considerations that exist in administrative guidelines. Veteran administrators maintain and refine methods of legal interpretation and case reasoning based on their evaluation of difficult cases over the course of their 10–20 years of administrative experience. This institutional knowledge creates the potential for very nuanced assessments of "what possibilities the law offers." It also means that a lot of what a caseworker needs to know to make decisions "is learned orally." Frontline staff are often initially socialized and receive ongoing training in these methods by so-called method developers, specialized staff who are responsible for the considerable on-the-job training of new caseworkers and who act as designated "discussion partners" for caseworkers after they have received decision-making authority.

Method developers are responsible for "everything around case processing itself. . . to make sure that cases are managed in a correct way." Their primary task is to stay abreast of current "practice"—the existing informal interpretive precedents for how regulations and court cases have been utilized in a wide variety of past claimant situations. This function requires collecting and familiarizing themselves with the various court decisions the office receives, which caseworkers generally know only cursorily. They have no cases of their own, but rather spend their time reviewing caseworker cases, doing background research, and consulting with staff. Their past experience and current focus on talking through claimant situations both gives them an available working knowledge and allows them to act more "neutrally," to consider different lines of reasoning without having an investment in the particular client. This kind of dedicated position ensures a higher degree of informal supervision and monitoring than would be possible if it occurred only in a hybridized supervisory role (as in the case of Germany).

Method developers assist caseworkers in two ways: (1) They draw caseworkers' attention to written interpretive aids with which they may not be familiar and inform them about how general regulations and principles have been interpreted for previous, similar cases. Most often fact patterns are new permutations of situations that have office precedents: "Since I am discussing cases the whole time, I have a good sense of what is approximately right and what is legally possible." (2) They also help caseworkers identify important client considerations in a particular kind of case and weigh the advantages and disadvantages of different possible decisions, "looking forward in time." The following illustrates the kind of discussion a developer might have with a caseworker for a situation of a claimant whose rent is excessive:

> They should think about how much the client has done to find out about cheaper apartments; are there any special circumstances that make it especially difficult for him or her to find one? If they can't get their own lease, perhaps they can get a relative to sign the contract, which is not the best situation because then the relative is also responsible for their rent. It could be we are the only possibility they have for signing a lease. That would mean the caseworker would have a lot more contact with the rental board which creates its own problems . . . But the most important issue, when one discusses this, is how difficult it is for the individual to find an apartment that is cheaper. For someone who is 18 or 19 years old who doesn't have a parent to sign for them, it can be very difficult. These are the kinds of things we discuss so they can think about them. If they have children then it is extra important to look at what is best for the children. How does it affect their surroundings, school friends and acquaintances? There is a lot. It isn't just money that one has to look at, because there is so much more.

Even after full delegation, administrators continue to develop caseworkers as independent experts. While there is little formal training, these collegial discussions are, as one supervisor described it, "a form of education that we have going on here the whole time."

Consultation persists as a central feature of social assistance casework in Malmö for several interrelated reasons. Through their background education and on-the-job training, staff come to understand collaboration as part of the "core task" (Johnson 1998) of social work. Consultation is also an important practice for managing the high level of uncertainty that appears to be an intrinsic part of the work.[12] Even for experienced staff the formal requirement to examine every case individually creates a heavy demand to justify and reason through cases. Discussing cases with another person—having someone to "bounce things off of" as it was repeatedly described—gives them more confidence in the decisions they ultimately take.[13] A dedicated discussion partner is also convenient[14] and "safe," lacking the ability to exert pressure on caseworkers that supervisors are able to do based on their positional authority. Caseworkers may therefore be more inclined to evaluate a difficult case carefully, rather than simply relying on their own impressions or forgoing a complicated assessment for a simpler, conventional approach.

Consultation is also a primary means by which supervisors develop confidence in their staff. Caseworkers are usually selected from among temporary summer workers. The close and frequent contact—the constant dialogue and checking in—gives supervisors a good sense of how their staff are making decisions. As a result, supervisors and method developers seemed relatively sanguine about the risk of inconsistent decision making among caseworkers.[15]

Additionally, as in Germany, some of the most important kinds of decisions are not left up to the voluntary consultation process. Caseworkers must consult with their supervisors on cases dealing with high rent debt; considerations of psychotherapy or other expensive treatment programs; special trips abroad, as in cases where a client's children still live in their country of origin; and situations where clients are living in a hotel. This practice minimizes the possibility for especially costly errors of judgment.

Interoffice consensus building and its limits
Malmö is divided into ten city districts, and each operates with considerable latitude. Supervisors and method developers from different city districts are therefore also in contact with each other in order to develop common interpretations of municipal regulations. These interoffice administrative discussions are intended to keep the conditions of eligibility similar, to create a "united net." But district offices still have the freedom to develop their own interpretations of communal regulations and court cases. As in Bremen, this discretion can create a problem of consistency at the next organizational level *among* offices within the same municipality.

The most extreme example concerns home furnishings for a young adult who moves out of his or her parents' home. This is a 6g application, and accordingly a caseworker has to determine what amount is "reasonable." In one city district (Havdal) the typical amount granted under these circumstances is 3,500 Kr (~$500), while in another (Lönnäng), it could be as much as 10,000 Kr (~$1,400). Whereas one office interprets a "reasonable" level to include only the most important things, the other office interprets it to mean "no worse off than someone who is not on welfare." As the supervisor there described it, "I think they should have a well-furnished apartment, one where they can be happy and take home friends, one that they are a little proud of." Although there is a court decision from the highest administrative court from five years previously stating that for young people who leave home 3,000 Kr is enough, the Lönnäng supervisor justified a more generous standard through a narrow interpretation of the legal case:

> I think that under normal conditions, [the court amount] is appropriate, if one hasn't been kicked out and has been given some things to take with them . . . But court decisions are just investigative practices. I mean they are made by lawyers. We are not lawyers, we are caseworkers. It is an individual assessment . . .
> Q: So there are other unit supervisors who use these court cases differently?
> Yes and it is actually not wrong. I follow the legal practice, it isn't wrong in a formal way. But I think the spirit of the judgment is wrong. The amount isn't nearly enough.

This example illustrates well how court cases, while providing "things that can be generalized," are not treated as regulations; how supervisors can have significant influence in how "lines of reasoning" are lifted from them; and that in at least some kinds of decisions, interoffice differences, "while not allowed by law," can and are allowed to persist.

Narrow program jurisdiction and limited accounting tasks

The ability of caseworkers to exercise their authority to make individualized assessments is facilitated by the comparatively "simple" features of the program they administer. Unlike the United States, Sweden has a single regulatory program. Unlike in Germany, the program is more circumscribed to the "traditional" welfare domain of daily living expenses. Thus, the greater demands created by program diversity (United States) and breadth of jurisdiction (Germany) are absent here. Additionally, assessing the precedential entitlements of the larger social security system does not appear to create the kinds of regulatory and task demands that are such a central and intractable part of German casework. While there are a considerable number of alternative forms of public support, program regulations in Sweden are generally simpler and assessment comparatively easier, with conditions of entitlement more like "double doors" rather than like Germany's "cubby holes."[16]

Division of labor—economic administrators

Another important facilitating factor is the division of labor in Malmö's offices. Much of the routine agency work that absorbs caseworker time in both Germany and the United States is handled by clerical staff known as economic administrators. Economic administrators carry out all routine processing of recipient cases, that is, monthly redeterminations, as well as standard 6b expense applications, which are generally automatically paid with submission of expense receipts (including bus cards, utilities, and minor dental care). Client contacts around basic support issues are also handled by these administrators, so that much of the effort needed for managing and responding to client demands is also diverted from caseworkers. Due to their regular contact with their cases they remain well informed about recipients' situations. Where a client requires special attention,[17] the economic administrator can refer them to the appropriate caseworker and provide important background information, especially regarding the client's current financial and family circumstances.

Thus, economic administrators play a crucial role in providing caseworkers the opportunity to consider difficult cases and to develop expertise in handling them. These supportive staff act not only as a work buffer, but also as a valuable source of client knowledge—an "information repository," which caseworkers are able to access whenever a task demands it. In contrast, this capacity for individualized assessments is not as easily maintained in Germany. While caseworkers there are not required to make monthly assessments, which itself limits the ability of the agency to control costs, they are still routinely inundated with routine questions and minor crises that require little technical skill to address, but which occupy much of their time.

Program Conditions that Limit Responsive Decision Making

Insulating effects of formalized eligibility and caseworker specialization

Several aspects of the organization of office work that simplify assessment and provide caseworkers the ability to focus on difficult cases also hinder their use of discretion. Intake is generally handled over the phone and via the mail—clients call in when they want to apply; a caseworker explains the process and the documents they need to submit, gathers some initial information, and sends them an application. Once the completed application and supporting documents are returned, the caseworker assesses the individual's case with follow-up telephone contact if any documents are missing or some information is unclear. Ongoing reassessments are also processed without face-to-face contact, and most of these interactions are handled by economic administrators. Caseworkers therefore have little direct or consistent contact with their clients. In general, they see comparatively few individuals in person for any reason, with an average of 0–5 per week.[18] This general arm's-length approach seems to be a result of both administrative reforms to limit the power of officials over welfare claimants (Johansson 2001) and high caseloads that prevent greater client contact. Such an approach, however, limits caseworkers' ability to familiarize themselves with the details of cases, and their investment in the decisions they make.

Caseload size

The downturn in the economy in the 1990s in Sweden increased the welfare roles dramatically, leading to much higher caseloads, estimated to be between 200 and 300, depending on the office and caseworker specialization. Almost universally, caseworkers and supervisors mentioned the lack of staff resources to meet current office caseloads. The pressure to make quick decisions on too many cases often demands superficial assessments—to look at things as "black or white"—and presents few opportunities for gathering potentially complicating and specific information that could affect decision making. As one supervisor commented, "there is a much greater need for limits and structure in the assessment process so that cases can be disposed of quickly, without too much time or uncertainty." Utilizing one's discretion to conduct an individualized assessment is often simply not warranted. The few veterans contrasted this loss of contact and client familiarity with an earlier time (the 1970s up to the mid-1980s) when caseloads were much smaller and caseworkers knew their clients well and had the time to "struggle more and think through their decisions more carefully."

Limited client knowledge also contributes to differential treatment of similar cases. When a caseworker knows a client well, she is likely to be more invested in the outcome and have more information to consider the possibilities of support that are justifiable under the law:

> If I am in close contact with a client . . . then I can have an entirely different perception than I do of another client who applies for the exact same thing, but who I don't know so well.

Short tenure and inadequate training

The largely administrative nature of the job under current work conditions also prevents most caseworkers from utilizing their skills as trained social workers. As a result, caseworkers are often very dissatisfied, contributing to high turnover rates. Of twelve caseworkers interviewed, three had worked in welfare less than 1 year, six less than 2 years, and only three had worked there longer (considerably so at 7, 12, and 20 years). One of the newest caseworkers said she could imagine doing the job for only one or two more years.[19] Agency contact and familiarity with recipients suffers under these conditions as clients often have several different caseworkers over time, each one starting on "the first page again."

The short job tenure and limited number of veteran workers also make it difficult for agencies to maintain and educate staff in the informal institutional knowledge that is crucial to the more complicated decisions. The lack of formalized office procedures was mentioned by several caseworkers as a significant problem. Often when new rules are promulgated there is inadequate operational detail, "and you have to go a little bit by your own head based on what you have understood about the discussion of the new rules." And novice staff's limited understanding of existing practices could easily lead to incorrect or superficial decisions. Several caseworkers commented that "many times it feels like you are not sure what you are doing."

The lack of regulatory guidance is also well illustrated by the difficulty faced in one district office after a reorganization of work. In this office caseworkers had specialized with particular client groups, including youth and drug addicts. With reorganization, caseworkers became generalists with a cross section of recipients. Staff who previously had childless clients were now dealing with families. This required them to learn how to assess a new set of additional issues around the "best interests of the child," a process that was poorly defined in the regulations. One supervisor at this office noted that since their reorganization last fall there had been frequent questions about rule interpretations and much discussion about whether there should be more extensive written guidelines.

Unauthorized use of discretion

The voluntary nature of the consultation process also limits how well administrators can monitor and control caseworker behavior. Those with full delegation can steer clear of it. The comments of an especially frank caseworker illustrate well the potential for avoidance and the unauthorized use of discretion. This caseworker stated that she and her supervisor had very different philosophies about client needs. Her supervisor was much more skeptical and tended to deny claims without much consideration of the merits. While this caseworker said she had no problem standing up to her supervisor, many colleagues were less secure. But because supervisors do not see most cases, it is relatively easy to make decisions that administrators would not agree with. And this was a common practice in her unit.

She went on to give an example where she used her discretion "to do things I'm not really allowed to do." One client uses her welfare payments to pay for private debts, which are not supposed to be considered in assessing a person's eligibility or the amount she receives. In order for the client to get by, this caseworker grants her emergency food aid on a regular basis. She continued: "This is bad because it means clients I like may get more, though even the black market creep would get what he was entitled to. I have tried to be more standardized in my treatment of clients, but it really comes down to trust. If I think someone is trying, I will help them."

Supervisors' perceptions that inconsistent decision making was not a significant problem may, in fact, be simply due to a lack of information (what Kagan (1978) calls "hierarchical insulation") about how caseworkers make decisions in many of their cases. The example above is not a case of uncertainty about how to apply the law, but an instance where a caseworker wants to help someone in a way that clearly violates program rules.[20]

Activation: The Lost Social Work Role and Organizational Efforts to Recoup It

Before the 1990s recession, the obligation to register at the Employment Office (EO), utilize their services, and accept available work was the only typical economic activation obligation for social assistance recipients, just as it was for all other unemployed citizens. At the same time, welfare recipients were primarily individuals with serious family and behavioral health problems who had difficulty finding work despite a full-employment economy. As such, it seemed relatively unproblematic that recipients were administered to by social service staff who granted support in the context of working toward clients' social integration and rehabilitation.

After the downturn in the economy, however, many long-term unemployed and increasing numbers of youth and immigrants who had never entered the labor market became dependent on welfare. As a result, "straight unemployment cases," for whom traditional social worker intervention was considered unnecessary (people with whom "we shouldn't have contact"), crowded out the needs of traditional clients ("those with drug problems and other personal problems"). Social assistance agencies had become responsible for a clientele that had largely altered the program's de facto function to one of pure economic assistance.

However, the increasing workloads for both welfare offices and EO branches, resulting from the economic changes of the 1990s, seriously limited the EO's ability to serve all unemployed, resulting in selective assistance generally for those already with unemployment benefits.[21]

Between the social service agency and the Employment Office there has clearly gone on a little war, because we are very overloaded here with cases, and they are overloaded with a lot of work, so that one tries to keep away as much work as possible. We refer clients to the Employment Office saying they are their responsibility and they send them back saying they can't work with these clients because they don't have the right qualifications.

To fill this gap, recently established municipal level welfare-to-work programs have become an alternative way to provide services to move social assistance clients toward self-sufficiency (see chapter 8 for more details). And changes in the law permit municipalities to require client participation in local programs as a condition of support. Reflecting this new local responsibility, Malmö's communal regulations outline an ambitious role for social assistance caseworkers in this process. They are to develop individualized activity plans, identify a client's goals and the means to achieve them; coordinate the provision of services from a variety of other agencies; and conduct frequent follow-ups to ensure client participation, program quality, and progress.

Some caseworkers consider these plans to be an important part of their daily work, using them as a means to convey to recipients that aid is conditional and to communicate clear expectations about their obligations. For most staff, however, workload pressures prevent them from engaging their clients in a substantive way on issues of employment or training.[22] Reflecting this fact, activity plans tend to be superficial, with standardized, simple content such as, "Client will register with the Employment Office and look for work." Many individuals also do not have activity plans. This "shadow group of clients" consists of individuals whom caseworkers have never met because they do not apply for additional kinds of support. Given high caseloads, staff have little time to proactively identify these individuals and call them in for meetings.

Organizational responses to the new reality—the return of the social worker?

District offices are reorganizing work to create greater opportunities for some welfare caseworkers to provide more individualized support services.[23] New divisions of labor are emerging that are meant to separate case responsibilities for the work capable from those for welfare's traditional clientele. Not only activation services but also all planning and follow-up are being shifted to welfare-to-work agencies for most referred clients. In addition, Malmö's city government has given district offices the option to delegate greater authority over economic decisions to economic administrators (continuing a trend toward increased authority for this level of staff), so that whole categories of economic support decisions or whole recipient groups could be transferred away from caseworkers.

Offices responded to these opportunities in different ways, leading to variations in the roles that caseworkers play in the area of activation. For some specialized staff, their work conditions and clientele allow them to largely fulfill the traditional social worker role; for others, they have become "super bureaucrats" focused almost exclusively on intake and referrals; many others fall somewhere in between.

In Boklunden, administrators had already created several kinds of specialized caseworkers—for drug addicts and young adults—in order to focus on those most in need of greater support and supervision. Their caseloads were much smaller than for those who worked with the more general recipient population (90 for drug addicts and 130 for youth as compared to around 200 for the general population). Caseworkers for both specialized groups thought they had more adequate time to meet clients regularly, become familiar with their situations, and develop more therapeutic ways of helping them — "to think about their future and how to organize themselves and maybe give them an ability to dare things they wouldn't have before." They also observed, though, that rapidly changing client situations and a lack of adequate referral resources made integration and rehabilitation more difficult.

One caseworker, who works with drug addicts, explained how the nature of her job allowed more opportunity to use her discretion in decision making in terms of activation support: (1) If an agency has made an earlier successful investment in a client for rehabilitation, then the caseworker is more willing to support them further with small sums—with clothing or a training course, for example, to help preserve what they have built up already, "commit ourselves a step further"; (2) Caseworkers generally have more information about these clients and know their situation better, both because they have fewer cases and therefore meet with them more often and because other agencies often provide them with additional information, in particular, the social services section. "The more you know about a client, the more you go with your own understanding about what should happen," that is, the more likely a caseworker is to actually make an individualized assessment and tailor support.

Another district (Havdal) presents the clearest example of the bifurcated organizational development that is occurring in welfare offices—to recoup spaces where traditional social work can still occur with more difficult clients, while sacrificing other caseworkers to the bureaucratic task of accepting and referring the unemployed. In this district office all work-capable clients have always been referred to the local activation agency since it opened in 1997, which is in line with this district's controversial, almost American philosophy of job search requirement as a primary strategy (see chapter 8). As the supervisor explained, a referral to the welfare-to-work agency is "the only tool we have." But often there were delays of a month or two before a client actually began attending, in part because a second assessment by another, welfare-to-work caseworker had to be completed to determine whether the referred individual should be in the employment or study section. In order to make this process more efficient, the district reorganized its welfare caseworkers into two units, distinguished by whether clients were judged to be "work capable" or not. The caseworkers in the work-capable unit receive all new intakes (referring the obviously non–work capable to the other unit for intake). If they determine a client to be work capable, they then assess whether the client should be referred to the job search or training section of the welfare-to-work agency and refer them that day. The responsibility for ongoing economic support (after intake) for such cases is moved to economic administrators. While this arrangement reduces caseworkers in the work-capable unit to intake workers, at the same time it creates opportunities for caseworkers in the non-work-capable unit to focus more on rehabilitation.

Conclusion

Swedish (Malmö) caseworkers, like their German counterparts, administer a single universal welfare program with a two-tiered system of support— a relatively rule-bound basic grant and a second discretionary area for exceptional needs. And, as in Germany, Swedish officials receive full decision-making authority after an initial traineeship period. Thus, in both countries caseworkers have considerable discretion to make individualized assessments of claimants' situations and provide tailored assistance. In contrast to the U.S. welfare program that narrowly defines the caseworker's task as determining a claimant's eligibility for a standardized amount, caseworkers in the two European programs have the more ambitious task of assessing whether the particular client's needs are sufficiently met to ensure their participation in societal life.

But whereas the discretion of German caseworkers is embedded in a highly developed system of regulations that attempts to exhaustively define basic need, Swedish caseworkers make discretionary decisions within a legal framework that is comparably "thin," with most formal guidelines existing in the form of general considerations. National legislation is minimal, a "frame law" that sets forth only basic program goals and principles. The lack of national regulation leads to considerable variation in rule development among municipalities, but such lack also likely leads to much less codification *in general* given the primarily consultative role that many policy-making bodies (health and welfare agencies, the court system) play in such a system. Malmö then provides one example of local response in a system marked by relatively sparse formal administrative guidelines.[24]

While welfare remains a legal institution, and caseworkers must be proficient in administering its laws, social assistance in Sweden is embedded within a social work tradition, with welfare administered by trained social workers in local social service agencies. Officials' vocational values and therapeutic expertise—to make holistic assessments of clients' social situations and look after clients' best interests—in applying program guidelines forms a considerable basis of their decision-making legitimacy. By contrast, the authority of German officials originates in their mastery of the complex regulations that govern their program—their ability to make individualized decisions in light of and through the use of all relevant constraints and considerations. They are, in effect, legal experts. U.S. caseworkers, on the other hand, have very little formal decision-making discretion, their role being defined as technical bureaucrats who simply "apply" the rules.

The limited articulation of legal requirements means that, in contrast to German caseworkers, Swedish officials have greater formal decision-making authority, falling far to the right on this dimension (figure 5.1). Their ability to exercise their authority to make individualized assessments is

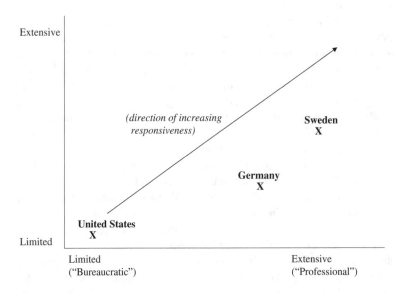

Figure 5.1   Comparing responsiveness among welfare caseworkers (U.S., German, and Swedish examples)

facilitated by their simpler work environment. They administer a single, unified program that deals only with cost-of-living expenses, without the burden of program breadth (Germany) or diversity (United States). They also have considerable clerical support to handle most routine aid decisions and client inquiries that absorb much of the time of German and American officials, allowing them to devote their attention to and develop expertise in difficult determinations.

Swedish caseworkers face a different decision-making challenge from their German counterparts, not a burden of too many rules, but rather one of "rule scarcity." The limited legal guidance provided by program regulations makes it difficult to develop confidence or consistency in the decisions they make. Staff therefore require considerable supplemental knowledge for determining what claimant information is relevant and how to think through cases. This decision-making uncertainty is aggravated by most caseworkers' short tenures. Program administrators cannot rely on careerist officials to maintain institutional interpretive knowledge, as is the case in Germany.

The inability of officials to rely on clear rules has both necessitated the development of substantial informal interpretive practices at the office level and created a more nuanced system of case evaluation than might occur where officials are more constrained by and can more readily rely on regulations. Veteran administrators have developed elaborate methods of legal interpretation and case reasoning, based on years of utilizing available interpretive resources from court decisions and national agencies to assess difficult cases.

Teaching caseworkers these approaches and the institutional values that underlie them is facilitated by specialized administrators known as "method developers," who supervise and train new staff and who act as "discussion partners" after caseworkers have received decision-making authority. The designation of expert advisers, separate from supervisors, allows these organizations to better maintain this crucial consultation function, unlike what occurs in Germany and the United States where supervisors are more readily overwhelmed by work conditions. Method developers also effectively act as an integrative force because caseworkers frequently confront new situations for which existing guidelines are inadequate. Additionally, due to caseworkers' initial training as well as the importance given to collegial exchange in the social work profession, staff seem to internalize advice-seeking as an integral part of the decision-making process.

But while there is a very active exchange among officials, it does not appear to fully address the problems of inconsistent decision making that one would expect in a system marked by decentralized authority and limited regulatory constraints. Staff's limited tenure also puts tremendous strain on the organization to continually educate its caseworkers, something not always successfully done. Many staff asserted that caseworkers make decisions based on different criteria because they were not sure how to handle the case. Thus, the greater dependence on informal guidelines creates potential for a sophisticated evaluative system but one that is also more difficult to sustain and put consistently into practice.

Caseworkers also do not have adequate opportunity to utilize this discretion under current work conditions, due to dramatic increases in caseload size during the economic recession of the 1990s. As in Germany these workload pressures have led to more routinized decision making, because caseworkers do not have the time to get to know their clients well or to make careful assessments of the legal possibilities available. Increased caseloads have impacted Swedish offices even more dramatically by significantly limiting caseworkers' ability to provide services directly in their capacity as social workers. This blending of "cash and care" organizational functions distinguishes Sweden from Germany and the United States, where these two activities are more clearly separated institutionally. And this inability to realize one's professional role has been one of the primary reasons for high staff turnover.

Thus, Swedish caseworkers, like their German counterparts, fall short of their responsive potential because agencies lack the organizational resources to create manageable work conditions and to instill caseworkers with the knowledge and values to make individualized, yet consistent assessments. However, the combination of significant clerical support, an integrated consultation process, and staff skills for assessing clients' social situations, has meant that, overall, Swedish caseworkers are able to evaluate clients more thoughtfully and tailor aid more carefully than German caseworkers (figure 5.1).

6

Welfare-to-Work Caseworkers in California, the United States: Institutionalizing the Search for Employment

We will go over resumes step by step and each of you will have a master application. Those who can't read, all you have to do is copy the material.

Think of the job you want to do most from the lists we made, look them up in the Yellow Pages, and start making phone calls.[1]

Introduction

The United States, as the ideal typical liberal welfare state, is distinguished by the limited role the state plays in regulating markets and the outcomes they produce. Insurance against most disruptions to working life is acquired through private provision in the market. Government spending on vocational and training programs, as well as on support resources, like childcare, is comparatively low, with most of these services provided by private for-profit and nonprofit actors. Employment offices and unemployment insurance[2] have a correspondingly marginal role. State intervention is generally limited to helping market losers via targeted, means-tested assistance.[3] The labor market is only weakly shaped by state regulations and union power, resulting in low fixed labor costs.[4] In the 1990s this weak regulation facilitated significant job creation in both well-paid, high-skilled jobs and in the unskilled private service sector. Such labor flexibility has meant that official unemployment levels in America have traditionally been lower than in many European countries, and standards of living generally higher. Yet, the U.S. economy has its unique and troubling side effects. According to Iversen and Wren's service economy "trilemma" (1998), while maintaining budget constraints and relatively low unemployment levels, the United States fails on the issue of wage equality. The result is a large class of households with full-time employment who live at or below the poverty line—the uninsured, working poor.[5]

Although welfare-to-work programs have existed in the United States for almost 40 years, ostensibly to move people toward substantive employment, low participation rates and chronic underfunding have resulted in little program development during the first three decades. But the passage of federal legislation in 1996, TANF, marked a watershed moment that eliminated the federal entitlement to welfare and required states to establish "work first" activation programs at an unprecedented level for welfare recipients.

In California, welfare-to-work administrators spent the first few years of CalWORKS, the state TANF program, rapidly expanding organizational capacity to provide supportive services and enroll large numbers of recipients into "Job Club," the central offering of the new program. This short-term program component teaches clients job-hunting skills, followed by several weeks of supervised search for employment. This simple, standardized activation activity became the agency's primary approach for assisting clients to become self-sufficient.

The role welfare-to-work staff in California can play in providing services tailored to participants' interests and needs is limited by this narrow construction of the organization's "critical task," one that is oriented almost exclusively to direct "labor market attachment" with limited program options (lower right quadrant, table 2.1). The jobs of activation caseworkers ("Employment Specialists") remain heavily regulated and oriented toward administrative tasks associated with enrolling and tracking clients' participation in activities. Client contact is infrequent, occurring primarily when a recipient changes activities or is out of program compliance, and focused on the technical requirements of these status changes. Thus, employment specialists have a very limited role to play in providing services, acting as "monitors."

"Job Club workers," the other major staff position, are able to interact with clients more frequently and continuously. As the program leaders for CalWORKS' primary activity, they may spend up to a few weeks in almost daily contact with participants, giving these staff members some opportunity to develop familiarity and rapport with their clients and provide them individual attention and encouragement. However, their role in responding to client needs is limited by the narrow focus of the program, so that they function as "facilitators" in assisting clients to remain engaged in job search activities.

Two counties also created a third type of staff position. "Job Developers" are specialized staff who focus on developing relationships with private employers interested in hiring welfare recipients. The introduction of this position was an effort by administrators to create a more direct interface between welfare agencies and private employers, sidestepping the Employment Development Department (EDD), which, while officially responsible for collecting job postings, was seen as limited in its ability to attract employers relevant to welfare beneficiaries. These staff were therefore the one kind of official able to assist clients in directly accessing tangible resources toward becoming self-sufficient—appropriate job leads. Most of their attention was devoted to developing job banks as a general resource for the computer systems in welfare lobbies and at Job Club locations. In some settings they also met with individual clients. Their contact was generally limited, though, usually one or two meetings, which did not give them opportunity for much personal impact on clients, so that in their capacity to provide client services directly they acted as "resource brokers." Additionally, the number of clients they met with directly was quite limited, as most of their attention was spent developing employment resources utilized at Job Clubs.

Welfare roles in California declined by 46 percent between 1996 and 1999, though the greatest reductions came before most clients had been enrolled in the new activation measures (Klerman, Zellman, and Steinberg 2001). The new Job Club approach also met with considerable resistance. Although recipients' failure to comply with program requirements led to reductions in their grant amount by the adult portion, an estimated one-third to two-thirds failed to participate. Thus, a considerable percentage of the welfare population was not enrolled in activation services at all, while continuing to receive limited assistance. As clients with more difficult problems failed to find employment, agencies struggled to develop more individualized services by establishing assessment and referral systems among a variety of government agencies, educational institutions, and nonprofit organizations. While there was considerable funding available, this process was very slow to develop. Agencies had initially focused almost exclusively on expanding Job Clubs, and they lacked a history of collaboration with a whole host of relevant organizations that had very different goals, funding sources, and cultures.

Research on the development of TANF programs in other states demonstrates several parallels to California's experience (Martinson and Holcomb 2002; Fossett, Gais, and Thompson 2003; Brock, Nelson, and Reiter 2002). Most states similarly focused on rapid expansion of a narrow range of job search and short-term job readiness activities. At the same time the reliance on a wide range of new service providers with whom agencies had little prior experience created significant implementation challenges. Poor quality services and improper sanctioning often resulted. This mix of a limited range of work first program options that were nonetheless difficult to implement and manage led to a situation of "complexity without variety."

Thirty Years of Welfare-to-Work Policy under AFDC (pre-TANF)

For the thirty years prior to federal welfare reform in 1996 there had been periodic efforts to shift the focus of the U.S. social assistance program from meeting the needs of poor families to an emphasis on adult obligations to prepare for and actively seek employment. Beginning with the establishment of the Work Incentive Program (WIN) in 1967, which required AFDC recipients to register with the national employment office, welfare policy has gradually evolved, increasing state options and available funds to develop welfare-to-work programs as an integral part of agency activities. Several federal initiatives were implemented during the 1980s, including a new welfare-to-work program called the Job Opportunity and Basic Skills (JOBS).[6] Unattractive federal fund matching rules and a lack of earmarked childcare monies meant that, while some states utilized this discretion and new funding to develop innovative small-scale programs, by the start of the 1990s, activation efforts were still minimal (Lurie 2006). As a result, less than 16 percent of nonexempt adults and 7 percent of adult recipients were participating in activation efforts in 1992 (Bane and Ellwood 1994). And even "successful" programs yielded only small gains in earnings and did not move most of those recipients out of poverty (Gueron and Pauly 1991). American welfare-to-work programs had been, up this point, "one of unfulfilled expectations that work programs and requirements would effectively mandate work and reduce welfare caseloads" (Lurie 2006, p. 14).

In 1992, however, a welter of state welfare reform activity commenced as the Bush administration began (and the Clinton administration continued) to allow states to experiment with their AFDC programs. In late 1992, California implemented the Assistance Payment Demonstration Project (later renamed the Work Pays Demonstration project).[7] The state intended to make working on welfare a more viable and attractive option. This programmatic goal was implemented through a combination of grant reductions and the introduction of more substantial income disregards, allowing clients to keep more of what they earned. This change in policy eliminated many of the disincentives that were seen to limit welfare recipients' efforts to find work. Together with additional legislation in 1993, California's statewide experiment included:

1. Reducing the maximum aid payment by 12.9 percent;
2. Eliminating the 100-hour per month work rule for two-parent (unemployed) cases. Under the then current AFDC regulations, two-parent families could work no more than a total of 100 hours per month to remain eligible for benefits, creating a serious poverty trap

where clients would refuse to take on more hours or reduce their work hours when threatened with cutoff;

3. Rescinding the four-month limitation on the $30 and one-third income disregard. Income disregards allow recipients to work on welfare and not have their grants reduced dollar-for-dollar. But under AFDC, the deductions of $30 plus one-third of the remaining earned income was only available for the first four months;

4. Increasing the need standard—the Minimum Basic Standard of Adequate Care (MBSAC). The MBSAC is used to determine whether individuals are income ineligible based on gross income. Raising it allows recipients to have more earned income without becoming ineligible. It is the first step in the eligibility assessment process (see chapter 3, endnote 8 for more details);

5. Introducing a childcare supplement to AFDC recipients who work. As part of the monthly grant calculations, working recipients could receive an automatic childcare deduction of $175/200 for each child depending on age;

6. Increasing resource limits for recipients; and

7. Expanding the Greater Avenues to Independence (GAIN) program (California's JOBS program) by 71 percent.

Up until the mid-1990s, most county GAIN programs emphasized long-term education and vocational training. Under this human resources development approach, the goal was for clients to acquire adequate education and skills to obtain employment that would get them off AFDC completely. However, a study of Riverside County's GAIN program (Riccio, Friedlander, and Freedman 1994) found that the agency's emphasis on immediate work led to measurable effects in recipient employment levels and reductions in benefits. In light of these findings, the California legislature further amended the GAIN program in 1995 to emphasize this "work first" approach by restricting the conditions under which recipients could enroll in education and training programs. "Job Club," the supervised search for employment, increasingly became the primary GAIN program offering.[8]

Slightly ahead of federal welfare reform, GAIN programs in 1996 and 1997 were already well underway in transitioning from education and training-oriented programs to ones in which the central focus was on Job Club participation, though the numbers of participants were still small compared to what they would become. In preparation for welfare reform, two counties developed new upfront Job Club presentations and streamlined referral processes targeted at applicants. By imposing job search obligations from the start, administrators intended to prevent many applicants from ever receiving aid. Claimants would presumably either find employment relatively quickly or would simply fail to complete the application process given the immediate demands made of them.

GAIN staff (pre-TANF)

The following section gives an account of three types of program staff that administered this standardized approach to activation—Employment Specialists (GAIN caseworkers), Job Club workers, and Job Developers.

Employment Specialists

When applying for welfare most clients were also registered with GAIN and were required to participate in this program when spaces became available. GAIN caseworkers (CW) assigned clients to welfare-to-work program activities, arranged supportive services to facilitate their participation (namely, coverage for transportation expenses and childcare costs), and monitored compliance. But GAIN CWs were limited in their ability to promote client employment, offering few services tailored to clients' particular interests and needs. There were insufficient welfare-to-work activity slots, often leading to long delays between completion of one activity and commencement of a new one. There were also only a limited variety of activities, consisting primarily of Job Club, unsupervised job search, and a few short vocational, general education, and language courses (see similarly, Brodkin 1997). And under the new "work first" approach, starting in the mid-1990s Job Club and job search became the primary, standard program activity.

Not only were GAIN CWs restricted in what they could materially offer clients, they also faced the onerous and unavoidable demands of work that, as for AFDC eligibility workers, was primarily organized around case processing. GAIN CWs' jobs were narrowly bureaucratic, with most of their time spent on routine administrative tasks, such as processing activity attendance records, calculating supportive service budgets, and keeping track of deferred and sanctioned cases. Noncompliance cases were especially time consuming because workers had to take the client out of her current activity, cancel services, and schedule a noncompliance appointment, rescheduling it if the client failed to appear at the first one. If a client subsequently complied, the worker had to then reenroll her and arrange for new supportive services. These tasks were especially difficult to manage given caseloads that typically averaged between 150 and 220 clients. Their knowledge likewise, centered primarily on program regulations that dealt with enrollment, service provision, and sanctioning. While there was generally a higher education requirement than for AFDC EWs (an associate degree or higher), GAIN CWs were not required to have any social work or similar skill set that would be important for engaging clients in individualized and motivational ways.

GAIN CWs' contact with clients was relatively infrequent and regulation-driven in content and occurred only when a recipient was out of program compliance or was starting a new activity. As in the AFDC setting, caseworker-client meetings were generally "high information" encounters. CWs had to explain to clients how to complete the complicated paperwork necessary to receive services, and these discussions absorbed most of the available time and attention of client and worker alike. Often intake and general caseload demands eliminated the possibility of communicating even these essential programmatic aspects.[9] In the context of heavy workload pressures and limited client contact, CWs focused on meeting paperwork requirements for case processing, the duty on which they themselves were evaluated.[10] These incentives were reinforced by automatic computer alerts that kept them (and their supervisors) aware of important case deadlines, for example, when an activity or deferral was ending.

An example from a welfare reform pilot program in one county illustrates well the importance of authority and knowledge, but also the overriding role that workload can play in GAIN CWs' relationships to their clients. In this pilot, regular GAIN CWs were given additional "client motivation" training and were not required to "keep track of every penny spent." The agency's intent was to create a new microclimate where staff encouraged clients to find work by increasing personalized contact with them. One pilot worker said, at first, the change in authority from "record-keeper" to "counselor" was difficult to make. However, at the time of this first interview, she had used her newfound discretion, complimented by her low caseload (approximately 70), to contact clients more frequently about the urgency of welfare reform, to inquire about their job search efforts, and to give them job leads based on a client card catalog she had created. Thus, changes in workload burden, authority, and knowledge were required to enable frontline staff to interact with clients in a relatively frequent and personalized way around employment issues. In a subsequent conversation nine months later, however, this worker's caseload had gone up close to "normal" levels of over 200. As a result, she no longer had frequent contact with her clients, and she found that her actual daily work had reverted to that of a traditional GAIN caseworker.

Thus, employment specialists in California's GAIN program played an important role in administering the complex regulations that governed the program. However, the narrow range of activation measures available to them and their infrequent and technically-oriented contact with clients limited their ability to offer services tailored to claimants' particular interests and needs and to personally assist them in the process of moving off welfare. Their role then was limited to that of a "monitor" (table 5.1 in conclusion section).

Job Club workers

In the GAIN program there were also specialized frontline welfare workers, the most prominent being the *Job Club (JC) worker* who ran the program component to which most GAIN participants were sent. JC workers supervised small groups of participants usually for the duration of the activity, which lasted between four and six weeks. During the first week, they led participants through a workshop focused on job search and interviewing skills for four to seven hours per day. This was followed by the "job search" component where recipients were monitored as they looked for job leads, submitted applications, and went on interviews.

Like GAIN CWs, JC workers viewed their role as helping clients find work, but the organizational conditions in which JC workers were situated facilitated their ability to interact with clients in a more sustained and individualized manner. They had authority to supervise clients' participation in employment-related skill building and job search activities over the course of several weeks. Their attenuated power over cash aid (only in their ability to report noncompliance to clients' GAIN caseworkers) also meant that benefit issues remained a subsidiary concern, allowing both workers and clients to focus on finding work. At the same time, their authority did not generally extend to the provision of any material benefits that would directly impact participants' prospects for finding employment, limiting JC workers' potential influence over client outcomes. Their work was not rule-oriented and did not involve much administrative work. Their caseload size was also small with 10 to 20 participants under their supervision at any one time, allowing them to interact with clients frequently and to become familiar with their situations.

This intense and prolonged contact doing job-related activities greatly facilitated a JC worker's ability to identify and address many of the barriers clients faced in their efforts to find work, including childcare problems, lack of professional clothing, and domestic abuse. An especially important part of a JC worker's role was addressing claimants' pervasive misconceptions and fears about working. For example, clients raised concerns about a dollar for dollar reduction of benefits, or being cut off AFDC and Medicaid when they found a job. In this setting, the worker could explain how program rules were supposed to operate, with income disregards and childcare reimbursements resulting in only partial grant reductions.[11] JC workers were also able to utilize the misgivings and experiences of participants as they came up in discussion to repeatedly illustrate to everyone the advantages of employment as well as recipients' abilities to overcome common work-related obstacles. JC workers' knowledge was oriented toward practical information and skills that would help clients in the labor market, and they had some training in teaching and motivating associated with learning the Job Club curriculum. In several settings, JC workers were also selected based on their reputation as exemplary GAIN caseworkers.

Ideally, then, Job Club provided a forum where clients were repeatedly exposed to new ideas, received positive affirmation, and given opportunities to learn certain job search strategies and to develop social skills through interaction with other participants.

Job Club workers, therefore, had a very different kind of job from ordinary GAIN caseworkers, one which allowed them to relate to clients more as whole people with complex problems. Their contact with clients was more frequent and flexible than that of caseworkers, and their main priority was achieving a particular outcome—client employment. They had greater opportunity, then, to *engage* clients, an important resource for an organization attempting to change clients' attitudes and behavior. Despite this level of interaction, however, the primary site of contact between the welfare-to-work agency and clients was in an activity exclusively aimed at enforcing recipients' search for work. This context structured the focus of interactions to a narrow set of client needs and interests, namely those most directly affecting participants' chances of finding low-skilled service jobs. Thus, the JC worker's role is at best one of a "facilitator" (table 5.1), having frequent contact, but under conditions of limited program choice.

Even with program components specifically designed for changing client attitudes and facilitating their efforts at seeking employment, these activities are time and labor intensive and can easily succumb to general agency pressures to increase the flow of clients through the program. While Job Clubs have great potential as settings for one-to-one communication between workers and clients, there were also significant differences among offices and between Job Club and job search components that substantially impacted the Job Club environment and experience. For example, it was often in the second week, when job search began and clients were expected to begin using skills they had learned for finding work, that problems first appeared. Continued worker-client interaction was crucial here for many clients' success, a situation that, unfortunately, was difficult to maintain at some program locations. Infrequent follow-up meetings, larger group settings caused by the merging of different classes, and the JC workers returning to the classroom to begin with a new group, often left recipients with little ongoing contact with their workers. Overcrowded facilities, poor materials, and inadequate worker training could readily lead to routinized, superficial, and ineffective interactions between workers and clients.

Job Developers

Two counties had also introduced another type of specialized worker, *Job Developers (JD)*, who became increasingly important in the interactions between the agency and many clients. These workers were responsible for developing relations with employers in the community who were interested in hiring welfare recipients, identifying recipients with the necessary qualifications, and matching clients to jobs. Like JC workers, their interactions with clients were individualized and employment focused. They viewed their jobs as primarily about client employment; their caseloads were small being mostly clients referred by GAIN caseworkers; and there were correspondingly few rules and regulations defining their work.

But due to other features of their work, in their capacity of promoting client employment they functioned less as counselors than as "resource brokers" (table 5.1). Whereas JC workers oversaw extended activities in which clients had to participate, JDs' authority stemmed from their access to a material resource, namely job leads, a powerful, concrete way for the agency to communicate the importance of finding employment while also having a direct effect on client outcomes. Their expertise derived from their knowledge of the constantly changing database of private and public employers and their ability to identify potentially appropriate vacancies. Their contact with clients was more limited than JC workers (no more than a few meetings generally), but with a narrower focus on a specific resource, their task was less complex. Their interactions with clients were less about motivation than identifying a recipient's abilities and interests in order to successfully place them in appropriate positions. The importance of client employment was further reinforced by supervisors' focus on placement numbers and a constant comparison of individual JD performances.

The role of Job Developers in providing client services was most significant in one county, where referral to these specialized staff was part of the regular program flow for applicants. JDs played a much more marginal role, however, in the normal GAIN process. While many Job Developers in GAIN offices also received referrals from caseworkers, the percentage of clients affected was small. Job Developers' main impact occurred through the arrangement of job fairs[12] and mass hirings for particular companies. Job Developers communicated these latter opportunities to GAIN caseworkers and Job Club workers, who were expected to identify and inform qualified clients—an arrangement that was chronically underutilized. A number of Job Developers complained that caseworkers would not inform their clients because the caseworkers considered it an extraneous task. At the same time, numerous caseworkers mentioned high caseloads as prohibiting their discussion of all but the essentials for paperwork processing. In order to work around this problem, many Job Developers also had tools for direct access to clients, primarily through the development of a client resume database.

Welfare-to-Work Policy under Temporary Aid to Needy Families (TANF)

TANF was a watershed event that dramatically altered the nature of welfare rights and the operational terms of activation programs. The federal entitlement to welfare was eliminated, and a 60-month lifetime limit was set for client receipt of federal monies. Federal funding for social assistance was block granted to the states, giving them greater discretion over spending priorities, while simultaneously imposing serious, new eligibility restrictions and ambitious activation goals.

Welfare-to-work participation requirements were increased substantially from those set by the previous JOBS legislation, requiring agencies to administer such activities at an unprecedented new scale. In the first year, 25 percent of lone parents and 75 percent of two-parent families were required to participate in a work activity for 20 hours/week. This rate increased to 50 percent and 90 percent respectively, and 35 hours/week during the following five years. Only parents with children under the age of one were omitted from the work participation rate calculations, and other exemption conditions were also substantially narrowed. A separate statute also required that all program claimants had to be in a work activity within two years of being on aid. These two work requirements had different targets—the first made work an increasingly prevalent obligation for anyone who came on welfare regardless of duration, while the second one was specifically aimed at long-term recipients.

Where many smaller JOBS programs once emphasized education and training, the new regulations required programs to have a strong "work first" emphasis. Education and training options were greatly restricted, as only 30 percent of the population could be in vocational education and counted toward work participation requirements, and individuals were only allowed to be in education activities for one year (Klerman, Zellman, and Steinberg 2001). But states had a range of employment-related activities they could develop, namely, unsubsidized employment; subsidized public or private jobs; work experience; on-the-job training; job search and readiness training; community service programs; vocational education (up to 12 months); job skills training directly tied to employment; education (General Educational Development (GED) credential only); and provision of childcare for a person in a community service program. States could also simplify and shorten the sanctioning procedures for noncompliance (which had required scheduling several follow-up "reconciliation" meetings) and impose much more severe punishments, including the elimination of the recipient's entire grant.

Penalties for states failing to meet work requirements ranged from 5 to 21 percent of the total block grant. States could exempt 20 percent of their caseload from work rate calculations, however, giving them room to avoid the high costs of moving the least employable into work. States could alternatively reduce their participation requirements by reducing their caseloads, though reductions through changes in eligibility rules were not counted. While this provision was meant as an incentive for states to develop effective welfare-to-work programs, it created an opportunity for states to develop other informal means of discouraging use, including via upfront work obligations as part of the application process (Lurie 2006; Martinson and Holcomb 2002; (see county case study below)).

California's CalWORKS program

California's state welfare reform plan—CalWORKS—was passed in August 1997. California was unusually "generous" in many of the policy choices it made in implementing TANF. For example, it is one of only six states that do not apply the limits to children's portion of the grant when the lifetime limit is reached, with the remaining grant being paid through state funds. It also has one of the highest benefit levels in the nation and one of the most generous income eligibility limits due to the high earned-income disregards.[13] Given the earlier shift in California's GAIN program to a work first model, the initial transition was primarily one of scaling up.

The new welfare-to-work program process is supposed to work as follows: In the first phase clients are informed of the new program requirements ("orientation"), screened for exemptions,[14] supportive services are set up (primarily childcare and transportation), and clients are referred to "Job Club," for between four days and six weeks. Those participants who fail to find adequate employment during the course of Job Club then enter the second phase of the CalWORKS process. Clients are evaluated for their skills and employment interests, and a welfare-to-work (WTW) plan is drawn up and signed ("assessment"). Clients are required to then choose among a variety of county-approved training and education possibilities that will meet the client's hour requirements and prepare them for employment. If the client is not sufficiently employed by the time they complete the plan, this cycle is repeated until 18 or 24 months have elapsed (depending on whether they applied before or after CalWORKS was implemented[15]) from the signing of the first WTW plan. At this point, the client must participate in community service or be sanctioned.

CalWORKS implementation

The relatively late passage of California's welfare reform plan (over a year after TANF), created very short timelines and considerable implementation pressures.[16] During the initial three years (1997–1999) after the passage of

CalWORKS, county welfare departments (CWDs) were focused on the most immediate demands of implementing a new quasi-universal welfare-to-work program. This new WTW program required rapidly increasing program capacity to a much larger scale.[17] CWDs had to hire or contract out for large numbers of additional staff to handle supportive services and sanctioning and operate Job Clubs. Many counties also colocated employment staff at eligibility offices in order to facilitate this process. Under such circumstances, enrolling all current clients and new applicants as quickly as possible created a bottleneck, though, in the first steps of the WTW process, orientation, appraisal, and Job Club.[18] A process that ideally would take under ten weeks often took over six months to complete. And CWDs, in prioritizing tasks in this period of initial mass enrollment, often neglected other functions, including quality control and noncompliance procedures against no-shows.

While *total funding* increased by 35 percent and quadrupled for social services from 1997 to 1999, *spending* did not increase nearly as fast and only rose substantially in the latter part of 1999. This delay reflected the lag in the ability of counties to build up staff and program capacity, as well as some reticence to committing too quickly to program expansion, given declining caseloads and a concern that the then-current state funding structures would not continue. This funding concern was validated in the 1999–2000 fiscal year, when the state recaptured all federal surpluses from the previous year (Klerman, Zellman, and Steinberg 2001).

At the end of 1999, entering the second phase of WTW ("assessment") appeared to be the least common exit from the initial phase. One-third to two-thirds of clients were in some stage of the noncompliance process and about 30 percent were working. Less than 10 percent were in assessment activities, with half of these in "self-initiated programs" (SIPs).[19] Thus up to the end of 1999, the CalWORKS program was characterized by slow capacity building—leading to slow movement through the WTW components; high no-show rates; relatively high levels of employment due to a robust economy; and a largely unused second WTW phase. Thus, actual program activity had only directly affected a small share of recipients and even then only in the form of job search obligations.

An illustrative CalWORKS county—Oakdale in 2000

Many of the transformations that CalWORKS brought to California's welfare-to-work program can be illustrated through a brief tour of one Southern California county in late 2000, "Oakdale."[20] In brief, CalWORKS had led to a more effective paternalism as called for by longtime welfare-to-work advocate, Lawrence Mead.[21] Enforcing claimant obligations to simply search for employment had become both more widespread and systematized (once an individual was approved), and more consistently supported.

Institutionalized Job Club and supportive services
After the introduction of CalWORKS in 1997, Oakdale County's welfare-to-work program, now titled simply CalWORKS, more than doubled in staff size. The number of enrolled had tripled, from around 8,000 to more than 25,000 (over 50 percent of the current recipient population). CalWORKS had taken "center stage," as one TANF eligibility caseworker explained. CalWORKS staff were outstationed at every welfare office, performing up-front orientations and personally handling the scheduling of client participation in the one week Job Club workshop (followed by five weeks of job search). In contrast to the pre-TANF days, when it often took months before people were called to attend, delays now appeared to be minimal, with most clients enrolled within the week. Unlike in many other states, requiring employment-related activities as a condition of eligibility was not allowed by California regulations, but county officials had effectively made it a prerequisite for aid by incorporating the first week workshop into the application process. While applicants had an initial meeting with an intake worker, they had to complete a second intake meeting on the last day of the workshop. As a result only an estimated 40–50 percent of initial applicants completed the workshop and attended the second meeting. The rest were denied on the grounds of having failed to complete the application process.

Employment counselors (the new title for GAIN employment specialists) had been divested of childcare responsibilities which had moved entirely to the TANF office, now called the Temporary Assistance Department.[22] After a rather shaky start-up, new childcare workers had been placed in every welfare office to ensure that all eligible recipients had access. The once-complicated and inconsistent supportive service structure had been expanded and simplified, providing all recipients who were working or enrolled in an employment-related activity with childcare support paid directly to the service providers of their choice. Childcare funding streams had been incorporated into a simplified three-stage system. Stage I was for welfare recipients who were working or participating in GAIN program activities. Stage II was for individuals who became income ineligible for TANF and was guaranteed (in Oakdale) for two years provided the former recipients were working during that period. Stage III was available when eligibility for Stage II expired, as well as for the general population. While funding for the first two stages was an entitlement, Stage III money was only available as long as there was funding, and a long waiting list had already developed to receive this subsidy.

The job development staff was expanded to 45 people (from eight in 1997) and had developed a strong reputation and presence in the county among private employers, overshadowing the lackluster, recently reorganized EDD, the traditional job bank and administrator of the unemployment insurance system. While Job Developers had been involved in screening clients for particular jobs (the draw for many employers), their main programmatic impact continued to be in providing online regular job postings to all Job Clubs.

Since the introduction of TANF-related changes, the county caseload had dropped by a third, from 62,000 to 44,000. The majority of remaining recipients were now employed.[23] Yet since these working individuals still received benefits, they continued to expend their "lifetime limits." While the philosophy was that employment would lead to better employment, it was still unclear whether this would hold true for the large numbers who had not yet become "self-sufficient." As of 2000, the county had very few recipients in community service (629 in August 2000), as very few had reached the 18/24 month time limit[24] without finding work, and community service was not offered as an option prior to that.

Noncompliance and sanctioning in Oakdale
Noncompliance was a significant problem, as a large percentage of recipients had opted to remain sanctioned (losing some benefits) rather than participate in the welfare-to-work program. The viability of this choice was likely due in large part to California's comparatively mild penalty for non-cooperation, which reduced a family grant only by the adult portion and was made up to some extent by increased Food Stamps payments. While in pre-TANF days there was no agency incentive to convince sanctioned recipients to comply with GAIN requirements, under TANF these individuals were incorporated back into the client population denominator after three months for purposes of determining program participation rates. The agency also had to begin vouchering rental payments directly to landlords for those under long-term sanctions. To contend with the chronic nonparticipant, caseworkers had increased their phone contact with truant clients and the county had developed a "home calls" pilot, where staff attempted to contact clients at their residence to determine the reasons for their failure to comply before sanctioning them. In so doing, they often found out information indicating the client shouldn't be sanctioned — "People will tell you stuff on their turf that they won't tell you in the office."

The harder-to-serve emerge—developing an assessment and referral process
As the agency had worked through its existing caseload with large numbers of recipients either finding part-time work or being sanctioned, those who remained increasingly represented the harder-to-serve. For these more challenging clients, a "softening of the work first approach" was necessary,

and assessments and referrals to other, more appropriate services—including mental health, substance abuse, domestic violence, and education and training—became an increasingly important agency task. Prior to the passage of TANF, interorganizational coordination with nonprofits, educational institutions, and other governmental agencies was extremely limited, not only because of the small size of the GAIN program, but also because clients with more difficult problems were simply exempted. With the new participation mandates, programs eventually had to contend with a whole new set of client needs. But this referral system remained in a very early stage of development in late 2000, requiring welfare-to-work agencies to develop working relationships with a variety of agencies with different funding sources, client groups, and program aims and cultures: "It took us the first year and a half of CalWORKS to convince ourselves of the need to develop a referral system, hookups in the larger community. But the decision-making process is much more complex. It's a slow process."

"Assessment" is the first step of the second phase of the welfare-to-work program flow and is typically intended for recipients who have not had success in finding employment. While in pre-TANF days there were often long delays between a participant's completion of Job Club and assessment, the urgency of time limits had led to assessment's integration into Job Club itself. After the second week of supervised job search, those clients with clear difficulties could be referred by a JC worker directly to an assessor, a task usually subcontracted out to community colleges. Recipients were evaluated using a series of standardized tests to determine their skills, and efforts were also made to discern other mental, behavioral, or family barriers to work. The outcome was a written report with three recommended occupations that was then sent to the client's employment counselor. From here, many clients went on to training or adult education. The resistance of many employment counselors to enroll clients in training, however, had created a major barrier to the education route: "There are some ferocious work first staff on-line." In addition, contracts with various education providers were still being drawn up. Further training was also being offered to recipients who were working, but with limited recruitment success: "We've turned their lives upside down already and they often have no interest in letting us interfere further." For all of these reasons, the numbers of participants in education and training activities was therefore still relatively small. In August 2000, of the 25,000 participants in CalWORKS in Oakdale county, 2,700 recipients were enrolled in vocational education, 300 in education related to employment, and 170 in adult basic education.

Referrals for behavioral or family problems had also been very low. In 2000, there were 689 mental health referrals, 252 drug rehabilitation referrals, and 140 domestic violence referrals, a large improvement over the previous year. These low referral rates were partly the result of relying on employment counselors to make these kinds of assessments. These staff did not have the appropriate training, and, due to the administrative nature of their work, they tended to frame clients' needs in terms of technical issues rather than broader personal issues. Many program recipients seemed hesitant to discuss personal problems in a welfare office setting: "Many just won't open up and you can only make the information available." Clients also often feared that any disclosures could lead their caseworker to cut off their aid or report them to child protective services (Klerman, Zellman, and Steinberg 2001). The agency had responded to the low referral rates by trying to station staff from mental health, addiction services, and domestic violence organizations to facilitate this process. It was also considering creating an "employment counselor II" position to be filled by trained social workers in order to develop some in-house expertise and keep staff focused on continuing to work with clients toward self-sufficiency.[25]

General Developments in the Post-TANF United States— "Complexity without Variety"

The advent of federal welfare reform in 1996 created a common challenge for welfare agencies in states across the country to convert what were often small, voluntary, educationally-oriented welfare-to-work programs into mandatory ones that placed a large majority of the recipient population into work or work-related activities. In effect, it attempted to shift the program orientation and budgetary center of gravity from cash grants to supportive services meant to move people into employment. A combination of factors created propitious conditions for such a programmatic transformation. State welfare reform was a policy issue with high salience to many state governors who had made it a crucial part of their political agenda (Martinson and Holcomb 2002; Fossett, Gais, and Thompson 2003). TANF provided states with considerable flexibility in how they designed their programs, while block grants based on funding levels from previous fiscal years with high recipient levels created significant funding surpluses to hire staff and develop services. A recent surge in the economy in most parts of the country also expanded the opportunities for recipients to find employment in the low-skill service sector.

At the same time the mandates on participation levels and the delimitations on appropriate activities required an unprecedented program expansion in particular directions. As in California, most states and local agencies relied primarily on job search and job readiness activities, a relatively simple, cheap, and direct method to obligate large numbers of recipients to look for work. In some locations this approach was supplemented with short-term vocational and education opportunities, but this was often limited in availability and duration due to the narrow restrictions on its use and the difficulty recipients had in balancing training with concurrent work requirements (Brock, Nelson, and Reiter 2002). A few locations also operated large-scale work experience programs, such as, Cleveland (Brock et al. 2002), Philadelphia (Michaelopoulos et al. 2003), New York City (Nightingale et al. 2002), and the State of Wisconsin (Robles, Doolittle, and Gooden 2003).[26] These programs were often the legacy of workfare programs that had been developed in the late 1980s and early 1990s for recipients of Food Stamps and local General Relief programs.

In order to develop program capacity rapidly, states contracted out for case management and employment services to a wide array of nonprofit, government, and some for-profit organizations. Outside organizations were used for several reasons including the slow process involved in state hiring, a lack of in-house expertise, and administrators' interest in maintaining flexibility to adjust future service capacity (Martinson and Holcomb 2002; Klerman, Zellman, and Steinberg 2001). While some states had experience with performance contracting and cultivating providers, in most cases there had been little collaborative history with organizations that could supply employment-related services. Relying on such incipient networks to deliver most of the program measures at the center of reform efforts thus led to systems that were considerably more complex.[27]

Creating new program structures was time consuming and error prone, and agencies experienced a wide range of common implementation problems. Vague role definitions and poor communication between agency and service providers often led to low referral rates, inadequate monitoring of clients' program participation, and wide variation in the application of sanctions (Martinson and Holcomb 2002; Robles, Doolittle, and Gooden 2003). Agencies also had trouble developing appropriate evaluation criteria for service providers and information systems for monitoring performance. Community-based organizations (CBOs), in turn, often lacked the infrastructure for data tracking demands or for large-scale service programs. As a result of this limited systems-level development, services were often unstable and of poor quality, and in some cases large numbers of recipients were cut off welfare due to administrative errors (Brock et al. 2004).

Problems implementing the new program also existed within welfare agencies. For example, exemptions to work participation requirements generally occurred at rates far lower than could be expected for the recipient population, reflecting inadequate procedural safeguards and frontline capacity for identifying those with serious health and family problems (Lurie 2006; Klerman, Zellman, and Steinberg 2001; Nightingale et al. 2002).There is also evidence that the incentive structures created by this performance-based "new managerialism" led to a numbers-driven process in which welfare-to-work caseworkers focused predominantly on work enforcement requirements and caseload reductions (Brodkin 2006). In the absence of evaluation measures for other aspects of performance, such as service quality or suitability, frontline staff readily redefined clients' needs to fit them to available program slots. Poor service that resulted in a client dropping out or their failure to comply could now be met in many places with a full-family sanctioning, a result for which both caseworker and agency were rewarded.

Thus, developments in recent American welfare-to-work policy can generally be characterized as one of "complexity without variety." The employment-related measure that most claimants were required to attend was a short-term activity geared toward facilitating independent job search efforts.[28] Yet despite the relatively standardized, low-intervention nature of this program component, massive up-scaling with little prior institution-building required the combined efforts of many small providers, leading to unwieldy new service systems.

More individualized service development is hindered by several structural features of the TANF program. Most states adopted new policies that significantly restrict the conditions under which they maintain responsibility for poor people as claimants of social assistance.[29] Full-family sanctioning can end the state-citizen relationship for large percentages of the recipient population for significant lengths of time. Fourteen states impose full-benefit sanctions for initial failure to comply; 36 impose full-benefit sanctions for continued failure to comply (Klerman, Zellman, and Steinberg 2001). Variations in state sanctioning policies are significantly correlated with caseload trends, with an estimated 36.2 percent of all declines directly attributable to changes in policies facilitated by the new welfare law (Wiseman 2000). Similarly in the context of low grant levels provided in many states, even with expanded disregards, relatively modest levels of wage income render clients ineligible for cash aid. And ultimately, time limits create a bright line boundary to agencies' involvement in claimants' lives.

In many states caseload reductions and recipient employment[30] meant the effective participation requirement rate for the current caseload was under 10 percent (Brock et al. 2002). Thus, there would be no clear and ongoing recipient demand for expansive new services. County and state agencies were also concerned that program budget levels would not be maintained, limiting their willingness to invest in new infrastructure. These fears were realized in many states when program expenditures were significantly reduced in the wake of many states' budget crises in 2001 (Polit et al. 2005; Martinson and Holcomb 2002).

Conclusion

From the years directly preceding major federal welfare reform to the first years after 2000, California's welfare-to-work program has grown into a large-scale operation still primarily aimed at requiring large numbers of recipients to simply look for employment. While the CalWORKS program is intended to provide a wide palette of services to address a variety of client needs that may be preventing them from finding employment, in practice the unprecedented participation requirements of TANF, as well as the lack of prior institutional collaboration with other service organizations, have led agencies to put most of their resources and attention toward the development of Job Clubs, short-term workshops to teach clients job-hunting skills and motivation, followed by several weeks of supervised job search. In a program with such a narrow repertoire of available activities, the ability of activation caseworkers to be responsive to recipients' needs was greatly circumscribed.

The role of the primary caseworker, the "Employment Specialist/Counselor," was largely focused on the administration of the complex rules involved in arranging supportive services and monitoring client attendance. Their contact with clients was infrequent and mostly oriented around technical requirements. Thus, their role was limited to that of a "monitor." Job Club workers, who administered the primary standardized activity offered by welfare agencies, had more frequent and continuous contact with clients for the duration of their activity, which gave them some opportunity to provide personal assistance to clients to keep them engaged and motivated in their efforts to find employment. However, the narrow focus of the activity (and the narrow focus of the

Table 6.1   Comparing responsiveness among activation caseworkers (California examples)

| | **Nature of client contact:** opportunity to develop rapport and provide direct services | |
Program offerings: range of options available to caseworker	Processing (short-term contact) −	Engaging (longer-term contact) +
Extensive +	"Resource Broker" *(medium)* Job Developer	"Counselor" *(high)*
Limited −	"Monitor" *(low)* Employment Specialist	"Facilitator" *(medium)* Job Club Worker

larger program) meant their efforts were primarily aimed at "facilitating" clients' meeting the requirements of the job search activity. A third position, that of Job Developer (in two counties), was exceptional in the CalWORKS program setting in that they were able to offer tangible additional resources to clients in the form of job leads. Owing to the program's "work first" strategy and a U.S. economy that had produced large numbers of low-skilled service jobs, this effort was the one instance where agencies had already had some success in developing contacts with other organizations, namely private employers. In their limited encounters with a small number of agency clients, they acted as "resource brokers," able to assist clients in identifying and applying for employment vacancies that fit their particular skill sets and interests.

While there are variations in how states built up their welfare-to-work programs, the high participation requirements generally led to similar responses. Like California, most initially focused on simple, cheap activities that could be upscaled relatively quickly, namely short-term programs intended to facilitate and enforce recipients' independent look for work. Limited prior program development in this area required that agencies often had to rapidly build new provider networks to supply these job search and job readiness activities. As a result, mechanisms for coordination and monitoring were often underdeveloped, leading to poor quality services and improper sanctioning. The new restrictions inscribed in most state welfare programs that have significantly reduced current and future service demands, and large expenditure cuts in many states, have also limited the incentives and capacity to cultivate more individualized programs.

Welfare-to-Work Caseworkers in Bremen, Germany: Resource Brokering into Vocational Training and the Secondary Labor Market

We have a pool of about 700 or more employers, projects, work places, not just private firms but all different kinds of institutions and organizations. That is why we can provide pretty individualized opportunities. It is a very differentiated structure that you have to keep in your head.[1]

Introduction

In the three worlds of welfare capitalism, Germany belongs to the conservative world. This type of welfare state is characterized by labor market structures and social security systems that assume and have created the "standard worker family," based on a male breadwinner and female partner who takes on most family responsibilities. In neither of the other two welfare state regimes is this form of familialism so deeply ingrained (Esping-Andersen 1996). An institutionalized occupational and apprenticeship system has maintained a protected, high-skilled core of "family wage," careerist, manufacturing jobs. At the same time, the Catholic principle of "subsidiarity" (promoted by the political hegemony of the Christian Democratic party) has led to comparatively limited funding for social services,[2] relying instead on voluntary and private (female) forms of caring. The lack of publicly-funded services, combined with tax disincentives for a second household wage earner, have discouraged married women's participation in the labor market, with levels of female employment below those found in the United States or Sweden.[3]

The institutional rigidities of these corporatist familial structures have made the transition to a postindustrial service economy very difficult for the German state. The high fixed labor costs of union jobs has retarded the development of the private service sector with its comparatively low productivity levels, leading to high chronic unemployment for decades.[4] The wide array of vested interests and dispersion of decision-making power in Germany's "semi-sovereign" state (Katzenstein 1987) has also meant that systemic reform has been virtually impossible. Rather than expanding public services or loosening employment conditions, unemployment has instead been managed by moving older workers into early pension and disability programs in order to provide jobs to some of the more recent and skilled labor market entrants. This labor-shedding strategy has only increased the ongoing fiscal burdens of Germany's insurance-based programs (Leibfried and Obinger 2003). The staggering costs of reunification have similarly contributed to massive increases in unemployment expenditures and work-creation schemes that have crowded out investment in business and human capital (Kitschelt and Streeck 2003). At the same time, low occupational mobility and a highly structured system of education (DiPrete et al. 1997) mean that apprenticeship certificates are almost essential for gaining access to most occupational fields.

High unemployment has predictably led to high rates of social assistance receipt. As municipalities in Germany are largely responsible for the financing and administration of social assistance, as well as local activation programs, these difficult economic conditions have created a heavy fiscal burden on local governments. Under such labor market conditions and fiscal pressures, the "paths to self-sufficiency" for welfare recipients are relatively narrow and limited. Prior to the Hartz reforms of 2005, local governments used the policy options available in the "Help to Work" (HtW [Hilfe zur Arbeit]) section of the federal social assistance law to pursue two primary strategies:

(i) *Scaling the divide to secure "insider" employment.* Protected union jobs are difficult to obtain in Germany due to a weak labor market and high training requirements. This option, then, is primarily available through the apprenticeship system where a vocational qualification is the ticket to a good job. As generally only individuals under the age of 26 are entitled to training, this avenue is primarily available to younger adults. However, the high demands of vocational programs require potential students to have adequate motivation and preparation that many young welfare recipients often lack. Welfare agencies can therefore assist these individuals in acquiring the work habits and basic skills to successfully enroll in such programs. On the other hand, for work-capable older recipients with adequate qualifications and employment histories, government-provided wage subsidies for the first year or two of employment may also be sufficient incentive for employers to hire them.

(ii) *Placing recipients in the "sheltered/secondary" labor market.* Work creation schemes instituted by federal and local governments, in response to the high unemployment levels, provide some employment opportunities in a small but thriving sheltered sector. Reflecting Germany's "dual welfare system" (Eardley et al. 1996), these "public welfare organizations" provide important services that the public sector does not and increasingly cannot provide itself (Bode 2003). Welfare agencies may arrange year-long employment contracts with these organizations for suitable recipients. This job experience and training in the "secondary labor market" may presumably lead to permanent private employment. Though this rarely happens, these placements serve another purpose as well. Recipients become entitled to unemployment benefits, allowing local governments to shift the costs of continued support onto the national government.

Despite difficult economic conditions, Werkstatt Bremen, the city-state's local welfare-to-work agency, has developed a wide range of these activation measures. To prepare recipients to enter full-time vocational training programs, and to provide many older recipients with sheltered employment in a variety of occupationally appropriate fields, staff have utilized their relationships with hundreds of such organizations in the secondary labor market to create career planning and work experience projects. Staff have also had some limited success in custom-placing some clients in private employment positions. Due to the variety of program offerings, caseworkers can arrange activities for clients tailored to their individual needs, skills, and interests, acting, in other words, as "resource brokers." In addition, those staff who work with young adults also have adequate opportunity and skills to meet with their clients frequently, personally assisting them as "counselors" with challenges that arise while making the transition off welfare. Yet limited funding resources mean that only a small percentage of recipients can be assisted.

This chapter describes activation policy in Bremen, Germany in 2000. Due to the significant changes that took place in 2005, it now likely serves more as a historical case study than a reflection of current practices. It discusses the program operations and work conditions of Werkstatt Bremen's various program divisions, as well as profiling one of their service providers, AUCOOP, a metal and electrical cooperative. It then compares Bremen's practices with other local welfare-to-work programs in Germany in the first years after 2000. Finally it concludes by discussing the more recent Hartz reforms that may radically change the municipal government's role in employment policy.

Regulatory Framework Activation Instruments

As part of the federal social assistance law, welfare agencies are required "to ensure that the assistance-seeker makes an effort to find work and actually does so" (Art. 18, Par. 2). It delineates three different policy measures activation agencies can use to move recipients toward self-sufficiency. Within these general parameters, though, local governments have considerable discretion regarding the level of funding and the range of choices they provide participants.

The primary fiscal measures include "19.2 contracts" (BSHG, Para.19.2, alt.1), one- to two-year government-funded employment contracts for full-time work in the "secondary labor market." Recipients receive regular wages, but at a reduced rate of the pay scale for equivalent private sector jobs. As part of these regular employment contracts, the government also pays for regular contributions to insurance funds (that employers usually make), thereby providing participants with various social security entitlements. The locality may also choose to include payments to service providers for supportive services, so that there is some degree of counseling and monitoring on-site. Secondary labor market employment must meet two requirements: it must be for the public welfare, that is, it must occur in the public or nonprofit sector; and it must be "additional" (zusätzlich), that is, it cannot be used to perform essential organizational functions or replace permanent personnel. Such work experience and skill development will lead to employment in the first labor market, so the rationale goes. Even if securing further employment fails, though, clients who find themselves out of work after this assignment ends will be eligible to receive unemployment benefits and, thus, costs of continued maintenance will shift from the local to the national government.

For clients who are already relatively work-ready, there is the "19.1 contract" option (BSHG, Para. 19). This instrument is to encourage private employers to hire welfare recipients in exchange for wage subsidies for the first one or two years of employment.

In order to test the ability or willingness of recipients to work (Para. 20), agencies may also utilize a more traditional workfare approach, known as "premium work" ("Prämienarbeit"—Para. 19.2, alt.2) or "blue card" work (due to the blue time cards). Recipients generally work for a shorter number of hours in return for their welfare grant, plus a small additional sum to cover work-related expenses. In Bremen it is generally 5 hours/day, 5 days/week, at 2 DM ($1)/hour, in addition to welfare benefits. This instrument is often used as a transition into a 19.2 contract, or it can become a regular way to structure the lives of participants who will never be able to sustain regular employment.

Werkstatt ("Workshop") Bremen

Werkstatt Bremen (WB),[5] Bremen's local welfare-to-work agency, was established in 1985, in response to the high unemployment levels and social assistance costs under which the city-state suffered. With relatively modest goals that have been increased incrementally from year to year, it has developed slowly over the past fifteen years. It currently houses several different divisions. There is a large 19.2 division, a smaller 19.1 division, both of which are formally voluntary, and a recently expanded and compulsory youth program, U27 (Under 27), for recipients through the age of 26. In 1999 there was also a, now defunct, one-year experimental project, known as BAVA, to assess the feasibility of placing recipients in private employment without wage subsidies. WB also operates two of its own public welfare projects in which participants refurbish old furniture, clothing, curtains, and other domestic items for use by welfare recipients.[6] While many of WB's clients participate in these in-house activities, most of the agency's offerings are provided by a variety of public welfare organizations.

The general process

WB caseworkers have a very different job from GAIN caseworkers in California. They have no responsibility for the supportive services that mire U.S. staff in so much administrative work. Support services are the responsibility of the social services agency, and childcare or other services must first be arranged with that agency before WB will assist the client.[7] In the compulsory U27 program there is no complicated, formal "reconciliation" process for noncompliance as in the United States. Rather, determining when to report a recipient for inadequate participation is left largely to the discretion of the caseworker. The 19.1 and 19.2 divisions of the program are ostensibly voluntary. Rules, in fact, play only a minor role in the work that WB staff do[8]— "It is not an administrative job, but it is very intense." Instead their role centers around advising and resource brokering, identifying and arranging for placements that best suit the participants' particular interests and qualifications.

In the mornings WB staff spend much of their time with clients[9]— assessing new participants' goals, skills, and limitations; following up with others on their progress; arranging for new measures and approaches for unsuccessful placements. The afternoons are devoted to updating case files based on the many meetings and to contacting other agencies, employers, and service providers. Because of the variety of measures offered through WB, caseworkers must devote considerable time to stay informed about existing programs—where there are available slots; the progress of their participants; and the work conditions at various sites. Beyond this general description of office operations and divisional responsibilities, the work of the three units varies considerably due to differences in program orientation, client needs, available resources, and work conditions.

19.2 division

The unit responsible for placements in the secondary labor market is one of the largest in the agency, with 9.5 staff positions. In 1999 they were responsible for ensuring that 1,000 participants successfully completed employment contracts. Staff here work with over 700 different employers and projects and therefore have the possibility of providing relatively individualized offerings. Approximately half of the 19.2 contracts are in group projects, sites with 10–60 positions for welfare recipients (several of which are operated by WB), and include activities in gardening, construction, restaurant services, recycling, and various cultural, recreational, and self-help groups. But there are also hundreds of public welfare organizations with one to several contracts offering opportunities for specialized client interests and qualifications.[10]

If, after assessing a client's qualifications and interests, an appropriate program slot is found, the individual will be sent for an interview at the organization. If both parties are still interested after this meeting, the client will work there on a trial "blue card" basis for between two weeks and two months. If the trial period is successful, an employment contract will be drawn up for one year (with the option to renew for a second year). For some clients for whom an employment contract is too difficult, and where daily structure is a sufficient goal, they may be employed on a blue card basis for a longer period, up to several years.

Work conditions
The work of 19.2 division staff involves two essential tasks: (1) identifying clients who are likely able to manage the demands of full-time work and becoming familiar with their particular situations; and (2) keeping up to date on the placement options among public welfare organizations. 19.2 caseworkers all had backgrounds in social work and social service projects, and as a result, a shared client-centered philosophy informed their work. They emphasized the importance of developing trusting relationships with their clients and of personally assisting them with the difficulties of being unemployed and the challenges of transitioning back into work. Brokering appropriate employment resources was intrinsically tied up with the process of counseling, helping clients to articulate their interests

and goals so the best employment match could be made, and helping them to address personal problems that could impede their ability to complete the work contract.

The vast number of potential employers creates an administratively complex environment, "a very challenging system," requiring extensive knowledge of the service provider landscape and sufficient time to monitor the availability of program slots. This information challenge is managed by assigning caseworkers responsibility for keeping up-to-date on all projects within a particular city sector and circulating their information within the unit. Because of the relatively unsophisticated computer system, caseworkers must keep a lot of information in their head and consult frequently with their colleagues about particular projects that might be appropriate for the client at hand. However, most of the 19.2 caseworkers are veterans who have a solid understanding of what is generally available.[11]

Managing the level of client demand, on the other hand, has not been so successful. While the resources devoted to employment contracts are considerable, they are a comparatively expensive program option, and as a result, can only serve a very small percentage of the welfare population (around 3 percent). What's more, these placements require that recipients do not have significant barriers to working and have a good chance of completing a year of regular, though "sheltered," employment. For many recipients the threshold is too high. In recent years, the program has become even more selective, as the increasingly inadequate organizational resources of service providers have hindered their placement of more difficult or disabled clients. Many organizations simply don't have the means to provide adequate supervision. Thus, for the agency, screening out the large portion of the recipient population they cannot help, as well as queuing and managing the large number of potential participants they cannot help immediately, creates a considerable organizational challenge.

The influx of clients has remained largely out of the agency's control. Welfare caseworkers regularly send clients who are not capable of working, often repeatedly and under threat of sanction (despite the "voluntary" nature of the program). This problem stems from the fact that WB is the only readily available means of imposing help-to-self-help obligations on clients without requiring much time or effort of welfare staff. One 19.2 staff member estimated that almost half of the clients referred to them are not capable of meeting their contract requirements. These inappropriate referrals, coupled with recent staff reductions, have meant that already high caseloads have increased significantly in the last year, estimated to be between 600 and 700 per staff member (an increase of 100 to 200 over the previous year).

These difficult conditions have resulted in a deterioration in the quality of casework. Workers have less frequent contact with clients or service providers than earlier and therefore generally insufficient time to adequately assess clients' abilities and identify appropriate slots. Their ability to develop personal rapport with recipients and provide direct counseling has been drastically reduced. The overburdened system is reflected in increased rates of broken contracts, as well as a large, inactive caseload. An estimated one-third of current clients are waiting for appropriate slots to be identified or become available, and one-third are simply inactive, being too difficult to be served by WB.[12] In 1999 the 19.2 division received 3,885 visitors. Of these, 1,040 were offered and completed 19.2 contracts; 198 were referred to the 19.1 division and were offered 19.1 contracts; 130 failed to complete their contracts; 1,445 (37 percent) received advising only because they could not be offered anything more at that time; and 1,006 (26 percent) could not be helped at all (Werkstatt Bremen, 1999). WB is currently working with the welfare offices to institute a system for categorizing clients according to their level of work-readiness, to limit the numbers of future inappropriate referrals.

The 19.2 caseworkers also complained they had insufficient funds and contracts for individual organizations (being limited to only three of the ten contracts each caseworker was allocated each month) and could place many more if funding were available. One caseworker noted she already had enough people lined up for all her individual contracts for the next year. To free up this money in the context of a fixed budget, though, would require shifting resources away from the group projects and would force the closure of many of them. Caseworkers also considered the low-paid, premium work to be a valuable resource for many of their clients who are incapable of finding private employment but who desire to participate in useful and structured activities. However, the agency is only evaluated on the number of successfully completed employment contracts, and so blue card work is not offered to the extent necessary to meet demand.

Comparing 19.2 caseworkers and California Job Developers
While both California Job Developers and 19.2 caseworkers function primarily as "resource brokers," helping clients to access employment resources, their way of providing services is quite different, in some ways fundamentally so, in large part owing to the different employment sectors with which they work and the different conditions of this interorganizational relationship. These two groups, therefore, are excellent examples of the contrasting collective welfare and individual client program orientations (Tweedie, 1989).

Job Developers' primary role is to continually develop working relationships with private employers. They offer employers an additional pool of potential applicants (in passing on job leads to Job Clubs) as well as pre-screening services for the clients they meet with personally. In their meetings with individual clients they can look through their data bank and find appropriate current vacancies to which the recipient can apply, and in this sense, the service is individualized. However, the developer's focus is only tangentially on the client insofar as he or she can only be assisted if they have the qualifications for which an employer is looking. The programmatic strategy is to move as many recipients as possible into the labor force, rather than to help the particular individual across the desk. Making job leads available and letting the market filter out the recipients with the best qualifications is an inexpensive means (the government does not pay for placements or services directly) to reduce the welfare population as a whole.

By contrast, in the 19.2 division, the resources are on the state's side; they are paying to place people in sheltered employment, in large part because the private labor market provides no cheaper alternative. This state funding creates a different dynamic between agency and public welfare organizations as these organizations have incentives to offer positions that can attract state funding. This financial clout has given staff the ability to focus first and foremost on the interests and needs of clients rather than on those of the potential employers (as is the case in the United States). Caseworkers are therefore primarily focused on assisting the individual client, rather than simply reducing the recipient population. Of course, this individualistic orientation is greatly tempered by the high qualification requirements 19.2 clients must possess in order to be offered assistance, and workload pressures have eroded the quality of this placement process. Nevertheless, caseworkers in California and Bremen operate in different fiscal contexts that establish profoundly different relationships with clients.

The viability of the secondary/sheltered labor market
The putative purpose of the 19.2 division is to provide a transition for recipients into the private labor market through the experience, contacts, and skill development they obtain from a year of employment in a public or nonprofit organization. A similar intent lies behind the work creation schemes (Arbeitsbeschaffungsmassnahmen) of the Federal Employment services (FES). Together, these government programs fund about 3,000 sheltered employment positions in Bremen each year.

But as one caseworker explained, integration into the private labor market has never been the predominant impact of the program. The combination of chronic high unemployment and the characteristics of most welfare recipients means that only about 10–20 percent of recipients ever find private employment. The program really serves more as a way of temporarily mitigating the effects of long-term unemployment, such as loss of self-esteem and personal initiative, for those who receive placements. The 19.2 positions also serve as a local political move in the back and forth cost-shifting efforts between different levels of government. While 19.2 contracts vest recipients with entitlement to unemployment insurance benefits, employment offices have simultaneously been reducing benefit levels and instituting more stringent eligibility requirements so that many unemployed become disqualified and must fall back on welfare (Bruttel and Sol 2006).

While Germany's welfare system emphasizes the provision of social services through private organizations, government job creation schemes also appear to facilitate a hollowing out of the public sector. Local governments, strapped for cash, have often utilized these public welfare measures to shift responsibility for many basic services from permanent public employees to temporary workers and nonprofit organizations. These fiscal pressures, then, have led to a degradation in the "additional" requirement for public employment contracts. One caseworker explained, for example, that in Bremen the landscaping department had been eliminated and replaced by 19.2 contract positions. A nonprofit project initially devoted to constructing extra buildings on school grounds for free-time activities was given responsibility for regular school renovation. In another project, unemployed academics started a program to help schoolchildren with difficulties; the public sector eventually did away with its own similar program, to save money. "That is the trick, that schools allow organizations to take over responsibility for areas which are actually among their core responsibilities."

At the same time, the unstable funding arrangements of one-year contracts makes it difficult for nonprofit organizations to develop their programs and offer quality positions. The scarcity of resources — "There are always more personnel requests by organizations than there are contracts" — also creates serious struggles among organizations, resulting in "in-fighting among left wing fighters." The head of the Association of Bremen Employers (ABE) (Verband Bremer Beschäftigungen), an organization of 17 public welfare organizations, which together employ 2,800 employees, a large portion through work creation contracts, surmised that the political opposition to creating more stable funding arrangements stemmed from a framing of these measures as a temporary solution to a labor market that would eventually "clear." More permanent arrangements would require a politically impossible admission that the private market is unable to provide adequate employment.

U27 division

The U27 division is an obligatory "youth" program for all welfare recipients under the age of 27, with most new young welfare applicants being sent directly to WB after their initial intake at the welfare office. U27's expansion into a quasi-universal[13] program is of recent genesis, following the Schroeder government's 2 billion DM 1998 effort to combat youth unemployment—the "Immediate 100,000 Jobs." This initiative increased funding for youth training measures and financed four new U27 positions in Bremen, for a total of 9.5. The participant population in U27 is mostly male (63 percent) and childless (90 percent).

By contrast to the United States, then, Germany (and as we shall see, Sweden) must address the problems of whole populations that do not fall under the purview of American welfare programs. Youth unemployment is not as politically visible, then, in the United States, but it is also not as large a problem. Where low-skilled, precarious jobs are relatively available, the material needs of the poorly paid employed make little demand for government intervention. By contrast, where the only available employment requires considerable training, and where untrained youth end up on government assistance, material need is a more politically tangible problem, and the solution requires considerably more effort.[14]

While the program also aims to move recipients off welfare, its primary focus is on education and training. Most (90 percent) young recipients have no vocational qualifications making it difficult to find adequate and lasting employment in a high-skills, certification-based labor market (DiPrete et al. 1997). As individuals up through the age of 25 have an entitlement to training, the program tries to exploit this window of opportunity to facilitate recipients' integration into the German apprenticeship system, where they would receive an education stipend rather than welfare.[15]

U27 staff occupy a position in which "several different information fields run together." The vocational system is complex, provided by dozens of different organizations, administered by different government agencies and with great variation in focus and level. The FES is responsible for the lion's share of information, access, and funding. U27 staff play a key role helping clients navigate this complex system through personal contacts that agency officials have developed with designated employment office staff in the areas of vocational counseling and disability. They also know "what is approximately available at the employment office," so they can advise clients, arrange appointments with staff there, and inform these caseworkers on the clients being referred.

Usually, though, information and employment office referrals are not enough, as clients often have multiple social and family problems, are not adequately motivated, or do not know what they want to do. For this reason, the U27 program provides a wide range of preparatory and transitional activities that address a broad spectrum of recipient capabilities and interests, a series of smaller, less demanding steps along the way to full-time education or employment. These projects reflect a mid- to long-term perspective to integration, giving clients opportunities to develop vocational interests, learn social skills and work habits, and become more confident. Some projects are designed for clients very far from the labor market and are meant simply to provide daily structure—a place to go and something to do. Others provide clients with opportunities to explore different careers, ending in an internship at an appropriate business firm. For those who have already expressed an interest in a specific occupation, there are projects in particular fields—including construction, gardening, restaurant work, metalwork, retail services, and health care—for first-hand experience to determine whether they would like to pursue it further in training. In some cases, clients can receive a training certificate for a particular skill, such as welding, which can lead more directly to employment. In all, there are approximately 20 different programs offered through WB itself.

If a client does not find something through the employment office, employment on his own, or some other activity (such as an optional civil service year for women), he is required to participate in one of U27's programs for six months on a blue card basis. Those who complete the six months may be eligible for a 19.2 contract, though these are relatively infrequent (59 in 1999), as most find other solutions by the end of their project. In 1999, U27 staff saw 1,563 welfare recipients. 220 (14.1 percent) could not be helped for various reasons (including no work permit, pregnancy, current drug or health problems, receipt of unemployment benefits). 446 (33 percent) were enrolled in various U27 programs. During the year, 757 left the welfare roles: 28 percent were denied benefits for failure to participate; 19 percent found their own employment; 21 percent enrolled in employment office programs; 10 percent enrolled in basic education programs; and 8 percent found employment through 19.2 contracts (Werkstatt Bremen 1999).

Work conditions
While U27 staff work with a much smaller number of organizations than the 19.2 division, keeping abreast of vacancies and client progress is even more important in some ways for this group. The unreliable behavior of many of their clients, as well as the demand to keep *all* recipients active in some way, means that most of the program slots are usually full and some participants are always dropping out. U27 staff must therefore constantly monitor the progress of their clients and identify openings for

the inevitable new clients they receive. In order to manage this rapid change, each staff member is a designated contact person for a handful of the group projects they monitor, and there is daily contact among caseworkers to update each other.

There is little overlap between the 19.2 and U27 projects. This separation was in part the result of differences in the blue card requirements between the two programs. 19.2 participants only have to do blue card work for approximately one month before receiving an employment contract, while U27 participants work for 6 months. As a result there were complaints from many service providers as well as 19.2 caseworkers that U27 clients were blocking slots for recipients of public employment contracts. U27 staff also felt their recipients needed more supervision than could be provided in some of the larger group projects. They therefore developed their own projects and continue to modify and expand their program repertoire as client interests and needs change.

The compulsory nature of the U27 program means caseworkers don't have the same capacity as 19.2 workers to control their caseloads and client types through formal filtering mechanisms, leading to a more heterogeneous and difficult mix of clients. They also must work with their cases until they leave the program, so that U27 staff have a more significant counseling function to play than in other sections that are more narrowly focused on employment placements for the more qualified. Often clients fail to participate in assigned programs. It is the caseworker's job to determine the causes and assist clients to achieve success, both through support and alternative measures, but also through the threat of sanctions to keep clients on track. (A U27 client can lose his entire grant if his activation caseworker reports he is failing to meet participation requirements.) Monitoring and follow-up are therefore central features of the U27 caseworker-client relationship. One caseworker estimated he saw clients an average of five times, though meetings varied widely between one visit up to fifteen.

While a compulsory program could lead to superficial treatment and inappropriate sanctioning because of a caseworker's difficulty in managing their caseload, U27 has sufficient staff and program resources to generally provide quite individualized assessments and services. The quadrupling of staff numbers since May 1999 has kept caseloads comparatively low, with approximately 50–80 active cases per worker. Caseworkers, who all have some social pedagogic training and experience in social services, report they generally have adequate time to meet with clients to discuss their situations, identify aspirations and barriers, negotiate particular assignments, and do follow-up. The U27 program appears to be a rare example where demands and resources are in relative equilibrium (as reported by workers).

Relations between U27 workers and welfare staff were also reported to be good, as WB became an integrated, automatic part of client processing, seen by social assistance caseworkers as an effective tool both for motivating clients and lightening their caseloads. U27 was also one of the few case examples where a strong relationship had been developed between historically noninteracting employment and welfare agencies.[16] Cooperation has also been successful because the Schroeder youth initiative has meant U27 had a tangible, more abundant resource to offer social assistance recipients, compared to WB's scarcer resources for other groups.

While caseworkers characterized their work as engaging and generally felt they had adequate time and resources, they faced several ongoing challenges. The work is intense and chaotic.[17] They spent a lot of effort calling employment office officials and various service providers to look for available program slots and book appointment times. Programs are often filled, and caseworkers have to scramble to find other activities or tasks for the clients before their next meeting, such as going to counseling at the employment office. Many times clients fail to attend their assigned program, so the service provider and/or the employment office will no longer work with them. Some clients become aggressive because they know their grant is on the line; others try to hide their addictions. Caseworkers said they were sometimes overwhelmed by the social problems clients presented, but they tried to refer them as best they could to social services and the employment office rehabilitation unit. One caseworker explained that she had to limit how involved she would get in clients' personal situations and that their focus on employment/education helped her maintain that boundary.

An illustration of a WB service provider—AUCOOP

AUCOOP (Handwerks- und Ausbildungscooperative— "Trade and Vocational Training Cooperative") is one of the relatively small nonprofit organizations that WB uses for both U27 and 19.2 placements. Established in 1976 by Green Party activists as an artisan cooperative that could offer unemployed youth apprenticeship opportunities, its small size gives it a more "personal touch" than many of the larger organizations. Currently it houses four independent workshops—in metalwork, electrical, heating, and carpentry—which provide goods and services on the private market. It also operates a three-year electrician's apprenticeship program[18] and runs a youth internet café.

For the past three years AUCOOP has also offered WB programs, with two social workers playing an important supportive staff role for participants on-site. A 19.2 program for 15 participants teaches basic skills in metal work, such as boring and filing, and may also lead to certifications in forklift operating and welding. They have a comparably high success rate, with 30–40 percent of participants finding employment or entering a formal training course.[19] The future viability of the program is uncertain, however, because metalwork is a glutted profession and because technology continues to reduce demand for skilled and semiskilled labor in this area.

AUCOOP has also offered a U27 metalwork program for the last two years. Class sizes are smaller (six students), less rigorous, "more fun" and meet only five hours/day for six months. The young adults in this program are much more difficult to work with than the 19.2 participants; they often have multiple behavioral and family problems, and there is considerable turnover. The agency director explained that the very success of Schroeder's "100,000 program" has meant that those left behind are therefore the ones with the greatest difficulties. Only one participant at AUCOOP so far has found employment afterwards. Two others enrolled in apprenticeship programs but subsequently dropped out. AUCOOP social workers were able to contact them and get them "stabilized," and both have since continued with their programs— "That's our success."

AUCOOP is a member of the Association of Bremen Employers, mentioned earlier. This organization was established in 1996 to better protect the interests of some of the larger nonprofits that are heavily dependent on local and federal work creation measures and "to keep competition among us at a certain level so we don't destroy each other." Among other things, they develop strategies for approaching funders like WB and the employment office. To strengthen their legitimacy they have collectively instituted a more professional "quality management" approach, by defining more clearly the service provision process and accounting methods. Through such means, they hope to assure politicians of the quality of their programs as they have become, in effect, "implementers of certain city-state programs." Still, funding for their projects is unstable, and contracts must be renewed annually. What's more, they must often struggle to find additional funds for administrative and supportive costs that are often not covered sufficiently by employment contracts. As a result, there is little opportunity to build up programs long term as "whole programs could be suddenly terminated."

19.1 division and BAVA

The 19.1 division and the separate BAVA project differ from the larger divisions of WB in their program orientation and method of placement. While 19.2 and U27 place participants in sheltered employment and training preparation, these groups attempt to place participants in private employment on the primary labor market. In contrast to 19.2 caseworkers, the role of 19.1 and BAVA caseworkers is more purely one of "resource brokering." The clients they work with are supposed to be the most work capable, who presumably do not need the more involved intervention 19.2 caseworkers attempt to provide, only a job. But, unlike the mass application process of the regular employment office, where the focus is on filling specific vacancies (the approach also taken by California Job Developers), staff here take a reverse approach. They start with the work capable recipient and look for employment that suits his or her particular qualifications and interests— "to find their niche in the market."[20] This individualized method has required slowly building up a network of contacts with businesses. Both projects offer employers the advantage of screening for qualified applicants, relieving firms of the time and costs of the selection and hiring process. They also both allow employers a free trial employment period before signing an employment contract.

The two programs differ in a number of ways that help to explain why BAVA failed and 19.1 remains. 19.1 is a small program (with 2.5 employees) that has been around for four years and therefore has had time to develop relationships with 250 employers willing to work with them regularly. It also has a large "carrot" in the form of wage subsidies for the first year or two of employment. As a division of WB, it provides assistance only to welfare recipients, usually through referrals from U27 and 19.2 sections who select their most work-capable clients. Still, it is a rather small endeavor given current labor market conditions, and in 1999 it placed 198 clients in private employment. While staff have become increasingly proficient at evaluating clients and identifying possible employment positions, the clientele has gotten progressively weaker. Most do not have the prerequisites for the general labor market.

BAVA, on the other hand, was a separate joint project of the Bremen government and the FES, receiving both welfare and employment office clients. While BAVA had a relatively large staff of eight, it failed due to the unreasonable demands of having to develop an entirely new project, establish the necessary contacts with businesses, screen clients, and place 300 into private employment within one year. What's more, it could not offer 19.1-like subsidies, being intended purely as a placement agency. By the end of the year caseworkers had been in contact with approximately 300 employers. However, program participants were unexpectedly weak. Most were not immediately ready for the shock and demands of full-time employment, requiring transitional, preparatory measures BAVA could not provide. While it was estimated they would be able to place one in four participants they interviewed, it turned out to be closer to one in seven.

In the end 1,200 were screened, 130 initially placed, with 80 still employed. While this project was dismantled at the end of 1999, several of its staff members were pulled into the 19.1 division that expanded to five workers responsible for 350 placements in subsidized and unsubsidized private employment in 2000. One 19.1 caseworker expressed serious doubt they would meet this goal.

The hidden low-skilled labor market
The modest results of efforts to place recipients into the private labor market seem to reflect the little room for maneuvering in a city-state with unusually high unemployment. However, the limited effectiveness of these measures may partially result from placement staff's inability to tap into the low-skilled areas of the labor market. One upper level administrator expressed deep frustration that Bremen had an estimated 6,000 unfilled low-paying jobs, the kinds of jobs not usually advertised in the daily newspapers or reported to the employment office. "There is no official channel of transmission. 70% of these positions don't show up officially in the labor market as offers." Needed was a more intensive, decentralized approach in which caseworkers became familiar with and known in particular neighborhoods and communities and were in regular contact with the various small firms there:

> These employers want convenience; they don't want to have to take out an ad. If a master artisan takes out an ad and gets 150 applications . . . he has to go through them all, invite people to interviews. This is two days' work. He is not going to do that. And he won't go to the employment office either, because they always send the wrong man, because the employment office doesn't care about this kind of work. So here is an important gap which needs to be filled. That's where our people come in. Of course, our clients are not always world champions, and are not always such hard workers; otherwise they would not be where they are.

Under current conditions, WB's private employment division does not have enough staff to develop this kind of community presence, and their efforts to find the right job for each referred client absorbs much of their available time.

Local Activation Practices in Germany

While there are no comprehensive studies of welfare-to-work programs, several surveys of practices in middle and large-sized German cities in the late 1990s and the first years after 2000 (e.g., Ahlrichs 2003; Hollenrieder et al. 2003; Empter and Frick 2000) provide a general picture of municipal activation programs during this time. During the 1990s, local governments in Germany began to play a significant role in employment policy. Between 1996 and 2000 the number of participants in HtW measures doubled to 403,000 (Schmid and Buhr 2002).[21] In 2002, it was estimated that approximately 24 percent of work-capable 15–65-year-olds on welfare were involved with their municipal activation program in some way (Hollenrieder et al. 2003).[22]

Like Werkstatt Bremen, municipal programs have tended to have three points of emphasis, namely, youth qualification measures, secondary labor market employment contracts, and direct placement in the primary labor market (with or without subsidies) (Schmid and Buhr 2002). One study of nine cities in the state of Nordrhein-Westfalen found that most programs focused equally on employment contracts and work-for-benefit, youth qualification measures, and to a lesser extent on primary labor market provisions (with an average of 9, 8.4 and 3.6 percent of all work-capable program claimants 15–65 years old enrolled in these respective measures [Hollenrieder et al. 2003]). Werkstatt Bremen appears to be unusual, though, in the variety of service providers it utilizes. By contrast, for example, the nearby city-state of Hamburg has relied primarily on a small number of large-scale, in-house group projects (Schaak 1997), while Stuttgart has depended on a half dozen public welfare organizations (Empter and Frick 2000).

Other studies have shown more substantial variations among municipal programs along many important program dimensions, including budgetary expenditures, participant levels, and mix of measures (Ahlrichs 2003). In many places in Eastern and Southern Germany, there are much higher levels of program participation among welfare recipients, especially on a premium work (workfare) basis. They tend to be enrolled in major public works projects, including road building and renovating public buildings. As many as 25 percent of municipalities use only this work-for-benefit type of program, an attractive option given how much cheaper it is compared to employment contracts (Leisering et al. 2001). In Southern Germany, which is a Christian Democratic stronghold, there is a tendency to prefer "workfare" for its disciplining effect on welfare recipients. There is also resistance to employment contracts for their potentially distorting effects on the market through the introduction of subsidized competition with private employers (Voges et al. 2000; also from interview with a Bremen administrator). By contrast, as a Social Democratic stronghold, Bremen has tended to place greater emphasis on "quality jobs" through employment contracts.

One of the most significant intranational variations is between programs in (former) East and West Germany. As part of the reunification effort, massive work-creation programs were developed by both the FES and local governments to limit the appearance and impact of open unemployment and to rebuild the public infrastructure.[23] Thus, for example, while in Hamburg the work placement level was estimated to be around 10 percent, in Leipzig it was near 100 percent of work-capable program participants (Adema, Gray, and Kahl 2003).

The effectiveness of HtW measures appears to be relatively limited, with estimates that 20–40 percent remain employed or enroll in vocational training afterwards. At the same time only 10–30 percent were still dependent on social assistance (Schmid and Buhr 2002). These discrepancies between successful integration and continued welfare receipt imply that these programs have continued to function primarily as a means to shift welfare recipients into the unemployment system.

Efforts to move recipients directly into the primary labor market (with or without wage subsidies) were the most successful and cost-effective policy instruments with anywhere between 50 and 100 percent remaining employed (Schmid and Buhr 2002). While these measures are most analogous to the American "work first" approach, they generally affected only a very small percentage of program participants (Hollenrieder et al. 2003). As in Bremen, a combination of weak labor market conditions and few recipients able to meet the demands of full-time employment has limited the general utility of this strategy in Germany.

A New Way? The Hartz Commission Reforms

While efforts in the 1990s to address the labor market rigidities and high nonwage labor costs failed (Leibfried and Obinger 2003; Aust 2003), a scandal involving inflated data from the FES created a window of opportunity to institute significant changes in employment policy and administrative arrangements. Between 2002 and 2005, the "Hartz" recommendations (named after the chair of the government commission) led to an alteration of the unemployment benefit system, organizational reform of the FES, and the introduction of new measures meant to "make work pay," changes which may significantly alter the role of local government in activation policy.

Until the adoption of the commission's recommendations for benefit restructuring, Germany was one of the few countries in the world with an income-based unemployment benefit of unlimited duration. It had consisted of a two-tiered system in which, after an unemployed claimant exhausted the first, most generous level ("unemployment benefit" at 60 percent wage level), he or she could receive a lower, means-tested, income-related benefit ("unemployment aid" at 53 percent) as long as the person was in need. This feature was viewed as a significant cause for the high level of structural unemployment in Germany as reflected in one of the highest levels of long-term unemployment in the OECD[24] (Adema, Gray, and Kahl 2003). As mentioned in chapter 4, the so-called Hartz IV reform led to a profound redesign of this system. Eligibility to the first tier (now called "unemployment benefit I (UBI)) was reduced from 32 months to 12 months. A new "unemployment benefit II" (UBII) replaced the lower, unemployment aid and social assistance for employable persons. It was structured as a needs-based, flat grant, fixed at the social assistance level, in effect altering it from a status-maintenance, insurance program to a poverty alleviation program. Recipients of the UBII were also held to a much stricter "suitable work" obligation, requiring them to take any job regardless of wage level. This change, then, represented a significant decline in the benefit conditions of unemployed workers who had previously had good jobs and who lost entitlement to UBI after a year (Kemmerling and Bruttel 2006).

All work-capable social assistance recipients (defined as able to work more than three hours/day) were also moved into this national, tax-financed program. In accordance with this new division of labor in which the federal government was responsible for all unemployed, HtW was effectively abolished as a component of social assistance (Aust 2003). Parts of it, especially the premium work statutes, were introduced into the new UBII program.

The organization and mix of employment-related services provided by the FES was also significantly altered. Following the examples of neighboring countries, the Hartz commission recommended the introduction of one-stop shops at which all unemployed individuals could access the whole range of available employment and social services. More individualized services were to be instituted through the introduction of "profiling," in order to identify claimants who needed intensive case management. A greater emphasis on activation was also reflected in a major shift in the active labor market policy (ALMP) mix of program measures from a traditional emphasis on long-term measures like further training and job creation (especially in East Germany) to short-term training and wage subsidies.[25]

The changes in the unemployment benefit system and the shift in ALMP mix were seen to represent a significant move of German employment policy toward a work-first model (Bruttel and Sol 2006). Yet the "active placement" service system envisioned seems far from reality, reflecting the impact of institutional inertia created by decentralized decision making in Germany's "interlocking federalism" (Kemmerling and Bruttel 2006). The profiling and intensive case management had not yet been enacted, as large numbers of new case managers still needed to be hired in order to reduce the typical caseload from 700 to 150.[26] One-stop shops had also not been implemented as intended. Recipients of UBI continued to be provided services at local FES offices, while recipients of the new UBII were handled by special job centers. What's more, a political compromise between the two major parties meant these centers were to be jointly managed by the FES and municipal governments.[27] Given the lack of collaborative history between those two different governmental systems, development of common management structures has been slow and complicated.[28]

Conclusion

In Germany, structural unemployment has made the task of moving welfare recipients into the labor market much more challenging than in the United States. The availability of low paying, low-skilled jobs in California has allowed agencies there to develop large-scale, standardized job search activities as a cost-effective means to move large numbers of recipients off the rolls. By contrast, in Bremen, where there seems to be a similar (though smaller) low-skilled sector, the welfare-to-work agency has not yet developed the capacity to tap into it. Rather Werkstatt Bremen has oriented its services primarily around other alternatives available given the existing labor market conditions and occupational structures.

19.2 division caseworkers are able to place a small percentage of older adult recipients in "sheltered employment" positions for one to two years in Bremen's diverse network of nonprofit organizations developed through government work creation measures. The wide range of public

Table 7.1   Comparing responsiveness among activation caseworkers (Bremen examples and a California comparison)

Program offerings: range of options available to caseworker	Nature of client contact: opportunity to develop rapport and provide direct services	
	Processing (short-term contact) −	Engaging (longer-term contact) +
Extensive +	"Resource Broker" (medium)	"Counselor" (high)
	X 19.2/19.1 Caseworkers	U27 Caseworker
	X (Job Developer—U.S.)	
Limited −	"Monitor" (low)	"Facilitator" (medium)

employment options gives caseworkers here an important role to play in matching clients with the most appropriate setting based on their skills and interests. Due to their social work backgrounds, caseworkers also aspire to develop substantive, personal relationships with their clients in order to be able to help clients move into suitable employment. Workload pressures created by excessive numbers of referrals, however, largely prevent sustained contact, resulting in a more truncated "resource brokering" function. While their role may seem similar to California's Job Developers, the orientation of the programs in which these two types of caseworkers operate are very different. Job Developers' primary purpose is to find private employers appropriate job candidates (with less attention to client interest), while 19.2 caseworkers' purpose is to help individual clients find an employment placement that is right for them. The difference in focus (on provider vs. client) leads to very different levels of commitment in the tailoring of services to the needs of participants, with the result that 19.2 caseworkers are much more client-centered, individualized brokers of their services (table 7.1).

Caseworkers in the small 19.1 division and the now-defunct BAVA project illustrate the differences in program orientation between the two countries even more clearly as they, like Job Developers, attempted to place clients in private employment. Whereas Job Developers start with their job listings and help clients apply for whatever may be appropriate, 19.1 and BAVA workers start with the client and then utilize their available employer connections to locate or design a job that suits them.[29] However, 19.1 and BAVA have had only marginal success placing clients in private employment, due to difficult economic conditions and limited staffing resources devoted primarily to customized employment placements.

U27 caseworkers help young adult recipients, mostly childless males, assume placements in Germany's apprenticeship system. This strategy represents a second, age-limited, alternative for moving clients off the welfare rolls (to training program stipends) and one that provides clients prospects of finding good-paying "insider" jobs if they complete their education. Unlike the other two divisions, program participation is mandatory for all adults under the age of 27, and this means caseworkers must continue to work with their clients until they no longer receive assistance. A federal initiative to combat youth unemployment has funded enough additional staff, though, that U27 caseworkers have manageable caseloads. Staff have utilized Werkstatt Bremen's connections to public welfare organizations to develop a wide variety of small group work experience and career planning activities to help clients identify their occupational interests and develop the necessary motivation and skills required for the demands of full-time training. They also meet with their clients frequently and are able to utilize their social work skills to provide individual counseling to assist clients in the transition between welfare and education. Thus, unlike 19.2 division caseworkers (who also aspire to develop substantive relationships but are hindered by the limitations of a small, locally funded program), national funding and a smaller client population have allowed U27 workers to act as "counselors" (table 7.1).

While WB provides an illustrative example of how local activation programs in Germany operated at the end of the 1990s, the major employment policy reforms in the first half-decade after 2000 have rendered it a bit of an historic artifact. It will take several years yet for researchers and policymakers to discern the kinds of program offerings and the nature of case management that develop in the new, large-scale job centers that have come to absorb municipal welfare-to-work programs.

8

Welfare-to-Work Caseworkers in Malmö, Sweden: The Emergence of Individualized Employment Services in Municipal Activation Agencies

I was quite displeased with the Employment Office. They forced a lot of recipients to go into computer training even if they didn't want to. They didn't have much to offer and so they didn't provide as much help as people needed. But those who come here, we can offer other solutions because there are a lot of other options. When you have a conversation with the individual and have a more complete picture of them, you can find other variations that are better for the person. It's not so much that there are now new resources; the difference is that you use them in a different way.[1]

Introduction

Sweden's world-renowned social security system—with its redistributive income policies, generous replacement rates, and relative equality among benefit levels (Esping-Andersen 1991)—has been made fiscally possible by the nation's ability to maintain high levels of work participation and an economy operating at close-to-full employment. This strategy has depended upon coordinated wage agreements, forcing less efficient firms out of business, and exceptionally high levels of spending on "active labor market" policies to retrain unemployed workers for the changing labor market. A second distinctive feature of the Swedish model emerged in the 1970s when, in an effort to combat unemployment and increase female labor force participation, Sweden greatly expanded public services, including public childcare.[2] This approach provided the means for women to juggle their responsibilities as mothers and workers, by socializing many of the responsibilities of family care, and by providing comparatively well-paying, protected state jobs. As a result, by the late 1980s, labor participation rates were the highest in the world at 75 percent of the working-age population in 1988 and 80 percent of working-age women (Esping-Andersen 1996).[3] But in 1990, with the onset of an unprecedented economic recession, the system began to unravel. Locally funded social assistance programs were inundated with large numbers of the "simply unemployed." And the Employment Office (EO) increasingly targeted its insufficient resources at the new demand for those with unemployment insurance benefits, leaving unemployed welfare recipients with little tangible assistance for finding work. By the mid-1990s, in response to the continuing high fiscal burden of their welfare programs and limited offerings of the EO, municipal governments entered the field of labor market policy by establishing their own "activation" programs.

In Malmö these projects were initially small, short-term, in-house measures. But by the late 1990s, more focused local government activation efforts and new national funding commitments were leading to greatly expanded and more institutionalized forms of service provision. In many district offices staff have built a network of contacts within the vast public service sector as well as increasingly with private employers to provide work experience and temporary job placements in a variety of occupational areas. In-house vocational counselors facilitate participants' entry into training programs. Free public education and the availability of student loans from the national government (considered a typical part of the Swedish career track) mean that further education is an important activation emphasis for all recipients. In an effort to broaden this focus on "competence" to those with basic education deficits, in the late 1990s the national government also greatly expanded adult education funding. Finally, the allocation of new state funding through the five-year "City Investment Initiative" (Storstadssatsningen) has also facilitated organizational innovation in the most adversely affected districts in Sweden's largest cities.

In this emergent setting, activation caseworkers in many districts have considerable resources to tailor services to the needs and interests of their clients, more so than in California or Bremen, and at a scale that is beginning to approach California's program. They also generally have enough opportunity and the skills necessary to develop familiarity with their clients and provide them individualized attention in order to personally help them through the process of transitioning into work or education. Thus, activation caseworkers in Malmö are able to be much more responsive to their clients than their counterparts in California and for a larger number and wider range of recipients than in Bremen.

Background—The Rise of Local Activation Programs in the 1990s

Up until the end of the 1980s there was a political consensus in Sweden that reintegrating the unemployed into the workforce was not a local task, but rather the duty of the national government. Part of the Swedish "Work line" (arbetslinjen) approach that began in the mid-1950s, employment was viewed as a social right. In order to give citizens the opportunity to work, the state was held to be respondible for expanding labor market participation and reducing the individual consequences of economic restructuring (Lindqvist and Marklund 1995). This strategy has demanded an exceptionally high level of national spending on "active labor market policies" (ALMP) at about 1.3–2.4 percent of gross national product (GNP),[4] including retraining, relocation, and other measures to adapt unemployed workers to the changing needs of the labor market (Johansson 2006). Local branches of the national EO play a central role in this system, overseeing the administration of ALMP programs and the distribution of unemployment benefits, as well as acting as a clearing-house for most job vacancies in the country. Work-capable welfare recipients were required to register with the EO, where staff were to provide employment assistance. Welfare caseworkers worked "actively" only with those clients who had additional social and behavioral difficulties that prevented them from being available for work. Thus, there was a clear interorganizational division of labor. For welfare clients who did not need additional social interventions, their behavioral obligations were indirect and similar in nature to those requirements made of social insurance recipients.

By the early 1990s, economic and social conditions had changed dramatically. Unemployment rose suddenly to an unprecedented 8 percent in 1990 from an average of 1.5–3.5 percent in the previous decade. Some of the unemployed lost their unemployment insurance entitlement and became recipients of local welfare programs. Many others who had never entered the Swedish labor market sought social assistance. Young adults were unable to find their first job after leaving school. A tremendous influx of immigrants from war-torn Yugoslavia, Iraq, and other countries during the economic downturn led to the rapid development of segregated ethnic enclaves in Sweden's largest cities, with populations that quickly became socially and economically marginalized.

In response to the economic downtown, ALMP measures were expanded, with participation levels rising from the usual 1.5 percent of the working population to 5.5 percent (Johansson 2006). But demand far outstripped available services, and the EO became increasingly restricted to individuals with entitlements to unemployment insurance benefits. New needs were also emerging among the unemployed, including cultural and linguistic deficits, low education levels, minimal or no job experience, and loss of self-esteem and motivation from long-term unemployment. EO services did not address these kinds of problems, being traditionally oriented toward "those who could take a job tomorrow."

As the inability of the EO to have much impact on unemployment rates (and local welfare costs) became apparent, local governments began to develop their own "activation" projects. Numerous court cases during this time sanctioned this expansion by allowing welfare offices to require social assistance recipients to participate in local projects as a condition of eligibility. And this position was later formalized in the 1998 revised national Social Service Law (Johansson 2001). This increased local activity in the area of labor market policy was further institutionalized by passage of the Development Guarantee (Utvecklingsgarantin). This national legislation transferred responsibility from the EO to local governments for adults under the age of 24 who were unemployed for more than 90 days, with the national government providing program support of 150 Kr/client/day (~$21). Required participation in local welfare-to-work programs (as opposed to EO program obligations) created a new status distinction that arguably enforced the second-class citizenship of social assistance recipients (Salonen 1999). Limited fiscal means and more direct political pressures to reduce caseloads often meant these programs were quickly developed, of varying quality (Hedblom 2004), and not clearly oriented toward employment-related skill development (Salonen and Ulmestig 2004).

During the first half of the 1990s in Malmö, a variety of small individual projects were developed, largely within the social assistance offices, in an effort to motivate particularly vulnerable groups—especially youth and immigrants (Giertz 2004). But it wasn't until 1997 that the General Plan for Work and Employment (GEFAS) was created, a specific local activation division with the aim of systematizing the expanding range of activation projects being developed. In 2000 there were ten separately administered, geographically defined GEFAS offices (corresponding to the ten district welfare offices).

The development of activation services was initially hindered by many problems typically associated with the creation of an entirely new program. GEFAS staff were "green" in that most had not worked in social services before, and it took time to develop services and establish procedures for referring and monitoring client participation. Due to unreliable funding, new projects were often operated for a year or two and then eliminated with little evaluation or learning. The decentralized organization of GEFAS also led to turf competition that undermined coordination among districts to offer the most effective array of services for recipients: "Is there any sense that each city district should potter about on its own? Shouldn't they be able to do something more as a whole?" (program administrator) Because it was introduced during a time of recession and targeted at those far from the labor market, it also served primarily as a way to keep many recipients participating in organized activities—"to have something to do." Clients were therefore often frustrated because the projects usually did not lead anywhere. The expansion of localities into activation policy, traditionally the jurisdiction of the EO, also created confusion about the specific roles each of the two organizations would play, as they "had gone into each other's areas."

GEFAS Activities in 2000—Three District Offices

The 1990s was the era of projects. Hopefully we have learned something from this and will develop a more systematic approach for moving people through appropriate programs that will lead to something.

(program supervisor)

Current activation efforts, however, appear to be evolving in a more organized and coordinated manner. Because of the decentralized nature of political authority in Malmö, each GEFAS program is somewhat different in size and program offerings, reflecting different political strategies and client populations.[5] The following section describes GEFAS offices in three city districts—Lönnäng, Boklunden, and Havdal—at the time this fieldwork was conducted in 2000.[6] Boklunden and Havdal are two of the three districts in Malmö with the highest welfare and immigrant populations in the city. Lönnäng is considered a less affected district with a smaller, but still substantial number of immigrants and welfare recipients and a more educated population than the other two.[7] Lönnäng has the most developed operational program in the city and is described first to introduce in some detail a variety of programs that are discussed in less detail for subsequent districts. Boklunden's office is undergoing major organizational change, anticipating the direction of activation programs in Sweden, so much of the discussion there focuses on these reforms. Havdal, by contrast, is in many ways a program outlier and illustrates how a large-scale American-style job search strategy can be both quite successful and politically controversial. An update of how activation programs have evolved in Malmö during the first few years of the new decade follows these case studies.

Lönnäng

Lönnäng's activation agency, the Work and Integration Center (WIC) (Arbete och Integration Center), is a quasi-independent program that primarily serves district welfare recipients but also provides services to clients from the EO, the social security agency (primarily those with lesser physical and psychiatric disabilities), and the national program for recent immigrants participating in "Introduction."[8] WIC has built a reputation as the premier activation program, having developed in a more systematic and comprehensive manner than many other GEFAS offices. In the first two years of operation it has grown from a staff of 2 to 20, with a range of in-house programs introduced gradually during this time. After Boklunden (see below), it serves the largest number and largest percentage of recipients of any district. During the first four months of 2000, 597 of the 1,390 welfare recipient households in Lönnäng (43 percent) participated in WIC programs,[9] and it is estimated that WIC gets about 60 referrals per month from the welfare office. The organizational goal is to place about one-third of clients into study/education programs, one-third into employment, and one-third into practica placements.

Each staff member generally has two functions. She is the "contact person" for between 50 and 70 clients and is responsible for following their progress at WIC, which is generally limited to one year. And she is jointly responsible with another staff member for one of the programs or services participants can utilize there. Almost all staff at WIC have some higher level of training and prior experience working in social service projects, though only about half are social workers. Participants initially attend a group information session where they are told about WIC, its various offerings, and the obligation they have to participate. Then clients choose among three different first activities, depending on their goals and abilities: "Workforce" (Arbetskraft); vocational counseling; or "Activity Gate." Those who remain after this first activity decide together with their contact person on the next appropriate measure, including a number of additional services (discussed below).

Workforce

This workshop is for those interested in finding employment directly. Fifteen participants spend three weeks learning how to write resumes and application letters; attending information sessions on topics such as the Swedish employment system (unions, unemployment insurance, employer associations, and employment opportunities in the EU); and visiting various temporary employment agencies—"to show them what exists for employment." Afterwards they are required to come into the office twice a week for eight weeks and use the computer system (with a link to EO job listings) and other office resources to look for a job. Generally they are expected to apply for five jobs per week.

This particular activity most closely resembles California's Job Club. However, Manpower is a more substantive, sophisticated version—three weeks of instruction rather than one week; better trained staff (who could make comments like, "it takes about five drafts usually to make an application letter right."); and more extensive employment resources, through access to the EO's job banks, where most job vacancies in the country are posted (rather than the limited number of postings collected by Job Developers).

Vocational counseling
Two caseworkers at WIC are trained in "study and occupational counseling." With their knowledge of the Swedish education and vocational systems, including the application process and financing possibilities, they can provide important information in both individual and group meetings to assist clients interested in additional training. The focus on training is especially important because, as the labor market improves, increasing numbers of vacancies are appearing that will be difficult to fill given the current low education levels in Malmö. Many immigrants with qualifications in their homelands may need to translate and validate their training in Sweden, and so may require additional courses or internships in order to become fully qualified.

The opportunities to pursue further education had also been significantly increased at all levels during the 1990s. In response to weak labor market conditions, the national government had shifted its traditional ALMP focus from a "work-first" to a "work-and-competence" principle (Hort 2001), expanding university capacities[10] and instituting a 5-year, adult education initiative in 1997. "Knowledge Boost" (Kunskapslyftet) was organized at the municipal level as a general skill development program, in particular to increase the number of adults with a three-year gymnasium degree, the prerequisite for enrolling in most studies at the university level. Thus it differed from traditional active labor market programs that were oriented to more work-related training. By creating an additional 100,000 slots in the adult education system, it represented "the largest and most ambitious skill raising program ever" (Albrecht et al. 2004, 1). The numbers of enrollees in adult education increased from approximately 130,000 in the early 1990s to over 300,000 in 1998 (Stenberg 2003). In Malmö in 1999, approximately 10,000 individuals, mostly unemployed, participated in this program.

One especially important topic caseworkers discussed with participants was student loans. In Sweden, most educational programs are public and therefore free to students. Adults over the age of 20 may continue receiving welfare to study for their basic school degree (ninth grade level), or their high school vocational or general education degree (twelfth grade) for up to two years. For education beyond gymnasium level, most students take out loans from the government for living expenses. This can add up to a considerable amount—one caseworker estimated that almost all staff at WIC had loans of between 200,000 and 500,000 Kr (~$29,000–71,000), but that this was typical for most educated Swedes. Loans are paid back at a very low, income-based rate for most of one's working life and often with the remainder forgiven at retirement. Many recipients had an inaccurate picture of student loans, imagining they had to be paid back at a rate comparable to bank loans, and this dissuaded many from considering higher education. All three GEFAS sites mentioned that dispelling these impressions so that clients "dared to take out loans" was a crucial role for activation agencies to play.

The vocational counselors saw their role as substantive, not simply a matter of "talking a bit and giving them a brochure." Clients who didn't know what they wanted to do often needed a lot of help in choosing the right occupation. Vocational counselors utilized their training in "conversation methods" to facilitate clients' thinking through what they really wanted to do, to imagine a particular job: "If they come in and say they want to be a bus driver, I don't simply say, 'Okay, you can apply here,' but rather, 'Why, what is it about that job that attracts you, perhaps you should consider a practicum there.' It is important they really have an interest so they don't go into a course of study that doesn't work."

Many clients also have additional problems and fears that have to be addressed before they are prepared to choose a course of study, and for these clients the "counseling" side of vocational counselor comes to predominate: "Many have fallen on bad times and so it can take some time before they are ready for studies or an occupation . . . Then our conversations are more therapeutic in nature . . . more about daily counseling."

Activity Gate (AG)

This project is for those "furthest from the labor market, who are the worst off." Its goal is to help participants become more involved in social life, to "get people going in a gentle way." AG lasts for four weeks, four hours per day with 10–12 participants in a group, half from the welfare office and half from the disability section of the social security agency.[11] Activities consist of a variety of "pleasant experiences," including lectures on health issues and field trips to places like the new bridge connecting Sweden and Denmark and the city library:

> Many of our participants have never seen the bridge even though they live here in Malmö. They have never been to the city library. They stand outside but are afraid to go in. They don't know how one behaves in a library. We can show them and help them get a library card, open a door for them.

AG also provides an opportunity for participants to develop friendships with each other that can be invaluable for many who are otherwise socially isolated. The AG caseworkers have also introduced an ongoing support group, now self-running, that meets in the evenings every week.

Employment opportunities in the public sector—practica and ARBIS positions
In Malmö, activation agencies have also developed a significant "work experience" program in the public sector that offers opportunities to place recipients in a range of occupational areas. Despite the recent genesis of GEFAS, staff there have been able to utilize this existing resource to rapidly develop a network of contacts and so place hundreds of recipients in municipal government agencies, either through 2–3 month internships (practica) or 6-month employment positions known as "ARBIS" positions ("work instead of welfare" (arbete istället socialbidrag)).

The caseworkers in charge of practica and ARBIS placements receive client referrals from other WIC staff (after the client has completed one of the three initial activities) and directly from the EO,[12] with a mix of about 70 percent welfare and 30 percent EO participants. Practica placements are seen by staff as a useful measure for "occupational orientation." They provide an introduction to employment areas in which recipients might be interested. For some, practica offer required work experience for vocational programs clients plan to begin at the start of the next school semester. For older adults, these kinds of internships can provide a fresh work reference and updated training in an area in which they may have work experience: "They may already have the education but not have had a job for a long time. Techniques may have developed so they have to practice a little, such as with the computer. And then if they look for a job, they have a little more in their suitcase." These positions are not suitable for all participants, however, because they make considerable demands on clients with "a lot of work and stress in these kinds of jobs." Practica rarely also lead to permanent employment at the same agency both because of limited agency funds and because most public jobs require considerable specific education that participants lack.

Placing referred clients in practica is a very dynamic process. Caseworkers have no placements set up in advance, but instead call their contacts throughout the city based on their impressions of a recipient after their first interview. But, as "veteran" staff (having both been at WIC for just over two years[!]), both caseworkers said the contacts they have built up during their time there are sufficient to place most clients relatively quickly, usually within one to two weeks. As one caseworker explained, most agencies understand the importance of these placements for the employment prospects of participants and are therefore willing to develop and supervise these positions. At the time of the interview, there were 34 in practica with 10 more waiting to be placed and an average of 2–10 new clients each week. It was estimated they would place about 160 during the course of the year.

Placements are relatively easy to find in the "traditionally female" public caring sector, especially in childcare centers and schools. There are also some civil engineering slots available in roads, water, and sanitation, but many (male) participants do not want to work there — "They all want to work in computers." It is also challenging to place people with occupational interests that occur primarily in the private sector (such as in auto repair), or where public organizations are not as able to develop simple jobs (such as in law or psychiatry). Practica caseworkers also had to contend with difficult cases from the EO. Unlike at WIC where clients were screened for suitability by contact staff members, there was no similar referral guarantee across agencies, and many EO staff found it easier simply to get rid of their more demanding clients. In addition, WIC is facing increasing competition from other GEFAS programs for placements. While earlier WIC had placed their clients all over the city, now they have found many district government agencies reserving their internship slots for recipients from their own districts.

ARBIS positions also occur in local government. But unlike practica they last longer (6 months) and are, in fact, real jobs with participants receiving wages and contributions to insurance programs. They are reserved exclusively for welfare recipients. As in the case of Germany, this form of employment contract, though shorter, entitles participants to unemployment benefits upon completion.[13] Being municipally funded they are expensive (about 100,000 Kr per placement) and therefore few in number, with about 75 currently planned for the year at WIC (and 526 in Malmö overall in 1999). Because ARBIS are "the best we have to offer," selection is more careful and generally reserved for those who have "attempted to find a job and nothing has happened."

Growth 2000 (Tillväxt 2000)
In addition to Workforce, WIC offers another, more intense employment-related project called Growth 2000. Like so many Malmö projects this one was originally started on EU money and shut down after only one year, but because of its success, the district government decided to reestablish it primarily with local funds. Participants from welfare and the EO attend an eight-week course from 8:30 A.M. to 4:00 P.M. that includes computer and math training, resume and application writing, and motivation. For immigrants it is especially important to learn to become proficient in writing associated with the job application process. The course is run "like a job" in order to acclimate participants to the hours and demands of work. At the same time, the project leader (who was formerly a small business owner) has been actively developing contacts with local businesses and employers associations, with the added incentive of wage subsidies from

the EO, in order to find suitable positions for individuals: "I know what businesses look for. I can imagine they survive on the basis of effectiveness and resources . . . and if you understand their problems it is easier to place people there." Once a client has been placed in employment, program staff maintain close contact with employers and participants to ensure that any problems are addressed quickly. Of 92 participants from the first two groups from the previous year, 70 were still in work currently. The next group was scheduled to begin in a month.[14]

Development Guarantee (youth program)
As mentioned earlier, with the introduction of the national Development Guarantee (DG) in 1998, local agencies became responsible for young adults under the age of 24 who had been unemployed for more than 90 days. One caseworker at WIC is responsible for all such EO referrals, and she currently has 35 youth under this program. According to her, DG was established because the EO became too involved in developing work preparation programs during the recession of the 1990s, moving away from its primary organizational function of job brokering between employers and potential employees. Practica in private firms increased dramatically, becoming an almost automatic measure for young unemployed adults, and it became easy for private firms to get free labor rather than hiring permanent employees. By shifting responsibility to municipalities and their placement resources in local government, practica could be more carefully targeted to those who needed it while minimizing potential distorting effects on the labor market.

Requirements for DG participants "can be very mixed, including job search activities, vocational counseling, different projects and practica." Most know what they want to do, and so practica offer clients a way to test possible occupations, gain some work experience, and perhaps "plant the seed" of the need for further education. Those unsure of their future career are referred to one of the vocational counselors. Many are also given time to study for their driver's license, something much more difficult to obtain in European countries than in the United States. While WIC is supposed to help DG participants find suitable employment or education within one year, none have remained that long, with the average being about six months before participants find employment or enroll in long-term education.

The relationship with the EO has improved dramatically since the program began. At first there was considerable confusion. "We didn't know what we were going to do and the EO didn't either. We were a little in their area." EO staff considered local activation agencies to be competition and referrals as compromising their own authority. However, with the recent reorganization of the EO along city district lines[15] the WIC staff member now works with only two staff from the Lönnäng EO, and they have developed a close collaboration, sometimes referring DG participants back who might be better served in a private training placement.

The caseworker's role as contact person
The contact person provides support and monitors their clients' progress and program participation. At their first client meeting they write up an "activity plan" setting out what the participant will do to secure employment or education. All caseworkers emphasized that they played more of an assisting role in the process and that the content was largely determined by the clients themselves. This client-centered approach was seen as important in order to make participation at WIC as "voluntary" as possible so that clients learned to take responsibility for their future plans. Subsequent meetings often focused on support and encouragement, helping clients to overcome fears and "dare to try," or help with a job or training application. On the other hand, some clients were not as enthusiastic about being there and would stop participating. Then the caseworker would have to make the "hidden control" more visible and reiterate their obligation to attend or lose benefits.

Staff generally felt they had enough time and flexibility to meet with their clients as needed: "Some clients I see twice a week, others who don't need as much assistance maybe once a month." They estimated they spent between one-half and three-fourths of their time in client contact. Frequent consultations with other staff, especially the program leader for their clients' current activities, allowed staff to keep close tabs on progress: "They can't ever really escape us."

Ongoing systemic problems
WIC staff (along with staff from other GEFAS agencies) identified a number of systemic problems that continue to hinder client success. Discrimination against immigrants, they said, was widespread. Staff hoped that the recent improvement in the economy and the impending shortage of trained workers in many sectors would make employers give more consideration to qualified immigrants. Staff also noted certain gaps in activation resources. There were insufficient Swedish language programs for those who needed very basic and gradual introduction to the language. There were also no funds for many private training programs that could easily lead directly to employment, such as truck driving school. Inadequate public childcare resources also often delayed recipients' participation in WIC programs and sometimes forced clients to miss a time-sensitive course or practicum. Several staff also thought welfare recipients who participated in programs should receive a little additional money, an "activity stipend",

both as incentive and reward, allowing them to save a little money, and giving them recognition for their self-help efforts: "It can be degrading to participate in an activity and not receive anything for it."

Comparing WIC caseworker responsiveness to caseworkers in Werkstatt Bremen and CalWORKS
The variety of in-house programs as well as the referral networks staff developed with the public service sector and some private employers allowed WIC staff to offer services addressing a very diverse set of interests and needs to a comparatively large percentage of district participants. The breadth and specificity of the program was unmatched by any other program in any of the three countries. What's more, their opportunity to interact with clients frequently, both as caseworkers and as program leaders, meant they could have a significant personal impact on agency participants. This combination of substantial program resources and the opportunity to personally engage participants gives caseworkers a very substantial "counselor" role to play in responding to clients' needs in assisting them to self-sufficiency.

By contrast, California's "employment specialists" have neither a range of services to offer nor the skills, opportunity, or job definition to affect clients' lives personally. While California's Job Club workers may provide some individualized encouragement and motivation, this contact occurs for a relatively short duration. Furthermore, participants have little choice in the matter as Job Club is the only activity offered. This lack of choice creates real problems of motivation and appropriateness (as many clients have other problems that could better be addressed by different services) that limit the capacity of JC workers to "engage" their participants effectively.

In Bremen, on the other hand, caseworkers have a considerable variety of activities to offer their clients. Like WIC, they too score well on program options. Caseworkers in the youth division are also able to provide personal counseling services to clients. WIC caseworkers, though, actually have an even greater role to play in providing services, because they also act as "service providers" themselves via their in-house offerings, while U27 staff utilize only off-site activities. This resource gives WIC staff an additional venue through which to know some clients and provide them important services. The U27 program is also a product of unique circumstances, made possible by the targeted efforts of the national government to combat youth unemployment and by the training entitlements available to those under the age of 26. U27 represents an exceptional pocket of responsive service provision in a system that otherwise has much more limited impact on recipients. More typical is the role 19.2 caseworkers play, where the small scale of the program limits the number of clients caseworkers can help, and where the gap between program demand and resources seriously constrains their ability to provide the kind of personalized direct services to which they aspire.

Boklunden

One of the most significant developments in Swedish welfare policy came at the end of the 1990s after the economy had begun to recover. Through the "City Investment Initiative" (CII) (Storstadssatsningen) the national government earmarked substantial new funding for five years to combat unemployment and social exclusion, especially among immigrants, in the most economically depressed areas of Sweden's largest cities, including Malmö.[16] While the initiative had an ambitious set of goals,[17] its most prominent focus was on increasing employment and labor market participation.

In 1999, a development agreement in Malmö was concluded to establish Work and Development Centers (WDC) (Arbets-och utvecklingscentra) in four districts in Malmö (two of which were among the districts studied here—Boklunden and Havdal). Compared to the earlier GEFAS programs, the number of staff was greatly expanded and professionalized. Ten staff from the EO and ten from the local social services, as well as one caseworker from the Social Security Agency (SSA) were to be allocated to each center. By colocating staff from three government agencies[18] policy makers intended to address the inefficiencies, role confusion, and cost/client-shifting that had occurred between different government programs during the past decade. Each office would be managed by a municipal level project leader, though EO and SSA staff would remain under the authority of their home offices. The new centers were to have at their disposal all programs and resources from the three agencies, including the additional funding provided to the municipalities through the CII.

The targeted population similarly transcended normal organizational boundaries as any of the three agencies could refer clients judged able to prepare for full-time employment or full-time study within one year. Priority was given to immigrants who were unemployed despite education and occupational experience, and young adults (20–24) who were either long-term unemployed or needed more involved motivation and guidance measures. Caseworkers from the two most relevant agencies were to jointly share clients in order to utilize the distinct skills and resources of the programs most appropriate to the clients' situations.[19] By separating the provision of activation services for those who need "extra support" from the overriding demands of home agencies—that is, high caseloads and routinized practices governed by regulations and authority over money—staff would presumably be able to assist clients in a more comprehensive, individualized, and continuous fashion than had been possible. An initial goal was set that each WDC should accept 1,250 participants each year and that within one year 30 percent should find work and 30 percent should be enrolled in study or education programs.

At the time of this fieldwork Boklunden's WDC was still in the very early stages of development.[20] While Lönnäng provides a good example of the kinds of services that are likely be offered at the WDCs, this new program takes a broader perspective on both the problem of social exclusion and the resources necessary for assisting victims of the last recession. It is on these organizational innovations that the Boklunden case study focuses.

The process
At the time of staff interviews (May 2000), intake meetings with potential participants had only been occurring for the previous month, and the first activities were scheduled to begin the following week. Much of the nature of the work and the program offerings were therefore still unclear. But a general approach to service provision was emerging (one that has been more substantially documented in subsequent research [see next section]). All clients were to have individualized activity plans that could include a variety of different measures the center would offer, depending on the individuals' needs and abilities and whether they were interested in employment or further training: "The thought is that it will be a program tailored to each individual, like at the gymnasium where students choose from among various courses."

At an initial three-party intake meeting, staff members assess the appropriateness of the referral[21] and, if so, whether the client is capable of looking for employment immediately or needs extra support and motivational work first. Those individuals already judged capable of obtaining employment (based in part on self-evaluation) begin working immediately with the EO staff member who assists them with job leads and perhaps finding a practicum in a private firm: "For example, you give them four job leads and meet with them again in two weeks." Most participants, though, require more help: "Of course, they should be looking for a job the whole time, but realistically to get a job and retain it, for many it will take more time before it is realistic to achieve this goal." These individuals are enrolled in a three-day introduction program. This course, purchased from an outside private firm, informs participants about the various projects offered and provides a "smaller form of advising," covering different ways of becoming self-sufficient, what demands employment makes, and reasons why many individuals fail to find work.

After participants finish this program their caseworkers hold a second meeting with them to determine whether the individual needs a more extensive general orientation to work and education by participating in the five-week in-house motivation course. Others may be ready for more individualized measures covering a whole range of potential program offerings, including practica in private firms or municipal organizations, vocational counseling, job search, computer coursework, and EO and old GEFAS projects.

Work conditions—WDC vs. welfare and employment offices

Staff from both agencies identified important differences in their work at WDC as compared with their home institutions, differences that give them greater opportunity to provide individualized services to clients. Former welfare caseworkers noted that while "working actively" with recipients was "the idea in social services too," welfare caseworkers generally did not know most of their clients well at all. The primary task of making decisions about money involved regulations, documentation, and deadline pressures; and given high caseloads, money decisions consumed most of their time.

By contrast, at the WDC, activities are more diffuse, not governed by extensive regulations and documentation, and staff have no direct decision-making authority. The job is about "having conversations, rather than making decisions." Clients also appear to be more forthcoming because their caseworkers lack direct authority over money: "I have already seen that there are certain differences in contact with clients, that they are open and report that perhaps they have been offered a job and declined it. They would never have reported that when I was a caseworker because they would have lost their money. So more openness here. At the same time, there is a connection to welfare, I must report not what they say, but what they do."

EO staff noted similar differences. The EO operates more as a self-service information center with computer banks for unemployed recipients to look for appropriate job vacancies. Very few of the people that utilize their services actually make appointments to have individual meetings with EO staff. High caseloads (of 300–400) lead to a very "mechanical" approach to casework, and, as a result, agency staff have very limited ability to respond to new needs—"There it was more difficult to change things. It is an operation that occurs continually and is always the same . . . By contrast, here in a project, changes can occur the whole time. We will build up based on what our clients need."

Advantages and challenges of joint case responsibility

Staff from both agencies extolled the benefits of working together under one roof with a common clientele. In three-party meetings involving the client, the social worker, and the EO officer, each staff member brought different resources and skills. EO staff are used to working with businesses and so "have knowledge about the labor market and the prognosis about it . . . and know what's needed and how to apply for a job." Social workers have their own skills and perspectives. They tend to "look more at the social and how it is all working, the client's environment. I look more about what's going on around." They are also more used to working with difficult clients—"how one works with those who say they want to but don't. How one deals with such practical issues."

Having two staff there also made such meetings richer in content and opportunity, as one caseworker could talk while the other observed. Or the EO staff could be looking for vacancies on the computer right there while the meeting continued. Afterwards staff members would have discussion partners to compare perspectives. Because both agencies are represented, they can also communicate a uniform message about the client's obligations and each staff member's responsibilities: "Everyone understands the expectations. It is clear."

Differences in training and work experience, however, also lead to organizationally distinct definitions of the client's problems, creating some challenges for collaboration and communication. This divergence stems in part from the difficulties of developing an organization with the employment-focused orientation of the EO, but with more difficult clientele like that from welfare. For example, one EO staff member expressed some skepticism about whether municipal social workers had any distinct contribution to make. While she had job-related resources to offer clients, social workers "cannot really articulate what they will do, when it comes to talking about motivation, which is supposed to be their responsibility. Nothing concrete . . . it is clear that [those from social administration] are to help people find work, but it isn't really their main task."

Municipal staff, on the other hand, felt EO staff lacked an appreciation for the impact of social circumstances on those further from the labor market. Their previous work at the EO had primarily involved providing information (job placements) to a clientele with work histories (unemployment insurance beneficiaries) and who voluntarily sought services. This prior experience often led to a somewhat naïve attitude toward clients and an implicit assumption by EO staff that everyone wanted a job. Having worked with clients who "strula" (persistently say they'll do something but don't and always have excuses), social workers are more attentive and skillful at pressing clients and testing their statements.

> It seems to me that EO are a little nicer, they buy more readily what the person says. 'I will wait and see if I get this job.' And I'm more like, 'You should

go into this project now and if you get a job then quit the project. Two variations, drive on two courses at the same time.' I am a little more used to dealing with youth and not ready to buy their arguments . . . Often the EO staff is like 'why did you say that in the meeting. I didn't understand that.' And then I explain my approach to her and she was like 'I hadn't thought of that.'

Still, overall, staff felt cooperation had worked well and that the advantages far outweighed the difficulties of talking across organizational worlds.

Havdal

Havdal is unique among district GEFAS offices in several ways that bring it closer to the U.S. job search approach than any non-U.S. agency in the study. Unlike other district offices that rely almost exclusively on permanent, skilled project staff, most caseworkers at the Havdal GEFAS are actually former welfare recipients in ARBIS positions. Additionally, while other offices may have no more than a few hundred GEFAS participants (and many less than 100), during the first four months of 2000, 2,797 of the district's 2,860 recipient households (98 percent!) were officially enrolled. Rather than focusing on various small projects and assisting clients only as slots become available, the former Havdal GEFAS director developed a large-scale, two pronged approach: (1) a "Job Search" Center ("Söka Jobb") at which recipients would be required to regularly look for employment; and (2) a study/education section in which clients with insufficient Swedish proficiency or low basic education levels were to take appropriate coursework. An ARBIS caseworker initially assesses new participants to determine whether employment or education is the most appropriate goal. Those who express interest in education are referred to the study section. Those who want to work and have adequate language proficiency are assigned to the Job Search Center.

The Job Search Center
The Job Search Center functions like "a little municipal Employment Office." Participants are expected to search and apply for relevant job openings using a computer system linked to the EO job banks. But unlike the relatively voluntary nature of the EO, individuals here have more substantive and specific behavioral obligations—they must visit the center three times per week and give proof of three applications per week or risk losing their benefits. At the same time, welfare recipients are meant to receive more active and individualized assistance than is available at the primarily self-service EO. All participants are assigned to one of the 15 ARBIS caseworkers (supervised by one full-time and one part-time social worker) who have caseloads of between 30 and 50 clients. They meet with

their clients once a week, providing counseling and encouragement, helping them identify potential jobs, and completing the application process. This U.S. style large-scale "labor market attachment" approach staffed by nonprofessionals has met with apparent success. One caseworker reported that of 650 GEFAS recipients in all of Malmö who left welfare for employment in the last year, 550 were from Havdal's job search unit.[22] While this strategy has "consistently shown the best results for the money," there are serious organizational problems and controversy associated with the program. Politically there have been objections to the use of ARBIS positions as the primary staffing resource. This expensive program option is generally utilized in other districts for individual cases where work experience is necessary to transition to employment or education. A caseworker from another district in charge of ARBIS positions commented on how "strange" Havdal's use of them was, and how few ARBIS recipients from Havdal found employment afterwards because they were not tailored to the needs of particular individuals. The local debate around the Job Search Center also consisted of a "moral concern" with the scale and stringency of the program—"People want more quality and not have clients treated like cattle. You push 1,100 in and require them to attend 3 days a week or they are denied. It is a very big process and a lot to demand of the client. Individuals disappear in this arrangement. I think that is the reason they (politicians) are so critical."

Organizationally there are several advantages to using welfare recipients as caseworkers. They are often innovative in their approach to clients, more so than social workers might be: "It would be more traditional and boring with only social workers who all have the same education and approach. Now it is more exciting, they come up with more creative solutions." They have knowledge of what it is like to be "on the other side" and share cultural and linguistic backgrounds with many of their clients. They therefore have some insights and a persuasive power with clients that social workers may not have.

The problems of ARBIS staff in their current usage, though, seem to outweigh the benefits. While their function should be primarily motivation and social work, they do not have the appropriate education and therefore tend to see their work in simpler terms of administrative tasks and control functions. This lack of training also makes it difficult for them to maintain boundaries, and they are sometimes easily manipulated by clients. ARBIS staff also know many of their clients, being from the same community and only recently recipients themselves. Such familiarity has raised concerns over the caseworkers' abilities to maintain professional relationships and confidentiality and to treat their clients in an equitable manner. As the primary contact for all program participants, they have considerable discretion in deciding when to report someone for noncompliance and when to seek additional assistance from a supervisor; and many seem reluctant to seek assistance, viewing the need for help as sign of defeat. One caseworker aptly summed up the problem, "It isn't good to lay that power on someone who is temporary with limited education."

On top of these shortcomings, the constant flux of new ARBIS staff every six months limits the ability to develop program structure and maintain continuity. This disruption has often led to low service quality and poor communication with welfare offices about client attendance, with many false reports of noncompliance. Also the one full-time and one half-time social workers employed at the program (one of whom was interviewed) quit (soon after the interviews), and as one staff member in the study section put it, "No social workers want to work here because it is so unstructured."[23]

Several staff suggested they needed a greater mix of social workers and former recipients employed more permanently in "project positions" which only cost 3,000 Kr more/year. With the recent firing of the GEFAS director, the program is apparently moving more in the direction of consolidation, "shrinking a bit and focusing on quality, making sure that those sent to job search can really be helped by it." Also the GEFAS office is giving up some of its ARBIS money so the welfare office can employ three additional caseworkers in order to assign clients to one of the two units and better inform participants about the program offerings.

Study section
Havdal has a high percentage of relatively recent immigrants who have never learned Swedish well enough to be employable. (About half of all Havdal recipients are registered in the study section.) Many are enrolled here because they could not begin to look for a job—"employers require you be able to speak Swedish well enough to be understood." The Job Search Center itself generally requires participants to have a certificate indicating basic Swedish proficiency. The EO has an even higher threshold, requiring two levels above basic proficiency. The study section has its own in-house "language school" (grundlyftet) requiring four hours/day for those with very low language skills, a relatively unique arrangement among district offices, reflecting the particular and acute needs of this district's clientele. The study section staff is very small, consisting of one social worker/program supervisor, a project position, and an ARBIS position. They initially help new referrals determine the appropriate language class, with in-house for beginners, and adult education schools and gymnasium courses for more advanced levels and faster tempos. While clients may also consider enrolling in other kinds of education, the office has no vocational counselor like the other districts to assist this process.

Most participants then enroll in programs without any further problems, having little ongoing contact with program staff, and are simply required to send in their semester grades. However, about 100 are left who need more substantive assistance—"where it doesn't work or where they refuse to go to school." With these clients staff focus considerable attention on motivation: "We work a lot with immigrants who have been at home for many years and been unemployed and are very afraid to take the first step to learn Swedish." Thus, staff in Havdal's study section also function as "facilitators," personally assisting those having difficulties even participating in the section's limited language course offerings.

Changes in Havdal—the introduction of a new work and development center
Alongside the current GEFAS office, Havdal was also developing its own WDC office, similar to Boklunden's. At the time of fieldwork, this program was in an even earlier planning stage with continuing major differences among agency staff about the center's primary purpose—EO staff seeing the WDC as primarily assisting those closest to the labor market and municipal staff considering it to be for those who needed extra help. There was also uncertainty about the new organization's relationship to, as well as the continued status of, the current GEFAS Job Search Center.

Subsequent Development in Malmö's Work and Development Centers

Considerable research has been done on Malmö's WDCs during their first few years in operation (e.g., Ahlstrand & Lindberg 2001; Bevelander et al. 2003; Lindberg 2003; Hedblom 2004; Oldrup et al. 2002; Tranquist 2001). These evaluations generally agree that after some early start-up problems, such as with program quality (Hedblom 2004) and poorly defined referral criteria (Tranquist 2001), these centers developed relatively successful, large-scale, and client-centered approaches to providing activation services. Several programmatic features are regarded as particularly innovative, namely assessment and resource synergies among colocated staff, and the conversational relationship that could develop between clients and their caseworkers.

Process

After some initial role confusions, staff from different agencies were able to develop a working rapport and become familiar with the distinct contributions each could make in collaborative casework. Smaller case-loads than were typically found at their home institutions greatly facil-itated this learning process (Tranquist 2001). Regular communication among caseworkers about common clients also allowed them to develop a more comprehensive perspective on individuals' situations than any would have been able to develop on their own.

Through this integrated approach to assessment and service provision, staff could largely avoid the problems of previous uncoordinated efforts of different agencies in which individuals were often either enrolled in over-lapping measures that were not well suited together, or endured long waiting times between measures. A WDC caseworker, by contrast, in consultation with their client, could draw up an activity plan that could take a long-term perspective on integration. Appropriate program measures could be selected that followed one after another in a logical way and that would be clear and agreed to by the participant.

At the agency level, there were and continued to be challenges to interor-ganizational coordination due to differences in funding streams, organiza-tional goals and cultures, and clientele (Bevelander et al. 2003). Yet concerns about cost- and responsibility-shifting appeared to be largely resolved within the centers as caseworkers from different agencies related to each other as colleagues with common goals, and the fiscal incentives of their home agen-cies were mediated by a setting in which clients were shared. Thus, making decisions about when a welfare client was ready to receive training support through the EO (representing a shift in financing) was considered by many staff to be made in a more careful fashion than previously.

Several studies noted that the WDCs were a dynamic and creative envi-ronment in which new ideas—about organizational processes or program offerings—could be tried and evaluated quickly. Information on promis-ing approaches was also readily shared both within and, later, among the centers (Oldrup et al. 2002; Tranquist 2001). Having maintained program operations for several years had also led to more significant program development (in terms of variety and quality) than had been possible in previous, shorter-term collaborations (Lindberg 2003). While there were some problems with the rigidities and often-changing priorities of the EO, leading to disruptions in individual client activity plans, the combination of resources from all three agencies, including the flexibility provided by CII funds, meant most caseworkers considered available resources to be sufficient for their current work conditions and clientele.[24] Such an assess-ment was characterized by one researcher as quite extraordinary for a social service organization (Tranquist 2001). In fact, the only problem identified was that the variety of measures available required efforts on caseworkers' parts to keep up to date.

Another crucial aspect identified by researchers distinguishing the WDC approach from previous activation programs was the ability of caseworkers to develop personal conversational relationships with their clients over a longer period of time. The initial assessment of a clients' educational and employment background and career goals and the development and updating of the individual activity plan formed a basis for this conversation. Some researchers argued that through this process of active listening, a client is able to develop trust in her caseworker (Lindberg 2003; Bevelander et al. 2003).[25] Subsequent discussions about how that individual should proceed are then viewed as a collaborative effort, allowing staff to help the client develop motivation and a realistic view of their goals and the steps to achieving them.

While the centers all have similar program targets and staffing resources, the goal-oriented, dynamic process has meant that offices often varied in how they designed various programmatic features. For example, offices organize their casework teams in different ways (sometimes with mixed EO and municipal staff, in other cases with teams separated by agency), offer introduction courses of different length and content, and utilize job search activities at different points in the process (sometimes as an obligatory and universal part of the first program component, in other places, as a voluntary option among the repertoire of available measures).

Internships/practica in municipal agencies and private firms were identified as a typical measure that was utilized for equipping clients to become employable (Lindberg 2003). While in the past, these placements had often not led to a real job and had often been experienced as useless or exploitative (Hedblom 2004), the centers have devoted considerable organizational attention to ensuring more consistent quality. These efforts include devoting staff to acquiring new internships, informing potential employers and supervisors about what is expected, and monitoring and providing support to clients once placed. This increased attention to work placements is also part of a larger effort to increase contacts with potential employers in order to be able to identify or create jobs that suit both clients and employers (similar to the approach taken by 19.1 division caseworkers in Werkstatt Bremen).

Outcomes

Early results indicated that placements in training were far below what had been anticipated (Tranquist 2001). This difficulty appeared to result from two sources—insufficient prior education that precluded many from enrolling in vocational programs; and "project/education fatigue." Because many participants' previous experiences with activation training programs had not been good, motivating them to enroll in further schooling proved difficult. As a result of these problems, the placement goals for each office were changed to 50 participants/month in either work or education. During the first three years in operation (2000–2002), though, the WDCs still fell short of registration and placement goals, with 8,864 registered in the four offices representing about 60 percent of the 15,000 intended (3 years x 4 offices x 1,250 registrants/office/year). Overall placement rates amounted to only about 20 clients/month (though there were some interoffice variations in effectiveness). However, by 2002, this rate had increased to nearly 30 per month with estimates that the rate would increase to 40 per month in 2003 (Bevelander et al. 2003). Despite falling somewhat short of policy expectations, Malmö's WDCs are generally considered a significant success due to the placement of a still-sizeable number of long-term unemployed, annual improvements in results, as well as innovations in service approach for this target group, especially as compared to earlier EO practices (Bevelander et al. 2003).

Ongoing challenges

Researchers also noted some ongoing challenges with the WDC approach. Staff turnover was a chronic problem from both the municipal side (due to short-term contracts for employees) and the EO side (due to significant agency control over staffing decisions), a situation that readily impeded the development of the caseworker-client relationship and common knowledge building in the organization (Ahlstrand & Lindberg 2001). There were also concerns that the centers weren't doing enough to assist long-term unemployed with more significant barriers to work. The one-year prognosis for employment or education created a clear selection filter that meant many individuals were sent back to the referring agencies without assistance. Centers could develop additional services or "steps before"[26] to assist clients with greater difficulties, especially those from the municipal social services. It also appeared that such a shift may be necessary because the more employable participants were becoming scarcer with the upturn in the economy (and presumably the success of the program).

Perhaps the most significant systemic problem for the future viability of the centers is their project-based nature as the WDCs arose out of a temporary, 5-year program. In order for them to be maintained in their current form, they will require additional state funding, as well as renewed agreements between the collaborating agencies (a very cumbersome and difficult process) (Bevelander et al. 2003). The time-limited, project-based nature of integrated activation services has been identified as an important weakness in recent Swedish policy development (Johansson 2006). This deficiency separates it from several of its Nordic neighbors—Denmark and Finland—who have gone much further in creating institutionalized forms of state-local activation service development since the late 1990s.

Conclusion

In Sweden local activation programs are a recent phenomenon of the mid- to late-1990s, brought on by the unprecedented economic recession of the last decade. Their emergence as an increasingly important site for integrating the unemployed represents in some ways a turn away from the Swedish welfare state model, with its traditional emphasis on nationally administered active labor market policy measures available to all unemployed citizens (Salonen and Ulmestig 2004). While the early years of development in Malmö were somewhat haphazard, by the first years after 2000 these programs were becoming increasingly well-funded and institutionalized, offering a wide array of services to a large percentage of clients. This rapid enlargement was facilitated by significant, available resources for a staff that could readily utilize them—a large public service sector for creating work experience placements; and comparatively accessible language classes, basic adult education, and vocational and university-level training programs. In neither California nor Bremen did agencies have a similar capacity to provide education and work experience resources to the general welfare recipient population. In California, program participation requirements and a "work first" mandate, combined with the limited prior development of relationships with community organizations, prompted agencies to focus primarily on their Job Clubs. In Bremen, while work experience through well-developed ties with public welfare organizations was their primary offering, limited local funding greatly restricted the numbers of clients they could assist.

Another distinctive feature of Malmö's programs was the large number of in-house services staff created that were tailored to welfare clients' needs. In neither of the other two national settings was a similar variety of internal service provision occurring. In California, while program offerings were also predominantly created by the agency itself, they were limited primarily to a single type of activity, job search. Werkstatt Bremen, on the other hand, depended on outside providers for almost all of their services. While GEFAS offices had often suffered from rapid program flux and limited integration success, in-house activities had taken on more stable forms in many offices and were now being better utilized as part of a larger repertoire of subsequently developed offerings. Caseworkers in one such setting—Lönnäng's Work and Integration Center—were therefore able to tailor services to client needs and interests using a variety of internal and external measures. Additionally, their training and experience in social service projects, and their limited caseloads, provided them the skills and time to know their clients and personally assist them in setting goals, choose program activities, and address personal problems. Thus, Lönnäng's activation caseworkers play a significant "counseling" role in providing client services (See table 8.1).

But not all district offices in Malmö have developed like Lönnäng. Limited local funding means many districts still operate very small programs, and district-level political control of activation programs has led to some considerable variation in program approaches. Havdal provides an illustration of this potential variation, having utilized its limited funds to develop a bare-bones, large-scale American style approach. Almost all welfare recipients in the district are enrolled in either a Job Search Center or a study section. Very similar in function to California Job Club workers, Job Search Center caseworkers are nonprofessional staff who help clients apply for jobs and monitor their participation. Similarly, in the study section, a handful of staff are charged with motivating clients to participate in Swedish language courses as a necessary first step to social and labor market integration. Caseworkers in both of these sections have the opportunity to meet their clients regularly. Personal assistance, however, is narrowly focused on clients' success in either job search or language class participation. Therefore caseworkers here have a more limited role of "facilitator" within a narrow range of client choice.

Such a stark choice between small individualized or large standardized programs might no longer have to be made in some of the hardest-hit urban areas. National funding commitments to local activation programs through the City Investment Initiative are allowing many district offices to increase staffing and offer programs to a broader recipient population than was possible when financing was strictly based on local (and limited EU) capacity. Through their Work and Development Centers, several districts in Malmö have utilized this additional financial support to bring the EO's focus back to unemployed welfare recipients by colocating EO staff with municipal social workers and assigning them joint case responsibilities. This organizational innovation restores to some extent the national focus on the unemployed regardless of their labor status or the agency under which recipients receive support. This move back toward universalism contrasts with the situation in Bremen, where, until very recently, the resources and staff of the federal EO remained inaccessible for most welfare recipients. The impact of the radical changes in 2005 in Germany (effectively merging unemployed welfare recipients into a new national unemployment system) are yet to be understood. In California, while there is sometimes

Table 8.1   Comparing responsiveness among activation caseworkers (Malmö examples)

Program offerings: range of options available to caseworker	Nature of client contact: opportunity to develop rapport and provide direct services	
	Processing (short-term contact) −	Engaging (longer-term contact) +
Extensive +	"Resource Broker" (medium)	"Counselor" (high)
		*Work and Integration Center Caseworker — Lönnäng
		*Work and Development Center Caseworker— Boklunden
Limited −	"Monitor" (low)	"Facilitator" (medium)
		*Job Search Center/Study section Caseworker — Havdal

coordination between welfare-to-work agencies and local branches of the Employment Development Department, this latter organization has traditionally had comparatively few resources to offer clients.

Malmö welfare participants in this new interagency organization have access to EO resources along with individualized attention from staff knowledgeable about labor market conditions, a rare situation even for unemployment insurance recipients. At the same time, social workers maintain agency focus on clients' often-difficult social situations. As a result WDC caseworkers have even greater opportunities to act as "counselors," offering individualized activation programs and personally engaging clients in the process of moving off welfare.

The WDCs therefore demonstrate the potential institutional development that can occur in Sweden—to create an activation service system with links to traditional EO resources while also developing an array of local resources aimed at those requiring additional kinds of lower-level competencies and support. Yet the continued importance of local governance in social services means that such municipal activation services are extremely varied across Sweden. About one-fifth of the localities have no activation program, and 70 percent of activation programs have less than

25 participants. There are also large differences in program costs with differences in quality that this implies (Salonen and Ulmestig 2004; Thorén 2005). While the Job Search Center approach was controversial in Malmö and significantly revised, it is a viable model in many urban settings, as is evidenced by the Skärholm and Uppsala programs (Thorén 2005; Ekström 2005).

This lack of a national development and integration of local and state programs also appears to have set Sweden apart from some of its Nordic neighbors (Johansson 2006). Even in Malmö, the rather successful Work and Development Centers are project-based and time-limited rather than reflecting any deeper institutional changes in the agencies that contend with employment services. In all four Scandinavian countries (Sweden, Norway, Denmark, and Finland) the 1990s were characterized by an increased focus on activating the long-term unemployed and the development of new local programs alongside the traditional state programs. However, in Denmark and Finland, these changes also included the development of new administrative institutions to integrate state and local program units as well as the establishment of requirements that these agencies provide services to all who need them. In doing so, these countries were seen as having shored up the rights of recipients alongside increasing their obligations (Johansson 2006).

Comparing Welfare Administration in the Three Worlds of Social Welfare

Designing public administrations to address claimants' financial and social needs while operating as responsive legal institutions is a weighty endeavor, especially for welfare programs. Welfare is a fraught and conflict-laden area of social policy, a site of economic and social breakdown, in which the market, family, and mainstream state institutions have all failed to adequately sustain and incorporate their members. The urgency of needs it is tasked to address, the heterogeneous reasons people end up on it, and its final jurisdictional responsibility (as the "program of last resort") mean that many tensions and contradictions in larger societal arrangements become manifest in this program. Fundamental issues about the levels and conditions of minimal public support that may be sidestepped in other areas of public policy must necessarily be dealt with here.[1]

Need as an organizing principle for the provision of services presents special challenges. Unlike many other income programs that have more delimited purposes, there are no straightforward formulas for determining eligibility and adequacy, as need is what's left over after all other available resources have been exhausted. What's more, as individualized embodiments of institutional failure, the etiology of recipiency is complex and varied and, therefore, constitutes an insecure basis for entitlement. Lacking legitimated justification for dependency on state aid, through contribution or deserving status for example, means that claims of need are treated with considerable political ambivalence. Individual responsibility for present and continued reliance on program support is a central focus of administrative inquiry and the basis for continued agency efforts to obligate and enable recipients to become independent.

Johnson's concepts of "individualized justice" and "institutional order" (Johnson 1998) offer a useful heuristic for analyzing the competing values inherent to the programmatic issues involved. The greater the ability of frontline officials to consider individual circumstances in providing support and services, the more likely they are to meet people's actual needs—to secure a basic level of economic security, to facilitate participation in economic and societal life. But as the number of circumstances and types of assistance multiply, so too does the complexity of the decision-making process and the difficulties for policymakers and program administrators to ensure consistency and fiscal control.

Since the 1990s, welfare has moved to center stage across the OECD. This increased attention has often occurred as part of a more general reconsideration of modern social security systems and concerns with their pacification effects on beneficiaries and other forms of increasing mismatch with the economic requisites of changing labor markets (Peck 2001). A common feature of this new era in social assistance policy across the developed world has been a shift in focus and locus to "local activation." First, the goals of labor market integration have been strongly incorporated into the operating principles of programs that had been more narrowly focused on material support, often to the detriment of stability and security in these forms of entitlement (Brodkin 2006). Secondly, policymaking in this area has been increasingly devolved to state and local levels of government, leading to a proliferation of program practices and forms (Theodore and Peck 1999). Activation and decentralization are not entirely new phenomena in many nations, but all three countries in this study have witnessed movements along both dimensions in welfare policy since the early 1990s.

Yet the limitations of much existing comparative social policy work make it difficult to know whether these developments have resulted in a convergence of administrative practice. Are we perhaps, instead, just seeing greater similarities in political discourse and policy aspirations, while diverse strategies and institutional forms persist? (Pollitt 2002)

Much of the current literature relies on comparisons of policy level information across a large number of countries, generally provided by different authors. The result is both too much and too little information. Case studies often provide a surfeit of program description, details which are not synthesized into forms that are comparable across cases. One is then left in an afterglow of confusion from the vast array of extraneous material. At the same time, paradoxically, there is often too little information. Because of the importance of context to the constitution of social services in general, and social assistance in particular, the scale of information—focusing primarily on formal program features—is often insufficient to characterize how different states contend with their able-bodied, nonworking poor.

This book has attempted to begin to fill in this gap in scholarship through detailed portraits of programmatic practices in welfare states from very different political traditions. Through case studies of welfare and welfare-to-work agencies in the United States (California), Germany (Bremen), and Sweden (Malmö), it identifies and elaborates the important ways state-level policy decisions and institutional features continue to impact the role officials play in assessing need and promoting self-sufficiency. Directly, states have utilized particular policy approaches and administrative arrangements that reflect different tradeoffs between programmatic control and responsiveness. Indirectly and inadvertently, through structuring labor markets, educational institutions, and the larger social security systems, states have influenced the general distribution of societies' resources and opportunities.

For both program types, the United States presents striking examples of caseworkers with very limited capacity to be responsive, where standardized grants, standardized activation obligations, and system complexity created by an array of narrowly targeted programs largely preclude individualized considerations. By contrast, in both European nations, caseworkers have greater authority and more choices, giving them a much more substantial role in tailoring aid to particular claimants' needs and interests.

Welfare State Traditions and the Administration of Needs Assessment

Despite the fact that TANF (United States), Sozialhilfe (Germany), and socialbidrag (Sweden) all serve similar functions as needs-based income programs of "last resort," the role caseworkers play in administering these programs through tailoring support to the actual needs of recipients varies considerably cross-nationally (figure 9.1).

This differential capacity is a product of both the formal authority caseworkers have to consider individual circumstances in assessing eligibility and the resources the organizations have to enable their staff to manage the requirements of their work and ensure they act in a consistent, timely, and legally correct fashion.[2] Program regulations may provide virtually no exceptions to standardized forms of support; they may provide latitude to consider unusual circumstances, but with substantial regulation to delimit the use of discretion; or they may give caseworkers relatively wide scope to evaluate when an individual requires additional assistance.

Work demands can vary both in degree and source. Various regulatory structures (from national, state, and local sources) define the program's goals as well as the core tasks involved in achieving them. They delineate the domain of official authority, the complexity of documentation and interpretive requirements (procedural) for making decisions, and the range and variety of claimant issues with which a program contends. The "regulatory environment" of the broader social security system may also significantly impact a program's function in delineating the availability

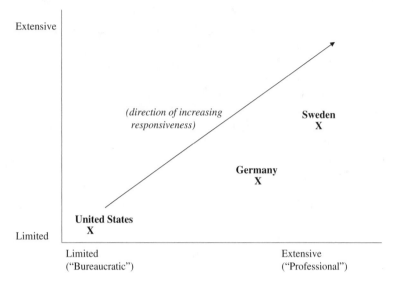

Extensive

(direction of increasing responsiveness)

Sweden
X

Germany
X

United States
X

Limited

Limited
("Bureaucratic")

Extensive
("Professional")

Horizontal Axis
Legal Authority for Responsive Decision Making: formal ability of caseworker to consider individual circumstances in assessing need

Vertical Axis
Organizational Capacity for Responsive Decision Making: ability of agency to enable and control official decision making

Figure 9.1   Comparing responsiveness among welfare caseworkers

and accessibility of other forms of public support that "precede" social assistance (figure 9.2).

While caseworkers retain some freedom in how they perform their work due to their positions as "street-level bureaucrats" (Lipsky 1980), agencies have various ways of affecting how staff implement program regulations. They can facilitate how cases are processed through worker specialization and the integration of information technology. They can influence how caseworkers make decisions through socialization and monitoring, including on-the-job training, supervision, and collegial consultation. They may hire staff with particular education or qualifications, providing some predictability to decision making based on common professional expertise and values. If they can retain staff, this can lead to the development and maintenance of informal institutional knowledge. And most directly (and bluntly), they may affect the workload by determining the number of cases assigned to each caseworker (figure 9.2).

U.S. welfare policy is characterized by a bureaucratic, flat-grant approach in which concerns with programmatic control are paramount. By contrast,

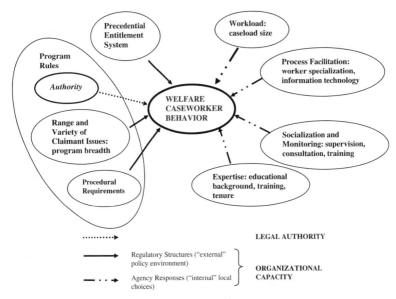

Figure 9.2   Factors affecting welfare caseworker responsiveness

social assistance programs in Germany and Sweden display features that make them potentially more responsive as needs-based programs, namely that aid is structured into a two-tiered system, authority is decentralized, and individualized assessments are a core organizational task. While these common formal features readily distinguish the European programs from those in the United States, the basis for trust in frontline expert judgment is based on very different professional foundations—in Germany on a long-established civil service tradition, in Sweden on a social work pedagogy.

In none of the three cases are the existing institutional safeguards fully effective at guaranteeing administrators' ability to enable and control how their caseworkers make decisions. In the United States, overregulation, caused by program fragmentation and the extensiveness of assessment demands, undermines bureaucratic predictability, as caseworkers are unable to process and administrators unable to monitor all program regulations (Diller 2000). Similarly, professionals can be reduced to technicians, unable to make use of delegated discretion, relying on informal shortcuts that can become as hard and fast as any technical procedures in more bureaucratically organized settings. While such potential for "dysfunctional" convergence is real and relevant, these composite programmatic case profiles, including both facilitators and hindrances, provide an unusual opportunity to trace how such practices relate to nationally-specific and, to some extent, welfare state regime-specific regulatory processes and governance traditions.

The United States, as a member of the liberal/Anglo-Saxon welfare state grouping, reflects an emphasis on means-tested benefits, both in terms of percentage of population who are recipients and percentage of social security expenditures devoted to these programs (Eardley et al. 1996). Associated with program salience is a comparatively high level of codification of rights to standardized benefits, arguably due to organizational and legal requirements that accompany processing large numbers of recipients (Bradshaw and Terum 1997; Lødemel 1997). At the same time, the safety net in the United States displays far greater variability, complexity, and fragmentation than many other liberal social assistance systems, reflecting an American "exceptionalism" (Skocpol 1988) both in the origins (and ongoing legacy) of its modern poverty programs and in the rise of a distinctly judicialized approach to regulatory development.

Scholars have written extensively about the early twentieth-century development of a U.S. "maternalist" welfare state in which a network of middle-class women's organizations provided the organizational resources to effect broad political alliances necessary to surmount the fragmented federated political system.[3] The result was a distinctly female-focused national form of poor support, a gendered and subsequently racialized design that would remain marginal, underfunded, and politically vulnerable in comparison to male- and worker-based programs (Orloff 1988; Nelson 1990; Mink 1990).

While this program could have remained a relatively localized and discretionary institution, it became highly regulated through another peculiarly American feature, a fragmented political authority that created a strong mistrust in official discretion and led to a reliance on the courts as an enforcement agent (Kagan 2006). This judicializing of administrative processes achieved its height in social welfare programs in the 1960s and resulted in well-developed procedural rights, imposed on a constellation of poverty programs that provided only very limited substantive rights (Melnick 1994). As a result, the caseworkers who implement American social assistance have very limited formal discretion in how they perform their work, while, at the same time, these same regulatory processes make it difficult for administrators to ensure that all of the technical requirements for eligibility assessment are done correctly and comprehensively.

By contrast, German social assistance was created and embedded in a national administrative civil service and broader Continental European legalism, centuries-old structures that were extended from earlier protective and economic functions of the state to social welfare services (König 2001). Within such a system, German caseworkers could be characterized as "regulatory entitlement scholars." Extensive legal constraints are both the primary method for controlling caseworker decision making and also the means through which officials legitimately use their discretion. Case-workers' authority is based on their mastery of a well-developed regulatory system and their proper utilization of the law to construct sound arguments. Their legal expertise in helping recipients access other entitlements also extends across the topography of the vast and intricate programs of the German welfare state. Such a highly structured and top-down policy approach also leads to distinct types of overload, through the ongoing efforts to operationalize and delimit the amorphous concept of basic need, and from the accumulated impact of all the other highly regulated precedential income programs with which caseworkers must be familiar.

Swedish social assistance reflects a long-standing tradition of local autonomy over social services, including welfare, and results in much more limited regulatory development nationally than in many other welfare states (including the United States and Germany). This lack of national regulation leads to considerable variation in rule development among municipalities, but also likely leads to much less codification in general given the primarily consultative role many policy-making bodies (health and welfare agencies, the court system) play in such a system. One explanation for this limited legal development is the actual success of the worker welfare state. Up until the 1990s, a well-developed social security system and full employment had kept social assistance receipt to minimal levels, usually limited to recipients suffering from multiple social problems. The low numbers of recipients allowed Social Democrats to focus on the continued expansion of more established entitlement programs, assuming that social assistance need would ultimately disappear (Johansson 2001; Lødemel 1997). Social assistance's residual place in the larger social security system also led it to be viewed in Sweden and other Nordic countries less in terms of legal rights and more in terms of individual eligibility and the needs of marginal populations (Behrendt 2002; Hort 2001).[4]

Malmö then provides one example of local response in a system marked by rule scarcity. Here, program practices are much less grounded in formalized guidelines than in the local working knowledge developed and maintained by experienced administrators. Structures of control and guidance are grown locally and organically from the bottom-up. Caseworkers are better characterized, then, as governed by a "social work ethos." While program regulations are an intrinsic part of decision making in a public institution like social assistance, legal expertise is not the primary basis of official proficiency or legitimacy. Caseworkers are trained social workers, and their program remains embedded in the practices and consultation culture of local social service agencies. At the same time, the lack of a firm foundation in rules makes the exercise of authority more obvious and weighty. Here, too, then, work overload manifests in system-specific ways. The short tenure of staff who seek less administrative work in other areas of the social service system, for example, creates problems maintaining the informal institutional knowledge base that is central to the decision-making process.

Trends Toward Convergence in Needs Assessment

Some observers have argued that high program demands were a driving force behind the centralization and bureaucratization of Anglo social assistance programs (Bradshaw and Terum 1997). A program with few clients has the resources to maintain a looser organizational structure based on caseworker discretion and individualized assessments, and localities are able to manage programmatic costs adequately. But as recipient levels and expenditures increase, the program comes under increasing political and administrative pressure to develop more standardized and controllable practices. This point is certainly illustrated in the U.S. case, with the turn away from the casework model in the early 1970s.[5]

With the persistence of high unemployment in Germany and its relatively recent development in Sweden (though followed by moderate recovery), high caseloads have eroded welfare agencies' capacity to act as responsive institutions. But are these fiscal pressures pushing European states to reform their social assistance programs toward an American style of administration—that is, one in which caseworker discretion is limited to the granting of standardized grants based on clear procedural rules?

Certainly regulatory and administrative changes underway in both Germany and Sweden point toward a more routinized approach to aid assessment, and the localized nature of financing makes the need for fiscal control all the more pressing. In Germany, very recent changes mark a significant move toward standardized support. At the start of 2005 the two-tiered benefit structure was largely consolidated. The range of nonrecurring forms of assistance was severely curtailed, while the standard grant rate was raised to reflect an incorporation of many of these one-time expenses into the average monthly recipient budget (Aust 2003). Such a radical change indicates how complicated and unwieldy regulating a program based on individualized need can become and the pressures such administrative complexity creates for simplified structures.

In Sweden, the introduction of national basic grant levels in 1998 demonstrates a development toward greater security of basic entitlement. And in Malmö at least, the increased delegation of responsibility to clerical staff for most economic decisions also moves Sweden toward a more decisive institutional separation between social work and a more purely administrative area of economic support.

Still, many distinct features persist. The programs in both Germany and Sweden remain oriented toward providing recipients a reasonable standard of living. The two-tiered structure of benefits and the principle of individualized assessment persist as basic features, and staff discretion over special needs seems to be an intrinsic administrative characteristic (though it remains to be seen whether the German reform has rendered these features largely a formality). Additionally, with the exception of Germany's introduction of a separate program for asylum seekers, in neither country does there appear to be any trend to restrict entitlements through status distinctions or time limits that contribute to the program fragmentation characteristic of the U.S. system.

Current European welfare practices emerge from quite distinct institutional and policy legacies that continue to exercise considerable influence. Sozialhilfe continues to remain a domain of public bureaucrats and as such is governed by complex regulatory processes requiring a high level of training. The German welfare state, too, will remain complex and financially strapped so that the system of precedential entitlements will continue to require considerable agency effort to navigate and recoup expenses.

In Sweden, localities retain considerable control, despite some moves toward greater national codification. Thus local variation in practices seems likely to continue to be a characteristic feature. So too will the loosely regulated structure, in Malmö at least; though with increasing delegation to clerical staff, perhaps functional demands will lead to increased codification at the local level. Social workers still have a considerable role to play in how welfare policy is administered, and this influence creates at least the possibilities for different, more individually oriented approach to services. While in the 1990s decision making became increasingly bureaucratic, a combination of organizational reforms to redistribute much of the administrative work to other staff and other agencies, as well as a recent upswing in the economy, may yet usher in a return of social work intervention for the most vulnerable welfare recipients, and with such a return, a reinvigoration of the program's dormant rehabilitative intent that is still unique among the three worlds.[6]

Welfare State Traditions and the Provision of Activation Services

For activation caseworkers, on the other hand, national styles of decision making are generally more difficult to discern, given that many institutional influences are more locally determined. The nature of this organizational work tends to be less rule-driven, therefore lacking the standardizing influence provided by a detailed legal framework. Rather than mediating

Table 9.1   Comparing responsiveness among activation caseworkers (California, Bremen, and Malmö examples)

Program offerings: range of options available to caseworker	Nature of client contact: opportunity to develop rapport and provide direct services	
	Processing (short-term contact) −	Engaging (longer-term contact) +
Extensive +	"Resource Broker" (medium)	"Counselor" (high)
	X 19.2/19.1 Caseworker— Bremen	U27 Caseworker— Bremen
	X Job Developer—California	Work and Integration Center/ Work and Development Center Caseworker—Malmö
Limited −	"Monitor" (low)	"Facilitator" (medium)
	GAIN/CalWORKS Caseworker—California	Job Club Worker— California
		Job Search Center caseworker; Study Section Caseworker—Malmö

regulations in order to release funds in the appropriate situations, activation depends more on utilizing available resources to change client situations and behavior. The capacity of activation staff to provide recipients with individualized services depends on two important dimensions: the range of program offerings; and the nature of caseworker-client contact. The work activation caseworkers perform and the ways in which they are able to assist recipients looks very different in California, Bremen, and Malmö (table 9.1).

Variations in caseworker functions and their ability to respond to client needs can be attributed to differences in a variety of institutional influences that impact their work. These influences include four sets of variables: program mandates and funding levels; labor market conditions and occupational structures; resource environments; and agency development (see figure 9.3).

Program mandates and funding levels
Mandates influence how agencies design their programs by setting politically visible goals, to which agencies must orient their operations. Program regulations may set specific participation and success rates that affect how

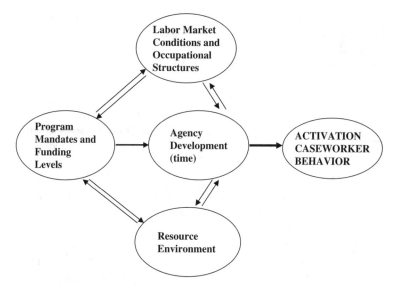

Figure 9.3   Factors affecting activation caseworker responsiveness

difficult it is for the agency to meet expectations. They may delineate the range of appropriate activities or give agencies considerable discretion over the design of service components and program flow. A program's goal may be narrowly focused on moving recipients directly into employment (the "labor market attachment" strategy) or on a broader approach to integration that relies on a wider repertoire of interventions including education, training, and work experience options (the "human resource development" strategy).

In relation to a program's intended scale, funding levels affect the amount of time staff can devote to clients and the quality of services that can be provided to them. Limited financial resources will likely result in very small programs; or, where high participation requirements create serious disjunctures between program capacity and political aspirations, to inexpensive, low quality, standardized activities, and increasingly limited contact with caseworkers.

Labor market conditions and occupational structures
Welfare state institutions are important determinants of how societal resources are produced and organized. They influence the kinds of employment opportunities that are available and the accessibility and importance of education and training for obtaining work. Where employment options are limited (due to high rates of unemployment or high qualification thresholds for available jobs, for example), the range of potential program options tends to be more limited because cheaper, short-term activities

aimed at integration into the primary labor market become less viable. Agencies must rely on activities in other sectors (public, nonprofit, education); client independence becomes more difficult to achieve; and program measures are more likely to degenerate into "make work" activities.

Resource environment
Program offerings may be developed in-house, but generally most relevant resources are controlled by other organizations. Support services, education and training programs, and job placements are often scattered among a diverse array of state, nonprofit and private actors. The variety and accessibility of other organizations' resources will affect the kinds of measures a caseworker can offer and how well they can tailor services to the particular needs and interests of their clients.

Agency development
These larger regulatory, funding, economic conditions, and program options set the parameters within which agencies develop their programs and, in turn, affect the jobs of staff and their interactions with clients. Staff attempt to facilitate participants' movement into available employment and education options; develop organizational linkages with available services and expertise; and utilize funds to meet program requirements. In order to carry out their work successfully, staff need time—time to develop program and referral procedures, to establish collaborations with various service providers, and to adapt and refine their offerings to the changing needs of their participants and labor market conditions. Where an agency is recently established (Sweden) or the program it implements is radically modified (the United States), the program is liable to operate in an amorphous state for some time before organizational development reaches a stable and recognizable form.

Trends Toward Convergence in Activation

The recent establishment of local welfare-to-work programs in many European countries in the 1990s, including Sweden, provides some evidence of a general movement of national approaches toward the Anglo-Saxon liberal strategy, that the social welfare states of old Europe are beginning to concede territory to the imperatives and principles of the market. But while activation programs in all three countries of this study share a common intent in facilitating client self-sufficiency through labor market integration, in practice the variety and directness of the paths that agencies make available to clients varies considerably, as do the roles case-workers play in the process.

Some parameters are beyond the immediate influence of policymakers or agency officials, stemming instead from historical legacies that determine the array of employment options and social service resources that can be utilized to assist recipients. One could characterize this set of "external" conditions as the potential responsiveness of the "system," the available means and difficulty of enabling citizens to live independently. Past political choices, crystallized in current institutional structures and processes, ensure that certain strategies are seen as more natural or better "fits" in a given system than others.

This naturalization process is where politics enters. Some combination of national and local level political choices determines activation agencies' mandates in light of economic conditions, which possible "paths to self-sufficiency" they should clear, how many recipients they will encourage down these paths, and what resources they will use to facilitate this process. And political choices for program goals and funding levels most directly determine the trade-off between program scale and service quality. The extent of local control in this policy area leads to considerable variation within each nation state, and these case studies each represent but one possible political/programmatic configuration. However, even with this qualifier, each agency site is marked by a combination of features that illustrate persistent, nationally distinctive activation approaches.

Bremen illustrates one program choice that is available within the constraints set by a difficult labor market and local funding—a small-scale employment placement program in a small sheltered labor market sector whose existence is due in large part to the government's use of work-creation measures as a response to chronic unemployment. A similarly sized nonprofit sector has never sprung up in Sweden due to the state's predominant role in providing social services. And while in the United States there exists a vibrant nonprofit world, a product in part of the lack of adequate public services, historically there has not been mandate or funding to incorporate them as an integral part of welfare-to-work measures at any scale. Only now are these interorganizational connections beginning to develop, but only to a very limited extent, reflecting the marginal, end-stage role they play in the current program design.

At the same time, the precarious nature of this alternative route to employment in Germany illustrates well the impact of prevailing labor market conditions on the room for maneuvering that agencies have to move clients toward financial independence. In attempting to create a genuine alternative or supplemental employment market as a way to integrate recipients, the emergent sector has begun to have corrupting effects on both public services and the private market. In a system like the United States with plentiful employment opportunities—even if wages for many are not enough to live on—politicians are not faced with the same kinds of difficult political choices that must be made in a system like Germany's where insufficient numbers of jobs highlight the economic losers so much more clearly.

Bremen's second, mandatory youth program illustrates how a new national funding commitment combined with a narrowly available, preexisting (training) entitlement for a specific group of recipients can quickly develop into a robust program that is able to circumvent the existing barriers to employment for most recipients. A similar youth training program is hard to imagine in the United States, in large part, because most of the young recipients on welfare in Germany and Sweden would never be eligible for benefits in the United States as they have no dependent children. Thus, the United States' more restricted programmatic reach puts many groups and social problems with which European programs contend beyond its jurisdiction.

Sweden has similarly made young adults (long-term unemployed under 24) a primary focus of local intervention, with a similar national funding commitment to local agencies (Development Guarantee) and a similar focus on education. However, the education system in Sweden is not so structured around employer-run apprenticeships, but rather around adult education, vocational, and university programs. And access is more generally available to all via inexpensive student loans, making education a more general strategy rather than one focused on a group with a time-limited entitlement.

A more interesting comparison is between California and Malmö. Both have relatively large-scale obligatory programs. California's program has had a longer institutional history and larger funding level in the context of a better performing economy in the mid- to late-1990s, but several of Malmö's districts have expanded rapidly, and the economy was improving rapidly at the end of 1999. Given somewhat more comparable conditions (than with Germany), the differences in approach are striking. California's almost exclusive job search approach is simple, relatively inexpensive, and a necessary short-term response to difficult federal political mandates in the context of the limited prior development of linkages with other organizations that would be necessary to provide a full-service program.

In Sweden, on the other hand, there were no national participation requirements or limitations on appropriate activities. Activation programs developed more organically but surprisingly quickly in some places, rapidly establishing ties within the large public sector, which was more accommodating to large numbers of internships and job placements, and channeling many recipients into adult and higher education programs. Many agency staff also had skills to develop effective in-house projects that have endured despite a general tendency for program flux from limited local governmental funding. In addition, an infusion of national funds in certain districts has allowed many agencies to overcome these local funding constraints and develop intergovernmental activation agencies, thereby tapping into the substantial resources and expertise of the national Employment Office (EO). In Germany, this interorganizational divide between local welfare and federal EOs remained virtually impenetrable (that is, until all unemployed welfare recipients were merged into a new unemployment benefit program). In the United States, on the other hand, the state Employment and Development Department (EDD) does not offer significant resources to be tapped. In contrast to the United States, then, Swedish programs have developed in a richer resource environment and have been able (and allowed) to utilize these social goods to develop a much broader array of services than is either available or politically viable in the United States.

The Possibility of Transcending the Service Quality-Program Scale Trade-off

In order to understand how responsive welfare-to-work programs are—whether conditioning receipt of welfare on self-help efforts has meant providing more or less to recipients (Lødemel and Trickey 2000)—it is important to look not only at how individual caseworkers make decisions, but also at the scale of the program. While needs assessment is an intrinsic part of welfare administration, activation is an optional, add-on intervention that may be designed to almost any size. But, given the limited amount of local resources typically available for such programs, policymakers generally must decide whether to focus on comparatively individualized services for a few or inexpensive, standardized measures for a larger number. This apparent trade-off between responsiveness and program magnitude also reflects the fact that oftentimes large-scale programs display considerable discrepancies between resources and program expectations. While services in these settings are typically limited in scope (job search programs for example), participant numbers from quasi-universal participation requirements often overwhelm administrative capacity, resulting in coordination, monitoring, and quality control break-downs. People often get sanctioned or cut off due to inappropriate referrals or administrative error, and frontline officials adapt predictable coping mechanisms to control the flow of their work, manage client demand, and maintain some sense of efficacy (Lipsky 1980; Brodkin and Thorén 2005).

Figure 9.4 provides a graphic representation of program responsiveness versus program scale, with the programs in this book placed in approximate locations. Other programs from the United States, Sweden, and Germany

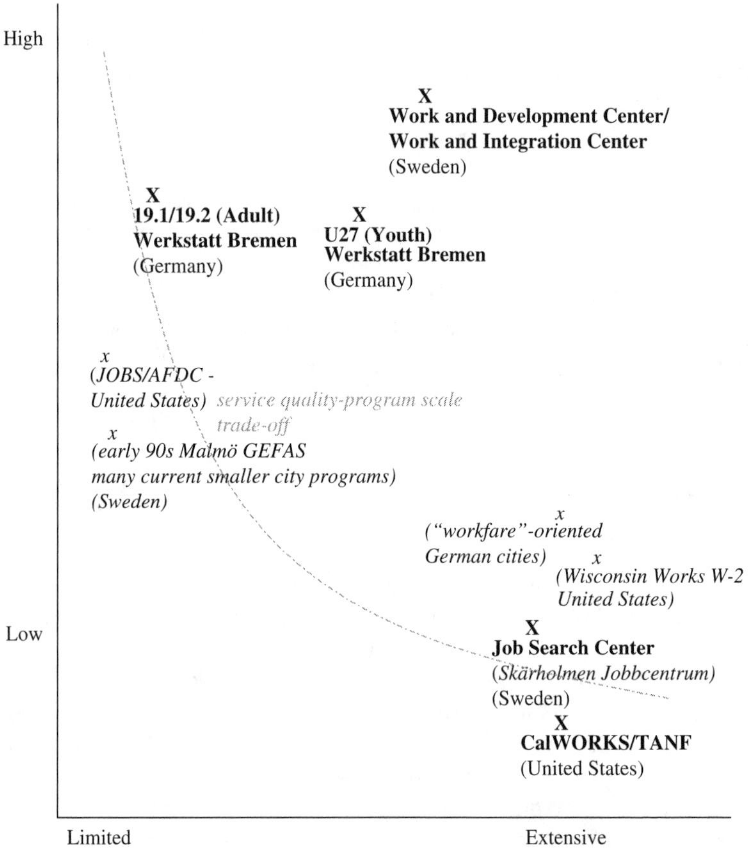
High
Low
X
Work and Development Center/
Work and Integration Center
(Sweden)
X
19.1/19.2 (Adult)
Werkstatt Bremen
(Germany)
X
U27 (Youth)
Werkstatt Bremen
(Germany)
x
(JOBS/AFDC -
United States)
service quality-program scale
trade-off
x
(early 90s Malmö GEFAS
many current smaller city programs)
(Sweden)
x
("workfare"-oriented
German cities)
x
(Wisconsin Works W-2
United States)
X
Job Search Center
(Skärholmen Jobbcentrum)
(Sweden)
X
CalWORKS/TANF
(United States)
Limited
Extensive

Horizontal axis
Program scale: proportion of social assistance population affected by activation program

Vertical axis
Program responsiveness: ability of agency to offer measures that are tailored to participants' needs and interests

Figure 9.4 Comparing responsiveness among activation programs

have also been added to provide comparative examples. The dotted line represents the service quality-program scale trade-off typically reflected in such programs. Most programs tend to cluster together on the high responsive-limited scale part of the curve or the low responsive-extensive scale end. There are also a few programs that seem to overcome this trade-off. These examples reflect the existence of organized societal resources that agencies do not have to generate themselves but instead are able to tap into. And it is this possibility of doing such institutional "linkwork" (Bevelander et al. 2003) that distinguishes those programs that are both highly responsive and that serve relatively large numbers of participants.

In Bremen, local politicians chose to utilize restricted resources under difficult economic conditions to provide individualized services to limited numbers of older adult recipients, a small pocket of responsiveness, building upon the network of public welfare organizations they helped create. Other German cities made a different choice, with massive workfare programs established to bolster a deteriorating public sector. By contrast, the rapid development of Bremen's mandatory youth program illustrates how these local constraints and limited choices could be overcome to some extent by national funding commitments and the existence of a vocational system to which a narrow segment of recipients had access.

In the United States, on the other hand, small-scale education programs were largely replaced in the mid-1990s when national political mandates effectively locked in agency and caseworker approaches in most states. Agencies were to move large numbers of recipients into work and work-related activities. A booming economy in the 1990s with large numbers of low-skilled jobs provided agencies with an administratively and financially easy route to move at least some recipients partly off welfare—by simply requiring them to make themselves available to the labor market. In a sense, comparatively plentiful employment is America's primary societal resource. Yet, the low-grade nature of much of it means most recipients who find work will be in unstable forms of employment and will remain poor (Brock, Nelson, and Reiter 2002).[7] Lack of earlier institution building with the range of organizations necessary to address the diverse needs of the recipient population led to a quick, standardized, minimal response fix. While German states and localities could choose their location on the "scale-service quality" curve, in the United States, federal welfare reform demanded the fast-food approach, with little room to develop or maintain boutique programs.

In Sweden many view the development of local activation programs, brought on by a downturn in the economy, as a degradation of a tradition based on equality of access to national active labor market policy measures. At the same time, this tradition has allowed some activation agencies to rapidly develop an array of services by accessing existing social resources that reflect Sweden's historical and ongoing commitment to promoting full employment and the right to work—a widely available education system, a large public service sector, and more recently (again through new national funding), traditional EO/ALMP resources. While these services may be cheaper and of lower quality than were traditionally offered under a full-employment economy, many activation programs have built a substantial response repertoire, tailored to the more challenging needs of large numbers of the unemployed on welfare.

At the same time, this is not a Swedish "style", more a national "predis-position," because continued local political and funding responsibilities mean there can be considerable variation in practices. Job Search Centers that provide limited services to large numbers of recipients therefore, do, exist in Malmö and in other locations in Sweden (Thorén 2005). But while an American labor market attachment approach can emerge in some situ-ations, the tendency can be in a different direction—toward the provision of individualized services on a relatively large scale that transcends the quality-scale trade-off.

Conclusion—The Difficulties and Discernments of Cross-National Street-Level Studies

Conducting a cross-national study of local program practices is tricky busi-ness. The method of inquiry (administrator interviews and observations) and the locus of interest (the individual, interpersonal, and organizational level) offer means for obtaining thick descriptions of how decisions are made and services provided in particular settings. Such detailed portraits are then intended to provide a meaningful basis for comparative analysis at the state level—to identify interesting features and variations in program operations and service delivery and relate these differences to nationally distinct institutional traits and political traditions. Yet the task of establish-ing and articulating these micro-macro links faces several challenges.

Intranational variations in both program content and the forces that shape them may be considerable, resisting generalizations across localities. Such concerns are especially pertinent in areas of social policy that, like welfare, are marked by decentralized policymaking and financial responsi-bilities and rapid change over time. National styles may simply not exist, or at least cannot be adequately characterized based on a few case studies. On the other hand, institutional aspects that might seem to represent fun-damental differences in program approach may, in fact, prove unimpor-tant due to the impact of chronic resource shortages that are an endemic feature of social services. This great leveler may lead to a kind of street-level functionalism in which most decision making in organizations suc-cumbs to process-oriented, paper-driven shortcuts that undermine any higher programmatic aspirations.

Comparative ground-level research is also difficult work for the indi-vidual scholar to do and especially to do well. It demands considerable time, resources, and persistence—to learn languages; collect and analyze data from different locations; to be comfortable residing on the steepest part of the learning curve most of the time, combing through primary data and large volumes of secondary literature in order to understand complex, interrelated systems; to become immersed in each setting in order to describe it accurately, but remain resilient enough to move back and forth between cases in order to do the necessary analytic work.

And yet there is no other way to understand the content of policy that, as in the case of welfare, involves fundamental issues about inclusion (state-citizen relationships), the terms of which are largely constituted in the actual, daily work that officials carry out. Between the Scylla and Charybdis of hyperlocalism and convergence-through-incapacity there is, in fact, a path the cross-national street-level research approach can follow. Case studies must be chosen carefully. Program officials must face real tensions and trade-offs in doing their daily work, yet must also have the potential to meet program mandates. The locations chosen, therefore, must not be too small or unusually poor, with organizational processes liable to be in an abridged form or simply besieged. The researcher must also be well informed about country-specific and comparative literature to properly situate the cases and to understand broader political-economic features and variations.

Having chosen theoretically and practically informed cases, then, the researcher will be in the best position to do the necessary comparative work—to inductively derive general concepts from the particular characteristics of case studies and to reframe intracountry differences in terms of nationally-distinct policy problems or approaches. Through such efforts, one can create a meaningful account of how the behavior of officials exemplifies and articulates aspects of national context—the basis of decision-making legitimacy, modes of governance and regulation, the organization of social resources, key policy choices. And it is only in the juxtaposition *across* cases that these distinctions and differences become so striking.

The generation of such "measured statements," tying national traditions to ground-level practices, is foundational work because of its ability to elucidate hidden yet profound facets of how states incorporate some of their most vulnerable citizens. Despite the challenges and pitfalls, it is research well worth the effort.

Appendix: Interview Data

Table A.1 Welfare (AFDC/TANF) interviews in California counties, 1996–1997; 2000

	Eligibility caseworkers	Unit supervisors	Specialized workers*	Administrators**	County totals	
Claremont County						
1996–1997	3	2	9	6	20	
Elmwood County						
1996–1997	4	2	0	3		
2000				1	10	
Oakdale County						
1996–1997	5	1	1	3		
2000	2	1	2		15	
Olathe County						
1996–1997	3	1	0	1		
						Total
2000	2			1	8	53

*Specialized workers include appeals workers, fraud workers, Child Care Coordinators, Work Pays coordinators, and child care workers.

**Administrators include program directors, office directors and deputy directors, staff development, and program specialists (responsible for writing and implementing county guidelines)

Table A.2 Welfare (AFDC/TANF) observations in California counties, 1996–1997

	Caseworker-client observations***	AFDC/Pilot presentations****	County totals	
Claremont County				
1996–1997	9	3	12	
Elmwood County				
1996–1997	6	n.a.	6	
Oakdale County				
1996–1997	4	2	6	
Olathe County				
				Total
1996–1997	3	1	4	28

***Caseworker-client observations include intake meetings, annual recertifications, and drop-ins.

****Presentations include clients' "rights and responsibilities," welfare reform, and, in Elmwood, the on-site, pilot GAIN program, GAP.

Table A.3 Welfare-to-Work program interviews in California counties, 1996–1997; 2000

	Employment counselors	Unit supervisors	Job Club workers	Job Developers	Administrators*	County totals
Claremont County						
1996–1997	6	3	4	3	1	17
Elmwood County						
1996–1997	4	3	4	n.a.	1	13
2000					1	
Oakdale County						
1996–1997	5	1	2	2	4	17
2000	2				1	
Olathe County						
1996–1997	3	1	0	n.a.	0	
2000	2					Total
						53
						6

*Administrators include program directors, office directors, and program specialists.

Table A.4 Welfare-to-Work program observations in California counties, 1996–1997

	Caseworker-client observations*	Job Club observations (times/total hours)	Job Developer-client observations	County totals	
Claremont County					
1996–1997	11	2/5	2	15	
Elmwood County					
1996–1997	4	13/17.5	n.a.	17	
Oakdale County					
1996–1997	2	4/4.5	1	7	
Olathe County					Total
1996–1997	2	2/1	n.a.	4	43

*Caseworker-client observations include GAIN employment specialists and GAIN pilot project workers in welfare offices (Claremont only).

Table A.5 Welfare interviews in Bremen, Germany, 1999–2000

	Eligibility caseworkers	Unit supervisors*	Program directors	City administrators		
				3		
City district					District totals	
Mittewest	5	5	1		11	
Sued	1	1	1		3	
						Total
Oest	2	1			3	20

*Unit supervisors also had a half client caseload each.

Table A.6 Welfare-to-Work interviews in Bremen, Germany, 1999–2000

Werkstatt Bremen		
Program director	2**	
U27 (youth program)	4**	
19.2 (public employment contracts)	4**	
19.1 and BAVA	3	
(private employment contracts)		
		Total
Public welfare organizations***	6	19

**Interview numbers include one follow-up interview with one staff member in the category six months later in July 2000.
***These included staff of two programs used by U27 and 19.2 staff for participant placements and the director of a public welfare organization association.

Table A.7 Observations (Welfare-to-Work) in Bremen, Germany, 1999–2000

	Total number of caseworker-client observations	
U27	17 (among three caseworkers)	Total
19.2	16 (among three caseworkers)	33

Table A.8 Welfare interviews in Malmö, Sweden, 2000

	Eligibility caseworkers	*Economic administrators*	*Method developers*	*Unit supervisors*	*Program directors*		
City district						District totals	
Havdal	4	0	1	1	0	6	
Lönnäng	3	2	0	1	1	7	
							Total
Boklunden	6	0	1	1	0	8	21

Table A.9 Welfare-to-Work interviews in Malmö, Sweden, 2000

	Activation caseworkers	Program directors		
City district			District totals	
Havdal	4		4	
Lönnäng	9	1	10	
				Total
Boklunden	5 (3/2)*	1	6	20

*In Boklunden there were both municipal social workers and employment office staff. Three interviews were with social workers and two with employment office staff.

Table A.10 Observations in Malmö, Sweden, 2000

Welfare

Lönnäng—3-hour visit with one caseworker. Observed daily work and meeting with one client.
Boklunden—3-hour visit with each of two caseworkers. Observed daily work and meetings with four clients.

Welfare-to-Work

Lönnäng—Two 3-hour visits to the job search program called Workforce. Observations included 5 caseworker-client interactions.
Havdal—One four-hour visit to the Job Search Center. Observations included 5 caseworker-client interactions.

Notes

Chapter 1

1. This is a policy-specific version of the general convergence argument that common exogenous and endogenous forces are compelling the scaling back of state institutions towards a more liberal, residual version (Mishra 1999; Swank 2000).
2. In this book, welfare in the United States refers specifically to Aid to Families with Dependent Children (AFDC) and its successor, Temporary Aid to Needy Families (TANF), the only national means-tested cash aid program for the able-bodied poor. For claimants without children, there are the more meager and stigmatized cash benefits provided by only some localities, known as General Relief.

Chapter 2

1. For example, an organization with a simple, dichotomous response and a transformative aim would be a regulatory agency that has few options except for applying the law and granting an exception, such as in the case of the U.S. price/wage freeze agency described by Kagan (1978); or where a regulatory agency enforces effluent limits for routine protection technology (Bardach and Kagan 1982).
2. Nonet and Selznick's (2001) well-known distinction between autonomous and responsive types of law also tracks these contrasting bureaucratic and professional administrative arrangements.
3. These features can also be seen as part of what is more generally referred to as an organization's "core technology," that is, the raw materials, activities, and skills an organization uses to produce a product or service (Glisson 2000; Johnson 1998; Carter 1974). Organizations that utilize established knowledge and are able to produce predictable and measurable outputs have "hard" technologies, for example, manufacturers and most benefit programs (Ochoa 1997). By contrast, where the processes central to an organization's work become more difficult to spell out in advance, and the outcomes less reliable, as is the case in human service organizations (HSO), an organization is said to employ "soft" technology. Whereas for organizations employing "hard" technologies, organizational structure is often strongly influenced by technological imperatives, the intrinsic uncertainties and complexities associated with the work of organizations with soft technologies means the conditions of implementation are a constitutive force of what workers in an organization *actually* do.

4. Rule interpretation is also known as "subsumption discretion," while consequential reasoning is also known as "means-end discretion" (Hvinden 1994).

5. By contrast, routinized interactions involved the provision of work-related information, but through the standardized recitation of program rules. Particularistic encounters involved an ad hoc interpretation of selective work-related information, often in an incomplete way based on the caseworker's perception of the client's needs. Instrumental transactions were ones in which caseworkers limited discussion of both work-related information and clients' personal issues that might interfere with efficient case processing (Meyers, Glaser, and MacDonald 1998).

6. The lack of alternatives for support (lack of an "exit option") and the limited knowledge clients have about an often Byzantine eligibility process means that social assistance claimants exist in a state of profound "dependency" (Handler and Hollingsworth 1971). The ability of caseworkers to make decisions based on arbitrary criteria is therefore especially worrisome in this type of program and makes agency oversight particularly important.

7. That is, individuals are more liable to seek and remain on assistance rather than making efforts to remain or become self-sufficient.

8. Similarly, discretion took a racially discriminatory form in the United States in the 1960s (Quadagno 1994; Piven and Cloward 1971).

9. Interview quote from a German administrator.

10. For example, the Anglo-Saxon world includes both generous (Australia, the UK) and meager benefit systems (the United States) (Gough et al. 1997); the most generous include not only Scandinavia, but also some other small countries such as the Netherlands and Switzerland (Bradshaw and Terum 1997).

11. The concept of distinct skills systems represents a narrower slice of the LME/CME "varieties of capitalism" literature that Estevez-Abe, Iversen, and Soskice (2001) refer to as "welfare production regimes."

12. Some of the criteria they considered were: the size of the recipient population, program costs and coverage levels; the program's relative level of benefits; the relationship between central and local government authority over regulations and administration; the extent of means-testing; and the degree of official discretion.

13. In this scheme, the United States was in its own class as a "public assistance state," with an extensive set of means-tested benefits, generally low benefit levels, but entrenched procedural rights. Germany was classified as an "integrated safety net," organized nationally, with average benefit levels, moderate means-testing, and low discretion. Sweden, like all the Nordic countries, was "residual," (or later modified to a "citizenship-based but residual" system [Gough et al. 1997]) with marginal costs and recipient levels; a single general scheme with relatively high benefits; a moderate role for local authorities; and the persistence of substantial links with social work and care. The conceptual slippage that occurs for the larger set of countries and the proliferation of categories highlights the greater challenges involved in identifying distinct "logics" as the level of analysis moves from a few, relatively stable, macro-level features of the state, to the many operational and more politically changeable details of a particular program.

14. In fact, much of the more recent literature in social assistance has focused exclusively on the move toward increased "activation" of recipients. While this represents an important policy development, such a focus has tended to eclipse the more "mundane" but fundamental "people-sustaining" role (Hasenfeld 1983) these programs play and the complex political and administrative issues such a function raises.

Chapter 3

1. Exchange between a welfare recipient and a caseworker at her annual redetermination interview. The caseworker is referring to the new case banking system in which a team of eligibility technicians is collectively responsible for over 2,000 recipients.
2. Food Stamps can be considered the only comprehensive safety net in the United States, being based primarily on income levels and with national standards. It is a federally funded program administered by the Department of Agriculture, Food and Nutrition Services created in 1964 by the Food Stamp Act.
3. For example, in 2004 Mississippi provided $170/month for a family of three, while Vermont provided $709 (Alaska and Hawaii provided higher amounts, but they also use a different poverty standard than the continental U.S.). The federal Food Stamps program has some modifying effect on these extreme differences, because its benefit levels are determined by available income, including TANF support. TANF plus Food Stamps' monthly benefit levels for a family of three varied among states from a low of $520 in Mississippi (40% of the poverty threshold) to $907 in Vermont (69% of the poverty threshold), with California weighing in at $904 (Walters, Falk, and Burke 2004).
4. These included a duty to provide benefits "with reasonable promptness to all eligible individuals" (402(a)(10)), income and asset limits for eligibility, and maintenance of benefit level requirements.
5. The courts developed "Condition X." Under this doctrine, a state-added eligibility condition was illegitimate if it was arbitrary and unreasonable in light of the purposes of the Social Security Act.
6. This represented a dramatic (though temporary) shift in the court's conception of its relation to administrative agencies over the claim to the power of statutory interpretation from one of administrative deference to increased scrutiny. The courts disregarded previous jurisdictional limitations to allow many recipient claims and made creative use of legislative history and statutory purpose to eliminate eligibility conditions that didn't exclusively address "actual need." However, the court's impact was limited. While its actions made AFDC benefits more widely available, the courts rarely addressed benefit levels. Setting grants still remained a state prerogative, highlighting the difficulty of crossing the procedural-substantive divide. In addition, Congress eventually passed major welfare reforms that overturned many of the courtroom victories (Melnick 1994).
7. This seemingly technical reform had significant effects on recipients' access to their entitlements. The program's exclusive attention on errors of leniency

(where an ineligible claimant is granted aid) led to increased errors of stringency (where an eligible claimant is denied), as many claimants failed to provide all of the necessary documentation to verify actual eligibility. These processing mistakes, however, were not measured or evaluated and therefore remained politically unnoticed and irrelevant (Brodkin 1986).

8. *Example—calculating the grant amount for an applicant with earned income under AFDC.* An illustrative example of this regulatory complexity is the task of identifying and assessing the group that will be receiving support. Under AFDC, the law distinguished between the "assistance unit" (AU) and the "family." The AU must include an eligible child and a caretaker relative, but there are extensive rules as to which other household members must be included (such as siblings living there), which are definitely excluded (such as convicted felons), and which may be included (such as grandparents). The "family" includes non-AU members. This distinction is important because income of family members are considered in calculating the initial eligibility and benefits of the AU.

There are also asset and income limits with distinctions based on source, who in the household receives it, and whether it is for an applicant or recipient. For an applicant with earned income, the income test is a three-step process: (i) The total gross income of the "family" (minus $90/employed person) must be below 185% of the state's "need standard," also known as the Minimum Basic Standards of Adequate Care (MBSAC) (which is the state's determination of how much a family needs to meet minimum survival needs). (ii) Then the "family's" net income (minus $30 and one-third of the remaining, but only for the first four months on aid, after which it is only $30) must be lower than the "maximum aid payment" (MAP), the highest grant level for an AU of that size. (iii) If both of these conditions are met, the benefit level is determined by subtracting net income from the appropriate MAP level. Note the relationship between the MBSAC and the MAP levels can vary considerably. For example (under AFDC), in New York, need and payment standards were both $577 for a family of three; in Florida the need standard was $965, while the payment standard was $303; in Texas need was $574 and maximum payment was $184. Thus, whereas families in similar financial conditions could both be eligible for AFDC in New York and Texas, the same family in Texas would receive less than one-third of the New York benefit.

In California, these calculations were further complicated by a distinction in MAP (and MBSAC) levels between "exempt" and "non-exempt" claimants based on an assessment of work capability. This distinction arose as a result of a state effort to reduce the grant level in 1992 as a putative "work incentive" that could be "earned back." However, a successful legal challenge (*Beno*) required the state to distinguish between those who were able to work and those who couldn't be expected to. As a result, exempt claimants receive approximately 10–12% more than the nonexempt (Snow et al. 1995; 1997).

9. For example, in AFDC in 1996, benefit levels changed four times as new laws and court orders went into effect.

10. There was no degree requirement to be an EW, and individuals interviewed indicated they had generally received 4–6 weeks of training before they began processing cases.

11. Pre-TANF, childcare expenses were generally addressed by automatic income disregards for subsequent grant calculations. This approach, though, did not subtract actual costs from earnings, but only a standardized amount of $175–200 per child depending on age. In recognition that these standard child-care deductions were often inadequate, a new resource was developed, supplemental child care (SCC). However, SCC was not designed as simply another automatic deduction, as this would mean clients would likely remain eligible for welfare longer (as they could earn more money before becoming income ineligible). Clients had to apply separately for it and were then paid directly as a supplement. But in order to access these benefits, two things had to occur: clients had to know about the new benefit and know how to apply for it; and caseworkers had to perform an additional complicated assessment. These conditions rarely were met, as clients didn't know about it (and caseworkers had no incentives to inform them), and so SCC was extremely underutilized.

12. In other counties, too, certain workers were being given additional responsibilities for doing group presentations, primarily to new applicants, on welfare reform and the new focus on employment. However, generally these new tasks were in addition to ongoing case management responsibilities and did not represent entirely new worker types like the coordinator positions in this county.

13. What is it about these workers and work conditions that led to such different client interactions than EWs could accomplish? Coordinators had authority that was limited to the discussion of employment-related issues with clients and understood this task to be their primary role. Some work pays coordinators also had access to additional material resources that added to these encounters. At the same time, coordinators did not have authority to approve benefits or sanction clients, allowing interactions to focus on counseling rather than rules and responsibilities. These workers generally had low or no caseloads, and their work involved very little administrative work, allowing them to work one-on-one with clients or to spend time on presentations and resource development. Their knowledge was technical but limited in scope, and their frequent discussion about these issues gave them opportunity to develop interpersonal skills and strategies for engaging clients. Opportunities for client contact was a mixture of short group presentations, which allowed the conveyance of information in a standardized form but did not allow much personalization; and individual meetings, which allowed more tailored interactions but were also generally one-time only (and affected far fewer clients) (for more information see Jewell and Glaser 2006).

14. Starting in 1992 the Bush administration began (and the Clinton administration later continued at an even more rapid pace) allowing states to experiment with their AFDC programs by waiving federal statutory requirements. The Secretary of Health and Human Services was given jurisdiction over the waiver

process under section 1115 of the Social Security Act, a statute that had existed on the books since the early 1970s but had not been utilized much by earlier administrations. Waiver policy changes occurred in three areas and premiered many of the elements of the TANF legislation: (1) Employment-focused policy both as carrots and sticks. Income disregards, income and asset limits, and transitional benefits were made more generous, but there were also increased work participation requirements and stricter sanctions for noncompliance; (2) New behavioral rules that involved the welfare agency in more direct oversight of client behavior, later incorporated into TANF; and (3) Time limits. By the time TANF was passed in 1996, 45 states had some kind of demonstration project in place.

15. State block grants were calculated by the most generous of three alternative federal expenditure formulas—the average of Fiscal Year 92–94, FY 94, or FY95—and froze at those rates until 2002.

16. Though there is a maintenance-of-effort requirement of generally 80% and numerous prohibited uses and penalties for failures to meet certain goals.

17. A consolidation of federal childcare funding into a companion block grant as well as availability of targeted welfare-to-work grants also increased the resources available to expand supportive services and transitional benefits like childcare and Medicaid (Brodkin 2006).

18. As one author has observed, "The issue of behavioral incentives of welfare—to discourage marriage or remarriage and to encourage teenage pregnancy and welfare dependency—appear to be a defining feature of the stigmatizing and divided public assistance system of the USA" (Gough et al, 1997, p.38).

19. Klerman, Zellman, and Steinberg (2001) report that staff estimated that the amount of work associated with a working client is two to three times as great as with a nonworking client.

Chapter 4

1. Quote from a district office director.
2. Welfare developed into a system of support provided by local authorities and voluntary organizations as early as the late nineteenth century and was regulated by law starting in 1924 (Eardley et al. 1996).
3. One distinctive feature of Germany (and Austria) is that familial obligations for support are more extensive than in any other OECD country, and include not only other household members and absent spouses, but also an adult applicant's parents and adult children who are living separately. The extent to which other family members can be required to support a recipient is left to the states to decide. Bremen is unusual in limiting this duty only to absent spouses, as is more typical in other countries.
4. The federal law is structured in terms of "must," "should," and "can" regulatory directives. A "must" directive is required by law without exception. For example, benefit rates cannot be reduced by local offices. Deviation from a "should" directive can only be justified if there are serious reasons, and these deviations

can be scrutinized by the courts. "Can" directives, on the other hand, provide wide interpretative latitude, discretion that is often narrowed and articulated through state and local administrative guidelines, including through the incorporation of administrative court decisions.

5. Among the 16 states, the monthly rate only varies from DM 522 to DM 548 for a single individual (Breuer and Engles, 1998).

6. Integration assistance serves to "prevent an impending disability, to eliminate or alleviate an existing disability or its effects, and to integrate the disabled person into society" (Art. 39, Para. 3, BSHG). It includes outpatient and in-patient treatment, special education for children, and assistance in obtaining suitable school education or assistance in completing training for a suitable occupation (Arts. 40, 43). The disabled have a right to employment in a workshop for the disabled, and funding for their employment is provided by social assistance agencies.

7. Care assistance is primarily intended for home care (Art. 69), old-age insurance contributions, and, where home care is no longer appropriate, institutional care. With the introduction of long-term care insurance in 1995 and 1996, the costs for this program in social assistance have gone down considerably (Adema, Gray, and Kahl 2003).

8. U.S. Medicaid represents one small area of overlap with Germany's HSC program.

9. In 1996 there were 2.7 million persons in private households who regularly received CLA, and 900,000 receiving HSC. While the number of recipients of HSC was only one-quarter of the social assistance clientele, it accounted for 60 percent of program expenditures (Breuer and Engles 1998).

10. The recipient is required "to exploit his ability to work to secure a livelihood for himself and his legally dependent family members" (Art. 18, Para. 1, BSHG). The agency is required "to ensure that the assistance-seeker makes an effort to find work and actually does so" (Art. 18, Para. 2).

11. Exemptions are made for individuals under certain circumstances, including physical or mental disability or where such efforts would endanger the proper upbringing of a child. Lone parents are not expected to work until the youngest child is three years old and then only part-time and only if childcare exists.

12. It is also regulated by the German Social Code, which delineates the legal right to public support (Ditch et al. 1997).

13. The purpose of social assistance in Sweden is worded somewhat differently—"to secure a reasonable standard of living" (Social Service Law, sec. 6b.1)—but the program is similarly oriented towards benefit adequacy (see chapter 5).

14. Support for each additional family member in a household was calculated as a percentage of the standard grant level based on age. Prior to the reforms of 2005, these rates were 50% or 55% in single-parent households for a child up to age 7; 65% for children 7–13; 90% for ages 14–17; 80% for adults from 18 and up. This "equivalence scale" is one of the highest in the OECD. Additional allowances of 20–40% of the basic rate are also automatically granted to individuals who fall in certain groups deemed to have greater needs,

including single parents and pregnant women. This targeted generosity high-lights what researchers have referred to as Germany's "active subsidiarity," in which the role of the family is supported by specific transfers and policies (Kazepov and Sabatinelli 2001).

15. "The things we pay on a regular basis are usually normed, we have a plan for that. It is indeed only the one-time applications that depend on the case-worker's decision and includes decision-making latitude" (caseworker). There are also other areas of decision making where discretion is important, including (1) whether housing or utility costs are "reasonable" or are too high and whether the claimant should be required to move; (2) the number of job applications a claimant must present and the frequency of doing so to show adequate self-help effort; and (3) whether assistance should be in the form of a loan or grant based on the prospects of becoming self-sufficient in the near future. Caseworkers also have the option of visiting a recipient at home to assess their need for particular items for which they have applied. Swedish casework-ers have a similar range of discretionary decision-making areas (see chapter 5).

16. Thus, unlike in the United States where client appeals have little effect beyond the case at hand (though lawsuits against specific regulations do (Melnick 1994)), in Germany, client appeals in the courts have an institutionalized influ-ence on policy development.

17. In Bremen, recipients applying for furniture are required to visit the local welfare-to-work agency's furniture refurbishment center to see if the items they need can be obtained there before they may receive cash assistance.

18. Reflecting the regular practice of intergovernmental conferral, the Bremen list had been recently revised after administrators surveyed other state practices (a "benchmarking" project in 1999) and found Bremen's amounts to generally be above average.

19. As mentioned earlier, caseworkers have the option to deviate from these amounts in individual cases, but these standardized payments act as presump-tive rules.

20. There are four main civil service categories—basic, intermediate, executive, and higher services—each with its own educational qualifications, pay scales, and career ladders.

21. Supervisors are supposed to review cases in three ways: (i) within three months of opening a new case; (ii) a randomly selected 10% of all cases per year; and (iii) random monthly inspections of four to five cases per caseworker.

22. However, the importance of the supervisor as an integrative force in their unit also limits the ability of the social service agency to ensure consistent behavior for the system as a whole. "When a supervisor is very restrictive in process and decision-making, many of the caseworkers do the same, of course. One can clearly observe that" (caseworker). "The topic 'floor coverings' for instance. Some offices approve it as necessary, and others don't" (caseworker).

23. For example, the guide notes that many caseworkers fail to make a legally required "concrete prognosis" in assessing whether an applicant should receive support only as a loan. A caseworker should determine that any expected

future income should be sufficient to allow a client to pay back the loan in a foreseeable time. They cannot simply assert that there are many jobs in the applicant's occupational field as a justification for granting aid in the form of a loan (AGAB 1999).

24. This booklet is over 100-pages long, reflecting the complicated nature and scope of social assistance law.

25. Caseworkers indicated that filing an appeal is a slow process and that few clients actually appealed decisions: "Yes, it is possible to appeal, but that is a very long process, which typically takes 1–2 years. Most clients accept the decision of the welfare worker. Maybe 10% appeal decisions." However, the high cost of a successful appeal still makes the threat an effective general deterrent to inappropriate uses of discretion.

26. In 1997, Bremen had an unemployment rate of 16.5%, with 9.5% of the population on welfare (Voges, Jacobs, and Trickey 2000).

27. Adema, Gray, and Kahl 2003 have noted that caseload sizes in Germany have increased during the 1990s to an average 120–180.

28. In the early 1990s in Bremen there was greater specialization in casework than there is currently. The so-called collaborative group consisted of a secretary, a first caseworker with midlevel qualifications who was responsible for the simpler decisions, and a senior caseworker, who dealt with the more difficult cases (more like Sweden, see chapter 4). This arrangement was changed to the "goal group" in which each caseworker is responsible for all work tasks associated with their cases. At least one justification for this change was that it minimized coordination problems and increased caseworkers' familiarity with their clients. But it also meant that lower qualified staff could no longer work there, raising the qualification threshold.

29. Clients are obliged to inform the agency if changes in living conditions occur. If clients receive more money than they are entitled to, they have to pay back the overpayment; however, this means more work for the case worker.

30. This administrator explained that a few other states, like Hamburg, have developed just such an online program.

31. Because other forms of public support are intended to take precedence over social assistance, they are sometimes referred to as "precedential" entitlements or programs.

32. Caseworkers are also supposed to be responsible for certain private sources, including assessing the alimony and child support rights of a recipient household if there is an absent parent (areas that are dealt with by officials from other programs in the United States and Sweden). Caseworkers are also responsible for keeping cases open in which clients were given support as a loan and must work to recover this money.

33. It should also be kept in mind this is the selective view of the caseworker. The "normal" case does not cause much trouble, but the few problem cases attract attention and will be remembered.

34. More recent assessments of program reductions have been far larger, with an estimate that only 400,000 persons will remain in the old social assistance

program (correspondence with Petra Buhr, Zentrum für Sozialpolitik der Universität Bremen).

Chapter 5

1. Quote from a unit supervisor.
2. It is important to keep in mind that outlays on social assistance benefits amount to a very small part of total social spending in Sweden compared to other countries. For example, in 1992 social assistance expenditures accounted for 6.2% of social security spending in Sweden, 11.9% in Germany, and 39.8% in the United States (Eardley et al., 1996).
3. This section is largely based on Håkan Johansson's dissertation work, *In the Shadow of Social Citizenship: The Right to Social Assistance During the 1980s and 1990s* (Lund: Arkiv förlag, 2001).
4. This variability in tasks and regulations (the added importance of local conditions) makes it more difficult to characterize typical behavior and is an important limitation to the Swedish case study.
5. "Support for daily living covers the reasonable costs for (1) food, clothing and shoes, recreational activities, nondurable goods, health and hygiene, and newspaper, telephone, and T.V. fees." (§6b.1)
6. "(2) living/dwelling, household electricity, work-related travel, home insurance, medical care, acute dental care, eyeglasses, and union and unemployment insurance group membership." (§6b.2)
7. "The local authority may provide support in another form than or in addition to what follows in 6b and 6f §§, if there exists a reason for it." (§6g)
8. One supervisor noted that as a result of this housing market change, she was much more inclined to grant rental debt relief than she would have been even a year before. "And that must have an impact. If we had a strict set of regulations, it would have been a simple no and ignoring how it is in the world around us."
9. "Every case should be examined individually. And it is that which is problematic, that you have to look at the whole picture ... It is difficult to say that there are things in particular they should be especially attentive to. Most everything is equally important."
10. "It can happen that you have a case where you didn't grant something and then you have another case where there is something unique that distinguishes it from the first. And even though they are so similar, based on this little difference you can justify approving the second application."
11. A more fiscally oriented approach to casework is well illustrated by a German caseworker's characterization of their relationship to social service workers. "As a rule, social workers are more generous. They are on the side of the client, one could say ... We are the ones who have to determine the money that is paid ... they describe the situation and what should be done and then we look to see if it works with the law."

12. It is also likely that the short tenure of most caseworkers—usually between one and three years—makes them more reliant on consultation than more experienced staff would be. New caseworkers are less confident in their decisions and therefore more likely to depend on expert advice during much of their employment time.

13. "If it was obvious that in this case it is always done this way, you wouldn't need anyone to talk to, you would find clear rules to follow. But you don't have that in the social service laws . . . So you need to discuss and reason through cases." (caseworker)

14. "While caseworkers could do their own research, they often find it more convenient to utilize my services."

15. "I think the overall (criteria they use) are the same because we have recommendations and court cases and we speak a lot about them." (supervisor) "I think they know on the whole . . . those who have full delegation, they should follow the same ways so that there are similar results in the end." (supervisor)

16. My thanks to Robert Kagan for suggesting this metaphor.

17. Caseworkers are responsible for "those things that are difficult . . . (and) those things that go to the court," that is, the initial intake, entitlements that exceed what is considered "reasonable," optional forms of support, and denial/sanction decisions.

18. These numbers are based on my informal survey of the caseworkers I interviewed.

19. As one social worker in a different agency (a friend of mine) explained to me, social workers generally go to the welfare office as their first job out of the university and stay for one or two years. To stay longer would seem odd because welfare work provides so little opportunity to be a social worker.

20. *Summer time.* Another distinct, apparently Swedish phenomenon is the very different condition under which welfare offices (and almost all other areas of the large public sector) operate during the summer. Caseworkers have (at least) six weeks of vacation time, and most of this time is taken during the short summer. As a result, from May until August, welfare offices are staffed with large numbers of "temp workers," usually students from the nearby school of social work. These workers have no delegation authority and know little about daily office operations, putting tremendous strain on supervisors, method developers, and remaining caseworkers to rapidly train and oversee the decisions of these temporary caseworkers. One method developer estimated she supervised 6–7 temps during the summer and spent approximately half an hour/worker/day overseeing their work. At the same time, summer is an especially busy time for new applicants, as many students have difficulty finding summer work between school terms and so apply for short-term aid. That this regular massive seasonal displacement does not lead to system-wide paralysis seems to indicate an organizational buffering capacity—from administrators' expertise and close supervision and from economic administrators' responsibility for core routine tasks. That the program is so resilient under such disruptive conditions may give us comfort. Or it may give us pause—that responsiveness is so limited already that using untrained workers has little

effect; or that the potentially drastic change in service quality is not politically or socially troubling.

21. The only exception to this minimal interagency contact came from a caseworker who specialized in youth recipients (age 18–25), reflecting the existence of an overlapping clientele.

> There exist opportunities for youth. They are a prioritized group so it is a little easier to work with them . . . the Employment Office, they are also oriented in the same way, they work with the same group, so youth are also prioritized there.

> The EO offers a variety of internships and trainings, generally lasting three to six months, to which youth are entitled. Most of this caseworker's clients had been referred to the EO and had been placed in some kind of program. However, there are still a number of ongoing problems. The low stipend levels for participants means they are still dependent on welfare. Most programs are short, and clients often end one without it leading to anything else. And, as in the general case, the EO will not work with clients who aren't "sufficiently motivated" (see chapter 8 for more details).

22. Supervisors and some caseworkers also mentioned other smaller, richer city districts where caseworkers had much smaller caseloads and less economic support decision-making responsibility and were therefore able to work more intensively with clients as social workers and were more effective in moving them off welfare.

23. Staff turnover is one reason supervisors were so concerned with changing work conditions: "It may be that you would remain as a caseworker if you had fewer cases. That you think it is a little more interesting to work, that you work as a caseworker and are able to use your social work skills."

24. Another well-known approach to local decision making in the context of limited regulation is the Uppsala model (Rönnlund, 1992; Thorén, 2005). This approach attempts to maintain decision-making consistency within the unit through a group variant of the consultation model, in which close monitoring of caseworker decisions occurs through regular peer group meetings and where atypical decisions must be clearly justified. Additionally, in many small municipalities, local social welfare committees still directly review cases, in some sense an institutional remnant of the poor law tradition (Salonen and Ulmestig, 2004).

Chapter 6

1. Quotes from two Job Club workers during classroom instruction.
2. Between 1990 and 1996, only about one-third of all unemployed received benefits (Vroman, 1998), reflecting a combination of comparatively restrictive eligibility conditions and the large numbers of precarious jobs that often do not entitle people to unemployment. On an index of *unemployment* protection (calculated as the average of net unemployment replacement rates, generosity of

benefits and the level of restrictions placed on the kind of job an unemployed person cannot refuse without loss of benefits) the United States scored 0.10 on a standardized scale of 0 to 1, the lowest in the OECD. By contrast, Germany scored 0.77 and Sweden 0.63 (Iversen 2005).

3. Social Security and insurance (Medicare) for the aged are major exceptions of a relatively broad-based redistributive program.

4. For example, on an index of *employment* protection (calculated as the weighted average of employment protection legislation, collective dismissals protection and company-based protections) the United States scored 0.14 on a standardized scale of 0 to 1, again the lowest in the OECD. By contrast, Sweden scored 0.94 and Germany 0.86 (Iversen 2005).

5. The income protection index, a third measure (see endnotes 2 and 4 above) developed by Iversen (2005) is intended to capture the variability of after tax and transfer income. Based on an average of total taxes and transfers (as a proxy for publicly mediated income protection), d9/d1 earnings ratios (as a proxy for protection of wages through the private wage-setting system), and after-tax and transfer Gini coefficients, the United States scored a 0.25 on a standardized scale of 0 to 1, clustering nicely with the other Anglo-Saxon countries in the bottom third of OECD countries. By contrast, Sweden scored 0.94 and Germany 0.52.

6. The Omnibus Budget Reconciliation Act of 1981 required mandatory job search, training, or community work experience for adults under certain circumstances. JOBS was established under the Family Support Act of 1988.

7. The following information is from the California Work Pays Demonstration Project Process Evaluation Phase IV: 1996 (Snow et al. 1997).

8. Many GAIN staff welcomed this change. Several program specialists and supervisors reported that GAIN's earlier human resource development philosophy turned out to be neither realistic nor sufficient. For many clients this approach led to years in vocational classes with no real expectations set by the agency for employment. Long-term students also consumed disproportionate amounts of childcare funds, in one county contributing to a virtual shutdown of new intake cases for months at a time during 1994 and 1995. Staff also discovered that many of the people who acquired marketable skills were unable to find employment because they lacked work experience, while many clients without even a GED were able to find employment if they had a job history.

9. For example, in one GAIN CW-client interaction observed, the worker spent considerable time explaining to the client how to get her childcare provider approved and how to fill out the reimbursement forms. Afterwards, he commented that if he had had more than one intake that day, which was the usual situation, he would have eliminated the entire childcare discussion. As another GAIN CW observed, when caseload demands reached a certain level, workers switched to "county mode". When this occurs the possibility of engaging in a conversational style of interaction becomes impossible and interaction is reduced to "read this, sign here."

10. A common complaint was that client tracking involved a lot of unnecessary paperwork, which made it difficult to keep one's caseload current.

11. Of course, often clients' perceptions were firmly grounded in reality. Cases with earned income have more complicated budget calculations, and as a result, welfare caseworkers are prone to higher error rates in these circumstances.

12. The impact of job fairs is unclear, as data for tracking was unavailable. Beyond the symbolic function, a number of JDs thought the impact was minimal because GAIN clients need more continuous supervision ("baby-sitting") and support than job fairs offer. "They just came in and took pens and left," said one JD.

13. California is one of only four states in which significant discretion has been further devolved to the county level for the welfare-to-work (WTW) component, and therefore county welfare departments (CWDs) had to submit their own plans to the state. Despite this implementation discretion, county CalWORKS programs have necessarily followed a "work first" model based on the state's general program guidelines. By contrast, eligibility regulation remains under the purview of the California Department of Social Services.

14. Clients who were already employed 32 or more hours or enrolled in an approved education or training program (self-initiated program [SIP]); had a youngest child under the age of one (in some counties the exemption was as low as 12 weeks); or had serious additional barriers that would hinder their success at job search activities, including very low skills, domestic abuse problems, mental health issues or drug problems could be exempted. Those with serious additional barriers could then be referred to additional support services, though screening and referrals for these barriers had been very limited through 1999 (Klerman, Zellman, and Steinberg 2001).

15. 18 months for new applicants; 24 months for ongoing recipients at the time CalWORKS was implemented.

16. The following information on implementation is based largely on the 1999 RAND study by Klerman, Zellman, and Steinberg *Welfare Reform in California: State and County Implementation of CalWORKS in the Second Year* (Santa Monica: RAND, 2001). This report utilized a series of field interviews with key informants in 24 counties in California. Six of these (the "focus" counties) were studied intensively; for the other eighteen ("follow-up" counties) the fieldwork was less extensive. Most data was collected between April and August 1999.

17. Another implementation issue that also absorbed significant administrative attention was the extensive and detailed federal reporting requirements for tracking clients' welfare receipt and program participation. There was no statewide system, and counties' computer systems were outdated and never designed for such tasks.

18. The scale of this process is illustrated by the experience of Los Angeles County where between April 1 and December 31, 1998, the agency had to enroll adults from 149,000 households for the first time (Polit et al. 2005).

19. A self-initiated program occurs when an applicant is already enrolled in an education/training program at the time their grant is approved and is therefore exempted from the Job Club requirements of the initial WTW phase. Some counties encouraged clients to enroll in SIPs before being called into their first meeting with their GAIN caseworkers.

20. Although most of the California fieldwork for this book occurred in 1996 and 1997, at the very beginning of the TANF revolution, I was also able to conduct 16 follow-up interviews in three counties in October of 2000. The most comprehensive survey was in Oakdale County, where I interviewed eight staff members—two TANF eligibility workers, one TANF unit supervisor, two childcare workers, two Job Club workers, and a program specialist for the new employment services division. What follows is based on their accounts.

21. According to Lawrence Mead (1997), the main reason welfare recipients do not work is that "people do not accept responsibility for themselves. They want to work in principle but they feel they cannot in practice." The paternalistic approach combines directive and supervisory measures to educate benefit recipients about their choices, sometimes known as "help and hassle."

22. The impact on caseworker service capacity of shifting supportive service responsibilities to other staff is unclear (as I had no opportunity to meet with employment counselors), but it is likely that with the tripling in the level of participants, this divestiture was offset by increased caseload size, as well as the large numbers of sanctioned cases, as sanctioning procedures remained complex.

23. The two TANF caseworkers interviewed in Oakdale in 2000 estimated that between 50 and 75% of their clients were now working. Klerman, Zellman, and Steinberg (2001) estimate that 40% of recipients in California were working at the end of 1999, up from 15% in 1993.

24. That is, after signing a welfare-to-work plan after Job Club and assessment, which is when this first time clock starts ticking and which didn't begin until 1998.

25. A more recent study from MDRC of Los Angeles County (Polit et al. 2005) further traces out policy and program development into the first years after 2000 in this part of California. By the first quarter of 2001, 47% of single parent cases were participating in a work-related activity. Working on welfare still remained the most significant way beneficiaries met program participation requirements (25,000). By this point only 2,000 clients were in Job Club while a larger percentage had progressed to short-term vocational training and basic education (8,000 and 2,000). A wide range of small innovative programs that had been in development for several years to assist claimants with more significant problems were largely eliminated in 2001 due to budgetary problems.

26. Wisconsin's program, Wisconsin Works (W-2), was exceptional in its program structure and offerings, representing the only state that had undertaken a large-scale, statewide, community service work experience program (Robles, Doolittle, and Gooden 2003).

27. As part of TANF there were also aspirations to create better coordination between welfare agencies and the traditional employment and training system, often known as the "Workforce Development System" (WDS) (Nightingale, Pindus, and Trutko 2002). Authorized under the Workforce Investment Act (WIA) of 1998 (previously the Job Training Partnership Act (JTPA)), these agencies provide a range of services and information about jobs and skills training in one-stop career centers primarily targeted at disadvantaged adults, youth, and dislocated workers.

The Welfare-to-Work (WtW) Grants Program, authorized under the Budget Reconciliation Act of 1997, provided additional funding through the WDS that was intended to assist long-term TANF recipients. There were, however, several challenges to the implementation of this program. Little past interagency collaboration in most places meant considerable time and resources were spent developing referral and coordination mechanisms. There were also basic differences in program goals. WDS has traditionally focused on career development through longer-term training, rather than placing people in low-wage jobs with little advancement potential. This focus as well as organizational performance standards also meant WDS was used to working with the job-ready rather than those with multiple barriers to work (Grubb et al. 1999). Many WDS agencies were also concerned that the strong push towards immediate employment was often inappropriate for many recipients, and could damage the agency's relationships with employers who depended on reliable referrals (Pindus et al. 2000).

The specificity of the group targeted by the WtW program (70% had to be spent on long-term recipients with 2–3 specific barriers) also made identifying and verifying eligible individuals time consuming and resulted in enrollment difficulties. The temporary nature of the funding (5 years) also had made it difficult to establish ongoing referral arrangements. Finally, due to the activity restrictions in the TANF legislation, even in those cases where WDS services were utilized, they were predominantly job search assistance and job readiness workshops (Nightingale, Pindus, and Trutko 2002).

28. Despite the strong push towards a work-first approach to welfare reform, there were still "pockets of choice" in which states have pursued more educationally oriented programs. For example, Rhode Island's program has an early emphasis on education and training with a range of basic skills and job specific training programs available for the first two years (Pindus et al. 2000).

29. For example, in a four-city study of Cleveland, Philadelphia, Miami, and Los Angeles by MDRC, researchers found that Ohio had one of the shortest interim limits (36 months then ineligible for 24 months) which it firmly enforced, but with significant efforts to ensure other benefits and supportive services were in place (Brock et al. 2002). Miami had similarly short interim time limits on aid, but little transitional help and the highest level of sanctioning ever seen by MDRC researchers (at 61%!) (Brock et al. 2004). Philadelphia had low rates of sanctioning and allowed extensions on time limits. California was a comparative lenient outlier in both of these areas, given its imposition of time limits and sanctions only on the adult portion (Polit et al. 2005).

30. The existence now of large numbers of working recipients also exposes the underlying contradiction of a program that obligates and, in some ways, facilitates working while on welfare, while causing those people who succeed to simultaneously use up their limited months of lifetime entitlement to aid. California is exceptional in that large numbers of recipients can work while on welfare, even after reaching time limits, while their children continue to receive state support. In the MDRC four-city comparison (Brock, Nelson, and Reiter 2002), the differences in various policies (time limits, grant levels, sanctioning policies) has meant that six times as many work while on welfare in LA than in Cleveland or Miami.

Chapter 7

1. "Quote from Werkstatt Bremen Caseworker".
2. For example, Swedish day care covers approximately 50% of children versus 1.4% in Germany (Esping-Andersen 1996).
3. In 1990, before a major recession hit Sweden, there was a 27% difference in female labor force participation between Germany and Sweden at 55.5% and 82.5% respectively (the United States was in the middle at 67.8%). By the year 2000 these differences had been cut in half, both from increases in Germany (at 63.8%) as well as a Swedish economy that had not returned to full employment (at 76.4%) (the U.S. was at 70.7%) (OECD 2005, Table B).
4. In Iversen and Wren's three horned service trilemma (1998), while Germany has succeeded in maintaining relatively equitable wages and limited budget deficits, it has failed to maintain adequate levels of employment.
5. Werkstatt Bremen has a main office and a smaller branch office in Bremen, as well as another office in Bremen Harbor (Bremerhaven) 20 miles north of the city, but still part of the city-state.
6. There are 60 participants in the sewing workshop and 48 participants in the furniture renovation workshop.
7. Childcare problems seem to affect relatively few clients. In 1999, 110 clients could not be helped because of child-rearing responsibilities (out of over 5,000 visitors). This low level may, in part, be due to filtering that occurs at the welfare office, as single mothers are not expected to participate until the youngest child reaches the age of three and only part-time after that (and in practice little pressure is placed on them until much later if at all). Being a single mother on welfare in Germany is a more viable (and legitimate) option than in the United States or Sweden. In both of these countries, single mothers are expected to participate in welfare-to-work activities when the youngest child reaches the age of one (and in the United States, in many states, mothers may be expected to participate when the child is even younger than this).
8. The employment contracts are highly technical, but this is not part of the client process itself.
9. There are regular visiting hours from 8:00 to 12:00 three mornings a week.
10. In 1999, 659 recipients were placed in 27 group projects; 212 were placed in 150 small public welfare organizations; and 169 were placed in a variety of government agencies (Werkstatt Bremen 1999).
11. Two of the three I interviewed had been there since the beginning 15 years ago, the other, 9 years.
12. One caseworker estimated that of her 580 cases, 120 were currently in contracts, 100 in daily structured activities (long-term blue cards), 50 in training, and 20–30 sent to the 19.1 division to try to get a private employment contract.
13. U27 like all of WB, cannot assist clients who are receiving any unemployment insurance benefits, even if only a very small amount, because officially such individuals are the responsibility of the EO.
14. The only comparable youth program in California occurs in a much more attenuated form. CalLearn is targeted at pregnant or parenting teens under the

age of 19 who have not completed high school, utilizing cash bonuses and sanctions to encourage school attendance (Klerman et al. 2001).

15. This incongruence between training entitlement and the age of the U27 clientele has meant that 26 year-olds have much greater difficulty finding appropriate training programs.

16. In California the Employment Development Department was sometimes contracted to conduct job readiness training but apparently had little else to offer clients (according to GAIN staff—see chapter 6). In Malmö, while employment and welfare offices had cooperated well together until the end of the 1980s, this was premised on a clear interagency division of labor in which the employment office dealt with all employment issues. With the end of full-employment economic conditions in the 1990s, this system deteriorated rapidly so that, in Germany, Swedish welfare offices were saddled with large numbers of unemployed who had no unemployment insurance benefits and whom the Employment Office had insufficient resources to assist. Only in the late 1990s has a better working relationship begun to develop between these two organizations (see chapter 8).

17. Based on observations with each of three U27 workers, and a total of 17 caseworker-client interactions.

18. Generally apprenticeships are provided by private employers themselves. But in some occupational areas, the firms fail to offer adequate numbers for the expected demands. In those cases the state steps in and finances additional programs (so-called industry-wide training ("überbetriebliche Ausbildung")).

19. 19.2 contracts, however, create financial disincentives for students to accept an apprenticeship slot before the year is up because the apprenticeship stipend is considerably lower than the close-to-market wages they receive while employed at AUCOOP.

20. This approach is known as the Maatwerk method, after the Dutch firm that developed it in 1985 to assist welfare recipients and the unemployed to find jobs.

21. It should be kept in mind, however, how small these programs are in comparison to the FES spending and participant levels. In 2001, there were 1.9 million participants in activation programs through the FES, with spending on such measures amounting to 1.25% GDP. By contrast, only 0.05% of GDP was spent on municipal activation programs (Schmid and Buhr 2002). Thus local activation measures represented about 17% of the activated population and 4% of the total costs.

22. It is unclear, though, how substantive these services were for many participants. Some studies with actual numbers indicate either that only a small percentage were actually enrolled in programs or that a large number of participants only received an initial consultation with a case manager, as was the case with Werkstatt Bremen. Stuttgart, for example, with a recipient population of 24,824, had placed 855 (3.4%) in 19.2 contracts, 430 (1.7%) in workfare work, and 259 (1.0%) in the primary labor market. In Krefeld, with a recipient population of 17,197, approximately 28% of recipients were seen for an initial consultation. However, in terms of placements in actual programs

the numbers were much smaller, with 446 (2.6%) in employment contracts, 791 (4.5%) in short-term projects, and 107 (0.6%) in the primary labor market (Empter and Frick 2000).

23. Former East German states have persistently been the site of a disproportionate number of federal job creation measures, including 145,500 of 203,600 placements in the public and nonprofit sector, and 98,100 of 109,800 in private employment in 2001 (Blien, Walwei, and Heinz Werner 2002).

24. In 2001, the incidence of long-term unemployment was over 50% versus the OECD average of about 30% (Adema, Gray, and Kahl 2003).

25. To increase the supply of low wage employment and income of employees in these jobs, a new classification of employment was also created. These "mini-jobs" were tax- and social-contribution free for employees for up to 400 Euros/month and required a flat 25% contribution on the employer's side. Additionally there were "Midi" jobs from 400–800 Euros/month with a gradation of employee contributions from 4–21%. Finally, to create market competition with the traditional job placement monopoly of the FES, unemployed individuals could receive a placement voucher which they could use at private employment agencies to find temporary employment as a transition to regular work (Kemmerling and Bruttel 2006).

26. It was estimated that 11,000 new staff needed to be hired, i.e., an approximate 12% increase in the organization's total workforce (Adema, Gray, and Kahl 2003).

27. While the Social Democrats wanted the FES to be fully responsible for the UBII benefit, the Christian Democrats wanted it fully administered by the municipalities. However, 69 municipalities were given full responsibility as part of a pilot project called "Optionskommunen" (Kemmerling and Bruttel 2006). There is a large-scale evaluation of the implementation and the effects of UBII (see e.g. http://iab.de/iab/forschung/sgbii.htm; http://www.iab.de/asp/info/dokSelect.asp?show=Forr; http://www. isg-institut.de/intern/HARTZ/); however, results are not expected before the end of 2007.

28. Other reforms have also failed to meet expectations. Temporary workers were incorporated into major collective bargaining agreements for fear that such positions would otherwise become a threat to core employment positions. This agreement between labor and business severely limited the utility of this new class of worker resulting in significant underutilization of the temp agency voucher plan. The mini-jobs were highly utilized, but evaluations indicate they largely acted as replacements for regular employment. These policy changes also failed to address the larger systemic problem of financing through employer-employee contributions rather than general taxes (Kemmerling and Bruttel 2006).

29. In table 7.1, the two dimensions of activation have been characterized as dichotomous variables with caseworker examples in each quadrant generally comparable to one another. However, the roles of California Job Developers and Bremen 19.1 and 19.2 caseworkers as "resource brokers" differ enough here that I have located them in relation to each other as if the dimensions

were continuous. 19.1/19.2 divisions' caseworkers have more resource options and provide more individualized services than California Job Developers, and this difference is reflected in the location of the German workers up and to the right of the Job Developers.

Chapter 8

1. Quote from caseworker at the Work and Development Center.
2. The Swedish emphasis on services is reflected by the ratio of social security expenditure spent on social services as compared to continental European countries (which emphasize income transfers): 0.33 in Sweden vs. 0.12 in France and 0.16 in Germany in 1990 (Esping-Andersen 1996).
3. See endnote 2 in chapter 7.
4. In 2002, Sweden spent 1.63% of GNP on active labor market policies. By contrast, Germany spent 1.22% and the United States, 0.18% (OECD 2005).
5. During the first four months of 2000, 4,484 social assistance recipients participated in approximately 43 different local labor market projects that were created through GEFAS city districts, representing approximately 36% of social assistance households. These projects fall into five categories—internships, programs for starting a business, training with internship, Swedish language courses, and "counseling and motivation" programs.
6. Note that the names of the districts have been changed for purposes of confidentiality.
7. In 1999, of approximately 30,000 inhabitants in Havdal, 46% were either immigrants or children of immigrants, and 32% of the population (in 1997) was on welfare. In Boklunden, of approximately 37,000 inhabitants, 45% were immigrants or children of immigrants, and 22% of the population was on welfare. In Lönnäng, of 35,000 inhabitants, 34% were immigrants or children of immigrants, and 15% of the population was on welfare. In Malmö as a whole, of 255,000 inhabitants, 35% were immigrants or children of immigrants, and 18% of the population was on welfare (Regional Facts for Malmö City Districts, 1999).
8. Introduction is an income support program for immigrants during their first three years in the country. Recipients receive support somewhat more generous than welfare and are obligated in turn to learn Swedish and "translate" their occupational skills and qualification in order to become employable in Sweden.
9. By contrast, of ten GEFAS offices, five had less than 100 participants during this time period.
10. The number of students in university or college level education doubled in the 1990s from 20% to 40% of the population between 20 and 24 years old (Hort 2001).
11. This program is to some extent a psychosocial intervention, as the majority of recipients from the social security agency have some form of mental disability, as do some welfare recipients.

12. There is a division of labor between the two agencies for practica reflecting their traditional domains. GEFAS organizations place clients in local government organizations, while the EO places clients in private firms.

13. The cost-shifting effects, though, are delayed in Sweden for six months because individuals cannot collect unemployment insurance benefits until they have been a member of the insurance fund for one year.

14. The Growth 2000 program is similar to 19.1/BAVA caseworkers in Bremen in terms of looking for employment that suits the particular client. However, unlike the Swedish program, in Bremen, there is no preparation and motivational course to offer clients. This lack of transitional services was a reason cited by several Bremen staff contributing to their limited success, as most clients simply were not ready to immediately begin full-time employment.

15. Earlier the EO had specialized its Malmö offices along occupational lines requiring WIC caseworkers to communicate with EO staff from all over the city about clients from Lönnäng.

16. Funding was provided to 24 districts in 7 cities (Malmö, Göteborg, Stockholm, Huddinge, Haninge, Södertälje, and Botkyrka) (Johansson and Salonen 2005).

17. The goals of the CII included: reducing welfare costs; increasing the use of Swedish in households; ensuring that no one left high school without sufficient knowledge of Swedish, English, and mathematics; improving the health of the population; guaranteeing residents comfort and security in all city districts; providing all individuals access to public and commercial services, as well as cultural and leisure activities; and increasing democratic participation. For a full evaluation of the program, see Johansson and Salonen 2005.

18. It appears Malmö was the only city that actually colocated staff. Other cities followed less integrated forms of collaboration (Tranquist 2001).

19. Which two agencies are involved depends on where the client is referred from. If they are from the EO or the welfare office, one staff from each is assigned. If they are from the disability program of the SSA, it is likely a municipal social worker and an SSA staff member initially. Clients from the SSA were expected to play a much smaller role in the program, reflected in the limited number of staff from this agency.

20. During the first four months of 2000, 247 of 2,645 households were enrolled in programs at Boklunden, about 9%, mostly in old GEFAS programs.

21. They would not help those without adequate Swedish or with current drug addiction, for example, problems more appropriate for social services.

22. I, however, could not confirm this assertion.

23. See Thorén 2005 for a similar assessment of the Jobbcentrum in Skärholmen, a suburb of Stockholm.

24. In one study (Tranquist 2001), an example of this flexibility that a caseworker cited was the ability to pay for a truck driver's license, the very example that staff at Lönnäng's WIC program had mentioned they were unable to do in describing the problems with the financial arrangements at that time.

25. Being listened to, and having a conversation with their caseworkers was also one of the things most appreciated by clients (Lindberg 2003; Bevelander et al. 2003).

26. Some offices have developed such services, including various special courses in language skills and a "second chance school" for youth who have had trouble succeeding at gymnasium. One particularly interesting example of this development was the apparent reorganization of the Job Search Center in Havdal (see Lindberg 2003 for more details). Once that district's WDC was well established, the clientele of the two programs overlapped significantly (i.e., long-term unemployed who were already relatively work ready), resulting in considerable duplicative work as well as referral problems for the new center. As a result, in Spring 2002, the Job Search Center was recast as a pre-WDC option that focused on a skill and motivation program that had been developed there (as well as a name change to Kompetens.kom). This program aimed at teaching participants to reflect on their skills and interests and translate these into a realistic activity plan, and in doing so, to strengthen their motivation and confidence. However at the time of that report, there still appeared to be a sense of competition between the two offices for referrals with suggestions that all referrals should go through the WDC and then those judged appropriate sent further on to Kompetens.kom.

Chapter 9

1. Welfare policy is certainly not the only boundary site of state action. Prison, public education, and immigration policy are other areas that raise fundamental issues about terms of inclusion.

2. At least in these three cases, as caseworker authority increases, so too do the necessary organizational commitments to managing it.

3. This is in contrast to European "paternalist" welfare states in which a class-based politics led to the establishment of male-, worker-based programs (Skocpol 1988).

4. Another, related argument is that discretionary schemes with comparatively generous benefits are common to small, affluent, homogenous countries. Such welfare states display a strong communitarian orientation in which pedagogical and paternalistic measures are viewed as appropriate conditions of aid (Bradshaw and Terum 1997).

5. An apparently similar transformation occurred earlier in the UK in the 1950s (Gough et al. 1997).

6. Such a return might also reawaken the tension in linking cash with care, the ambivalent back-and-forth between the therapeutic value of social work and the second-class citizenship of potentially conditioning help on unwanted interventions.

7. The current substantial investment in services for social assistance recipients also throws into even sharper relief the disincentive structures and equity problems targeted benefits can create. While individuals on welfare now have access to some considerable resources (especially childcare) to help them transition into employment and support their remaining there, much of the current working population at the low end of the socioeconomic spectrum have almost no access to similar kinds of aid.

References

Abrahamson, Peter. 1999. The Welfare Modeling Business. *Social Policy & Administration* 33 (4): 349–415.

Adema, Willem, Donald Gray, and Sigrun Kahl. 2003. *Social Assistance in Germany.* Paris: Directorate for Employment, Labour and Social Affairs. Organisation for Economic Co-operation and Development.

Adler, Michael. 2000. Special Educational Needs and Competing Policy Frameworks in England and Scotland. *Journal of Education Policy* 15 (6): 621–35.

AGAB. 1999. *Sozialhilfe in Bremen.* Bremen: Aktionsgemeinschaft Arbeitsloser Bürgerinnen und Bürger e.V. (AGAB).

Ahlrichs, Jan. 2003. *Benchmarking in der kommunalen Beschäftigungsförderung.* Gütersloh, Germany: Bertelsmann Stiftung.

Ahlstrand, R, and Göran Lindberg. 2001. *Arbets- och Utvecklingscenter i Malmö.* Lund: Sociologiska Institutionen, Lund Universitet.

Albrecht, James, Gerard J van den Berg, and Susan Vroman. 2004. *The Knowledge Lift: The Swedish Adult Education Program that Aimed to Eliminate Low Worker Skill Levels.* Uppsala, Sweden: Institute for Labour Market Policy Evaluation.

Aust, Andreas. 2003. *Policy Map Germany: Labour Market Policy, Social Assistance and Women's Employment, Long-term Care.* Canterbury, England: University of Kent—Welfare Reform and Management of Societal Change (WRAMSOC).

Bane, Mary Jo, and David Ellwood. 1994. *Welfare Realities: From Rhetoric to Reform.* Cambridge, MA: Harvard University Press.

Bardach, Eugene, and Robert A. Kagan. 2002. *Going by the Book: The Problem of Regulatory Unreasonableness.* Cambridge, MA: Harvard University Press.

Behrendt, Christina. 2002. *At the Margins of the Welfare State: Social Assistance and the Alleviation of Poverty in Germany, Sweden and the United Kingdom.* Hampshire: Ashgate.

Bevelander, Pieter, Per Broomé, Benny Carlson, and Göran Lindberg. 2003. *Storstadssatsningen i Malmö. Utvärdering av locala arbets- och utvecklingscentra.* Malmö: Malmö Stad.

Blau, Peter. 1963. *The Dynamics of Bureaucracy.* Chicago: University of Chicago Press.

Blien, Uwe, Ulrich Walwei, and Heinz Werner. 2002. *Labour Market Policy in Germany.* Nürnberg, Germany: Federal Employment Services.

Bode, Ingo. 2003. The Creeping Disorganization of Welfare Capitalism or What is the Future of Germany's Social Sector? *Review of Social Economy* 61 (3): 341–63.

Bonoli, Giuliano. 1997. Classifying Welfare States: A Two-Dimensional Approach. *Journal of Social Policy* 26 (3): 351–72.

Bradshaw, Jonathan, and Lars Inge Terum. 1997. How Nordic is the Nordic Model? Social Assistance in a Comparative Perspective. *Scandinavian Journal of Social Welfare* 6: 247–56.

Breuer, Wilhelm, and Dietrich Engels. 1998. *Basic Information and Data on Social Assistance in Germany.* Federal Ministry of Health.

Brock, Thomas, Claudia Coulton, Andrew London, Denise F. Polit, Lashawn Richburg-Hayes, Ellen Scott, and Nandita Verma. 2002. *Welfare Reform in Cleveland. Implementation, Effects, and Experiences of Poor Families and Neighborhoods.* New York: MDRC.

Brock, Thomas, Isaac Kwakye, Judy C. Polyne, Lashawn Richburg-Hayes, David Seith, Alex Stepick, and Carol Dutton Stepick. 2004. *Welfare Reform in Miami. Implementation, Effects, and Experiences of Poor Families and Neighborhoods.* New York: MDRC.

Brock, Thomas, Laura C. Nelson, and Megan Reiter. 2002. *Readying Welfare Recipients for Work: Lessons from Four Big Cities as They Implement Welfare Reform.* New York: MDRC.

Brodkin, Evelyn. 1986. *The False Promise of Administrative Reform: Implementing Quality Control in Welfare.* Philadelphia: Temple University Press.

———. 1997. Inside the Welfare Contract: Discretion and Accountability in State Welfare Administration. *Social Service Review* 71 (1): 1–33.

———. 2006. Does Good Politics Make for Good Practice? Reflections on Welfare-to-Work in the United States. In *Road to Where? The Politics and Practice of Welfare to Work,* edited by G. Marston, C. McDonald, and P. Henman. Brisbane, Australia: Social Policy Unit, School of Social Work and Applied Human Sciences, The University of Queensland www.uq.edu.au/swahs/welfaretowork.

Brodkin, Evelyn, and Katarina Thorén. 2005. *Work Activation in the "Model Welfare State": The Swedish Experience: Project on the Public Economy of Work.* Chicago: University of Chicago Press.

Bruttel, Oliver and Els Sol. 2006. Work First as a European Model? Evidence from Germany and the Netherlands. *Policy & Politics* 34:69–89.

Byberg, Ingrid. 1998. *Work Methods and Social Assistance. A Study of the Significance of Various Factors on Municipal Welfare Costs.* Stockholm: Department of Social Work, Stockholm University.

Carter, Lief H. 1974. *The Limits of Order.* Lexington, MA: Lexington Books.

Diller, Matthew. 2000. The Revolution in Welfare Administration: Rules, Discretion, and Entrepreneurial Government. *New York University Law Review* 75 (5): 1121–223.

DiPrete, Thomas A., Paul M. de Graaf, Ruud Luijkx, Michael Tåhlin, and Hans-Peter Blossfeld. 1997. Collectivist versus Individualist Mobility Regimes? Structural Change and Job Mobility in Four Countries. *American Journal of Sociology* 103 (2): 318–58.

Ditch, John, Jonathan Bradshaw, Jochen Clasen, Meg Huby, and Margaret Moodie. 1997. *Comparative Social Assistance: Localisation and Discretion.* Aldershot: Ashgate Publishing.

Eardley, Tony, Jonathan Bradshaw, John Ditch, Ian Gough, and Peter Whiteford. 1996. *Social Assistance in OECD Countries.* Vol. 1: Synthesis Report. London: Stationery Office Books.

Edin, Kathy, and Laura Lein. 1997. *Making Ends Meet: How Single Mothers Survive Welfare and Low-Wage Work.* New York: Russell Sage Foundation.

Ekström, Veronica. 2005. *Individens Eget Ansvar och Samhällets Stöd. En Utvärdering av "Skärholmsmodellen" vid Jobbcentrum Sydväst.* Stockholm: Institute for Labour Market Policy Evaluation.

Empter, Stefan, and Frank Frick. 2000. *Beschäftigungsorientierte Sozialpolitik in Kommunen.* Gütersloh, Germany: Bertelsmann Stiftung.

Esping-Andersen, Gøsta. 1991. *The Three Worlds of Welfare Capitalism.* Princeton: Princeton University Press.

———. 1996. Welfare State Without Work: The Impasse of Labor Shedding and Familialism in Continental European Social Policy. In *Welfare States in Transition: National Adaptations in a Global Economy,* ed. G. Esping-Andersen. Thousand Oaks: Sage Publications.

Estevez-Abe, Margarita, Torben Iversen, and David Soskice. 2001. Social Protection and the Formation of Skills: A Reinterpretation of the Welfare State. In *Varieties of Capitalism: The Institutional Foundations of Comparative Advantage,* ed. P. A. Hall and D. Soskice. Oxford: Oxford University Press.

FMH. 2005. *Sozialhife.* Federal Ministry of Health (Germany).

Fossett, James, Thomas Gais, and Frank Thompson. 2003. New Systems of Social Programs? Local Implementation of Health Care, Food Stamps, and TANF Programs. *Focus* 22 (3): 44–49.

GAO. 2000. *Welfare Reform—State Sanction Policies and Number of Families Affected.* Washington, D.C.: General Accounting Office (GAO).

Garcia, Marison, and Chiara Saraceno. 1998. Introduction. In *ESOPO—Evaluation of Social Policies at the Local Urban Level: Income Support for the Able Bodied,* ed. C. Saraceno. Turin: University of Turin, Department of Social Sciences.

Giertz, Anders. 2004. *Making the Poor Work. Social Assistance and Activation Programs in Sweden.* Lund: Lund University, School of Social Work.

Glisson, Charles. 2000. Organizational Climate and Culture. In *The Handbook of Social Welfare Management,* ed. R. Patti. Thousand Oaks, CA: Sage Publications.

Goetz, Klaus H. 2000. The Development and Current Features of the German Civil Service System. In *Civil Service Systems in Western Europe,* ed. H. A. G. M. Bekke and F. M. van der Meer. Cheltenham: Edward Elgar.

Gornick, Janet C., Marcia K. Meyers, and Katherin E. Ross. 1997. Supporting the Employment of Mothers: Policy Variation across Fourteen Welfare States. *Journal of European Social Policy* 7 (1): 45–70.

Gough, Ian, Jonathan Bradshaw, John Ditch, Tony Eardley, and Peter Whiteford. 1997. Social Assistance in OECD Countries. *Journal of European Social Policy* 7 (1): 17–43.

Grubb, Norton W., Norena Badway, Denise Bell, Bernadette Chi, Chris King, Julie Herr, Heath Prince, Richard Kazis, Lisa Hicks, and Judith Combes Taylor. 1999. *Toward Order From Chaos: State Efforts to Reform Workforce Development Systems.* Berkeley, CA: National Center for Research in Vocational Education.

Grunow, Dieter. 2001. Public Services. In *Public Administration in Germany,* ed. K. König and H. Siedentopf. Baden-Baden: Nomos Verlagsgesellschaft.

Gueron, Judith, and Edward Pauly. 1991. *From Welfare to Work.* New York: Sage Publications.

Gustafsson, Siv 1994. Childcare and Types of Welfare States. In *Gendering Welfare States*, ed. D. Sainsbury. London: Sage Publications.

Hagen, Jan L. 1987. Income Maintenance Workers: Technicians or Service Providers? *Social Service Review* 61 (2): 261–71.

Hall, Peter A., and David Soskice. 2001. An Introduction to Varieties of Capitalism. In *Varieties of Capitalism: The Institutional Foundations of Comparative Advantage*, ed. P. A. Hall and D. Soskice. Oxford: Oxford University Press.

Handler, Joel. 1997. *We the Poor People: Work, Poverty, and Welfare*. New Haven: Yale University Press.

———. 2004. *Social Citizenship and Workfare in the United States and Western Europe. The Paradox of Inclusion*. Cambridge: Cambridge University Press.

Handler, Joel, and Ellen Hollingsworth. 1971. *The "Deserving Poor": A Study of Welfare Administration*. Chicago: Markham.

Hanesch, Walter, Christine Stelzer-Orthofer, and Nadine Balzter. 2001. Activation Policies in Minimum Income Schemes. In *Social Assistance in Europe*, ed. M. Heikklä and E. Keskitalo. Helsinki: National Research and Development Center for Welfare and Health (STAKES).

Hasenfeld, Yeheshkel. 1983. *Human Service Organizations*. Englewood Cliffs, NJ: Prentice-Hall.

———. ed. 1992. *Human Services as Complex Organizations*. Newbury Park, CA: Sage Publications.

Hauschild, Christoph. 2001. Qualifications and Training for the Public Service. In *Public Administration in Germany*, ed. K. König and H. Siedentopf. Baden-Baden: Nomos Verlagsgesellschaft.

Hedblom, Agneta. 2004. *Aktiveringspolitikens Janusansikte. En Studie av Differentiering, Inklusion och Marginarlisering*. Lund: Lund University, Department of Social Work.

Hollenrieder, Jutta, Petra Bolte, Corinna Wilfling, Jan Ahlrichs, and Helmut Hartmann. 2003. *Benchmarking der mittelgrossen Grossstädte in Nordrhein-Westfalen. Kennzahlenvergleich 2002. Hilfe zur Arbeit*. Hamburg: con_sens Hamburg. Consulting für Steuerung und soziale Entwicklung GmbH.

Hort, Sven E.O. 2001. Sweden—Still a Civilized Version of Workfare? In *Activating the Unemployed: A Comparative Appraisal of Work-Oriented Policies*, ed. R. Van Voorhis and N. Gilbert. New Brunswick: Transaction Publishers.

Hvinden, Bjørn. 1994. *Divided Against Itself: A Study of Integration in Welfare Bureaucracy*. New York: Oxford University Press.

Iversen, Torben. 2005. *Capitalism, Democracy, and Welfare*. Cambridge Studies in Comparative Politics. New York: Cambridge University Press.

Iversen, Torben, and Anne Wren. 1998. Equality, Employment, and Budgetary Restraint: The Trilemma of the Service Economy. *World Politics* 50 (July): 507–46.

Jewell, Christopher J., and Bonnie E. Glaser. 2006. Toward a General Analytic Framework: Organizational Settings, Policy Goals, and Street-Level Behavior. *Administration & Society* 38 (3): 335–64.

Johansson, Christina, and Tapio Salonen. 2005. *Storstad i Rörelse—Kunskapsöversikt över Utvärderingar av Storstadspolitikens Lokala Utvecklingsavtal*. Stockholm: Statens Offentliga Utredningar.

Johansson, Håkan. 2001. *I Det Sociala Medborgarskapets Skugga. Rätten till Socialbidrag under 1980- och 1990-Talen* (In Social Citizenship's Shadow. The Right to Social Assistance during the 1980s and 1990s). Lund: Arkiv förlag.

———. 2006. *Svensk Aktiveringspolitik i Nordiskt Perspektiv.* Stockholm: Finansdepartementet, Expertgrupp för Studier i Samhällsekonomi (ESS), Swedish Government.

Johnson, David. 1998. The Organization of Prosecution and the Possibility of Order. *Law & Society* 32 (2): 247–308.

Kagan, Robert A. 1978. *Regulatory Justice. Implementing a Wage-Price Freeze.* New York: Russell Sage Foundation.

———. 2006. The Organization of Administrative Justice Systems: Center for the Study of Law and Society Jurisprudence and Social Policy Program. Paper 38. JSP/Center for the Study of Law and Society Faculty Working Papers. http://repositories.cdlib.org/csls/fwp/38.

Katzenstein, Peter J. 1987. *Policy and Politics in West Germany: The Growth of a Semisovereign State.* Philadelphia: Temple University Press.

Kaufman, Herbert. 1967. *The Forest Ranger: A Study in Administrative Behavior.* Baltimore: Resources for the Future Press.

Kazepov, Yuri, and Stafania Sabatinelli. 2001. How Generous Are Social Assistance Schemes? In *Social Assistance in Europe,* ed. M. Heikklä and E. Keskitalo. Helsinki: National Research and Development Center for Welfare and Health (STAKES).

Kemmerling, Achim, and Oliver Bruttel. 2006. "New Politics" in German Labour Market Policy? The Implications of the Recent Hartz Reforms for the German Welfare State. *West European Politics* 29 (1): 90–112.

Kitschelt, Herbert and Wolfgang Streeck. 2003. From Stability to Stagnation: Germany at the Beginning of the Twenty-First Century. *Western European Politics* 26:1–34.

Klerman, Jacob, Gail L. Zellman, and Paul Steinberg. 2001. *Welfare Reform in California: State and County Implementation of CalWORKS in the Second Year.* Santa Monica: RAND.

König, Klaus. 2001. Public Administration in the Unified Germany. In *Public Administration in Germany,* ed. K. König and H. Siedentopf. Baden-Baden: Nomos Verlagsgesellschaft.

Leibfried, Stephan. 1993. Towards a European Welfare State. In *New Perspectives on the Welfare State,* ed. C. Jones. London: Routledge.

Leibfried, Stephan, and Herbert Obinger. 2003. The State of the Welfare State: German Social Policy between Macroeconomic Retrenchment and Microeconomic Recalibration. *Western European Politics* 26 (4): 199–218.

Leisering, L., B. Hilkert, F. Berner, K. Krug, S. Intrup, M. Gorotheer, and C. Lidzba. 2001. *Strategien des Umbaus im lokalen Sozialstaat. Chancen und Risiken der kommunalen Sozialhilfereformen (Hilfe zum Lebensunterhalt) unter besonderer Beruecksichtigung neuer Informationssysteme.* Bielefeld: Hand-Boeckler-Stiftung.

Leisering, Lutz, and Stephan Leibfried. 1999. *Time and Poverty in Western Welfare States: United Germany in Perspective.* Cambridge: Cambridge University Press.

Lewis, Jane. 1992. Introduction: Women, Work, Family and Social Policies in Europe. In *Women and Social Policies in Europe: Work, Family and the State*, ed. J. Lewis. Aldershot: Edward Elgar.

Lindberg, Göran. 2003. *Individcentrerad arbetsförmedling i samverkan. Processutvärdering av Arbets- och utvecklingscentra i Fosie, Hyllie och Södra Innerstaden.* Lund: Sociologiska Institutionen, Lunds universitet.

Lindqvist, Rafael and Staffan Marklund. 1995. Forced to Work and Liberated from Work. *Scandinavian Journal of Social Welfare* 12:224–37.

Lipsky, Michael. 1980. *Street-Level Bureaucracy: Dilemmas of the Individual in Public Services.* New York: Russell Sage Foundation.

Lødemel, Ivar. 1997. *The Welfare Paradox: Income Maintenance and Personal Social Services in Norway and Britain, 1946–1966.* Oslo: Scandinavian University Press.

———. 2000. Discussion: Workfare in the Welfare State. In *"An Offer You Can't Refuse": Workfare in International Perspective,* ed. I. Lødemel and H. Trickey. Bristol: The Policy Press.

Lødemel, Ivar, and Bernd Schulte. 1992. *Social Assistance: A Part of Social Security or the Poor Law in New Disguise?* Leuven: European Institute of Social Security.

Lurie, Irene. 2006. *At the Front Lines of the Welfare System. A Perspective on the Decline in Welfare Caseloads.* Albany, New York: Rockefeller Institute Press.

Martinson, Karin. 1999. *Literature Review on Service Coordination and Integration in the Welfare and Workforce Development Systems.* Washington, D.C.: Urban Institute.

Martinson, Karin, and Pamela A. Holcomb. 2002. *Reforming Welfare. Institutional Change and Challenges.* Washington, D.C.: Urban Institute.

Mashaw, Jerry. 1983. *Bureaucratic Justice.* New Haven: Yale University Press.

Maynard-Moody, Steven, and Michael Musheno. 2003. *Cops, Teachers, Counselors. Stories from the Front Lines of Public Service.* Ann Arbor: University of Michigan Press.

Mead, Lawrence. 1997. The New Paternalism. Supervisory Approaches to Poverty. In *The Rise of Paternalism,* ed. L. Mead. Washington, D.C.: Brookings Institute.

Melnick, Shep. 1994. *Between the Lines: Interpreting Welfare Rights.* Washington, D.C.: Brookings Institute.

Meyers, Marcia, Bonnie Glaser, and Karin MacDonald. 1998. On the Front Lines of Welfare Delivery: Are Workers Implementing Policy Reforms? *Journal of Policy Analysis and Management* 17 (1): 1–22.

Michaelopoulos, Charles, Kathryn Edin, Barbara Fink, Mirella Landriscina, Denise F. Polit, Judy C. Polyne, Lashawn Richburg-Hayes, David Seith, and Nandita Verma. 2003. *Welfare Reform in Philadelphia. Implementation, Effects, and Experiences of Poor Families and Neighborhoods.* New York: MDRC.

Mink, Gwendolyn. 1990. The Lady and the Tramp: Gender, Race, and the Origins of the American Welfare State. In *Women, the State, and Welfare,* ed. L. Gordon. Madison: University of Wisconsin Press.

Mishra, Ramesh. 1999. *Globalization and the Welfare State.* Cheltenham: Edward Elgar.

Munger, Frank. 1998. Immanence and Identity: Understanding Poverty through Law and Society Research. *Law & Society Review* 37 (2): 283–94.

Nelson, Barbara J. 1990. The Origins of the Two-Channel Welfare State: Workmen's Compensation and Mothers' Aid. In *Women, the State, and Welfare*.

Nightingale, Demetra Smith, Nancy Pindus, Fredrica D. Kramer, John Trutko, Kelly Mikelson, and Michael Egner. 2002. *Work and Welfare Reform in New York City During the Giulianni Administration: A Study of Program Implementation*. Washington, D.C.: Urban Institute Labor and Social Policy Center.

Nightingale, Demetra Smith, Nancy Pindus, and John Trutko. 2002. *The Implementation of the Welfare-to-Work Grants Program*. Washington, D.C.: Urban Institute.

Nonet, Phillipe, and Phillip Selznick. 2001. *Law and Society in Transition: Toward Responsive Law*. New York: Harper and Row.

Ochoa, Michael. 1997. A Culture of Law: Street-Level Decision Making in the Social Security Administration, Jurisprudence and Social Policy Program. Dissertation. University of California, Berkeley.

OECD. 2005. *OECD Employment Outlook 2005*. Paris: Organisation for Economic Co-operation and Development (OECD).

Oldrup, Kaj, Hanna Ershytt, Åsa Karlsson, and Göran Holmberg. 2002. *Arbets- och Utvecklingscenter (AUC) i Malmö. Granskning av de Kommunalt Anställda Handläggarnas Arbetsformer och Deras Informationsutbyte*. Malmö: Stadsrevisionen.

Orloff, Ann. 1988. The Political Origins of America's Belated Welfare State. In *The Politics of Social Policy in the United States*, ed. M. Weir, A. Orloff, and T. Skocpol. Princeton: Princeton University Press.

———. 1993. Gender and the Social Rights of Citizenship: The Comparative Analysis of State Policies and Gender Relations. *American Sociological Review* 58: 303–28.

Patton, Michael Quinn. 2002. *Qualitative Research and Evaluation Methods*. Thousand Oaks, CA: Sage Publications.

Peck, Jamie. 2001. *Workfare States*. New York: Guilford Press.

Pindus, Nancy, Robin Koralek, Karin Martinson, and John Trutko. 2000. *Coordination and Integration of Welfare and Workforce Development Systems*. Washington, D.C.: Urban Institute.

Piven, Frances Fox, and Richard Cloward. 1971. *Regulating the Poor*. New York: Pantheon.

Polit, Denise F., Laura C. Nelson, Lashawn Richburg-Hayes, and David Seith. 2005. *Welfare Reform in Los Angeles. Implementation, Effects, and Experiences of Poor Families and Neighborhoods*. New York: MDRC.

Pollitt, Christopher. 2002. Clarifying Convergence. Striking Similarities and Durable Differences in Public Management Reform. *Public Management Review* 4 (1): 471–92.

Prottas, Jeffrey Manditch. 1979. *People-Processing. The Street-Level Bureaucrat in Public Service Bureaucracies*. Lexington, MA: Lexington Books.

Puide, Annika, and Renate Minas. 2001. Recipients of Social Assistance. In *Social Assistance in Europe*, ed. M. Heikklä and E. Keskitalo. Helsinki: National Research and Development Center for Welfare and Health (STAKES).

Quadagno, Jill. 1994. *The Color of Welfare: How Racism Undermined the War on Poverty*. New York: Oxford University Press.

Riccio, James, Daniel Friedlander, and Stephan Freedman. 1994. *GAIN: Benefits, Costs, and Three-Year Impacts of a Welfare-to-Work Program.* New York City: MDRC.

Riccucci, Norma M. 2005. *How Management Matters. Street-Level Bureaucrats and Welfare Reform.* Washington, D.C.: Georgetown University Press.

Robles, Andrea, Fred Doolittle, and Susan Gooden. 2003. *Community Service Jobs in Wisconsin Works. The Milwaukee County Experience.* New York: MDRC.

Rönnlund, Eileen. 1992. *Socialt arbete – att se möjligheter.* Stockholm: Almquist & Wicksell.

Rothstein, Bo, and Sven Steinmo. 2002. Restructuring Politics: Institutional Analysis and the Challenges of Modern Welfare States. In *Restructuring the Welfare State: Political Institutions and Policy Change,* ed. B. Rothstein and S. Steinmo. New York: Palgrave Macmillan.

Sainsbury, Diane. 1994. Women's and Men's Social Rights: Gendering Dimensions of Welfare States. In *Gendering Welfare States,* ed. D. Sainsbury. London: Sage Publications.

Salonen, Tapio. 2000. Outsiders and Activation in Swedish Labour Market Policy. Paper read at The Activating Welfare States. New Ways of Fighting Poverty and Social Exclusion in Europe, at Lund University, Sweden.

———. 2001. Sweden—Between Model and Reality. In *International Social Policy: Welfare Regimes in the Developed World,* ed. P. Alcock and G. Craig. New York: Palgrave Macmillan.

Salonen, Tapio, and Håkan Johansson. 1999. Youth and Workfare—a Case Study of Youth Unemployment Policies in Sweden. Paper read at European Sociological Conference, at Amsterdam, The Netherlands.

Salonen, Tapio, and Rickard Ulmestig. 2004. *Nedersta Trappsteget. En Studie om Kommunal Aktivering. Växjö.* Sweden: Institutionen för Vårdvetenskap och Socialt Arbete, Växjö Universitet.

Schaak, Torsten. 1997. *Die "Hilfe zur Arbeit" nach dem Bundessozialhilfegesetz.* Hamburg: Behörde für Arbeit, Gesundheit und Soziales (BAGS).

Schmid, Achim, and Petra Buhr. 2002. *Aktive Klienten—Aktive Politik? (Wie) Lässt sich dauerhafte Unabhängigkeit von Sozialhilfe erreichen? Ein Literaturbericht.* Bremen: Center for Social Policy (CeS).

Schwarze, Uwe. 1996. *Social Administration and Clientele—on the Relevance of Time and Processing Dimensions in Welfare Practice. Results of an Empirical Analysis on the Basis of Expert Interviews.* Bremen: University of Bremen.

Simon, William. 1983. Legality, Bureaucracy, and Class in the Welfare System. *Yale Law Journal* 92: 1198–250.

Skocpol, Theda. 1988. The Limits of the New Deal System and the Roots of Contemporary Welfare Dilemmas. In *The Politics of Social Policy in the United States,* ed. M. Weir, A. Orloff, and T. Skocpol. Princeton: Princeton University Press.

Snow, Barbara West, Bonnie Glaser, Christopher Jewell, and Karin Mac Donald. 1995. *California Work Pays Demonstration Project. Process Evaluation Phase III: 1995.* Berkeley: University of California Data Archive and Technical Assistance (UC DATA).

————. 1997. *California Work Pays Demonstration Project. Process Evaluation Phase IV: 1996.* Berkeley: University of California Data Archive and Technical Assistance (UC DATA).

Stenberg, Anders. 2003. *An Evaluation of the Adult Education Initiative Relative Labor Market Training.* Umeå, Sweden: Department of Economics, Umeå University.

Streeck, Wolfgang. 1991. On the Institutional Conditions of Diversified Quality Production. In *Beyond Keynesianism,* ed. E. Matzner and W. Streeck. Aldershot: Edward Elgar.

Swank, Duane. 2000. Social Democratic Welfare States in a Global Economy: Scandinavia in Comparative Perspective. In *Globalization, Europeanization and the End of Scandinavian Social Democracy?* ed. R. Geyer, C. Ingebrigsten, and J. Moses. London: Macmillan.

Taylor-Gooby, Peter. 2005. Ideas and Policy Change. In *Ideas and Welfare State Reform in Western Europe,* ed. P. Taylor-Gooby. Houndmills: Palgrave Macmillan.

Theodore, Nikolas, and Jamie Peck. 1999. Welfare-to-Work: National Problems, Local Solutions? *Critical Social Policy* 19(4): 485–510.

Thorén, Katarina Hjertner. 2005. *Municipal Activation Policy: A Case Study of the Practical Work with Unemployed Social Assistance Recipients.* Uppsala, Sweden: Institute for Labour Market Policy Evaluation.

Titmuss, Richard. 1970. *The Gift Relationship: From Human Blood to Social Policy.* Oxford: George Allen & Unwin.

Tranquist, Joakim. 2001. *Samverkan Med Individen i Fokus: En Processutvärdering av Arbets- och Utvecklingscentra i Malmö.* Malmö: Arbetslivsinstitutet Syd.

Trickey, Heather. 2000. Comparing Workfare Programmes: Features and Implications. In *"An Offer You Can't Refuse": Workfare in International Perspective.*

Tweedie, Jack. 1989. Discretion to Use Rules: Individual Interests and Collective Welfare in School Admissions. *Law and Policy* 10 (2): 189–213.

Univation. 2004. *Pauschalierte Leistungsgewährung in sozialen Sicherungssystemen. Erfahrungen und Konsequenzen. Abshlussbericht der wissenschaftlichen Begleitung zu den Modellvorhaben zur Pauschalierung von Sozialhilfe in NRW.* Cologne, Germany: Univation—Institute for Evaluation Dr. Beywl & Associates GmbH.

Van Voorhis, Rebecca, and Neil Gilbert. 2001. Activating the Unemployed: The Challenge Ahead. In *Activating the Unemployed: A Comparative Appraisal of Work-Oriented Policies,* ed. R. Van Voorhis and N. Gilbert. New Brunswick: Transaction Publishers.

Voges, Wolfgang, Herbert Jacobs, and Heather Trickey. 2000. Uneven Development: Local Authorities and Workfare in Germany. In *"An Offer You Can't Refuse": Workfare in International Perspective.*

Vroman, Wayne. 1998. *Effects of Welfare Reform on Unemployment Insurance.* Washington, D.C.: Urban Institute—Assessing the New Federalism.

Walters, Meridith, Gene Falk, and Vee Burke. 2004. *TANF Cash Benefits as of January 1, 2004.* Washington, D.C.: Congressional Research Service.

Weaver, R. Kent. 1998. Ending Welfare as We Know It. In *The Social Divide: Political Parties and the Future of Activist Government,* ed. M. Weir. New York: Russell Sage Foundation.

Weir, Margaret. 1988. The Federal Government and Unemployment: The Frustration of Policy Innovation from the New Deal to the Great Society. In *The Politics of Social Policy in the United States,* ed. M. Weir, A. Orloff, and T. Skocpol. Princeton: Princeton University Press.

Werkstatt Bremen. 1999. *Hilfen Zur Arbeit: Jahresbericht* (Help Towards Work: Annual Report). Bremen: Werkstatt Bremen.

Wiseman, Michael. 2000. Making Work for Welfare in the United States. In *"An Offer You Can't Refuse": Workfare in International Perspective.*

Yin, R.K. 2003. *Case Study Research. Designs and Methods.* Thousand Oaks, CA: Sage Publications.

Laws Cited
Germany
Bundessozialhilfegesetz (Federal Social Assistance Law). 1961.

Sweden
The Social Service Law. 1998.
Malmö Communal Regulations. 1999.

Index